THE BIBLICAL HERO

University of Nebraska Press

Lincoln

The Biblical Hero

Portraits in Nobility and Fallibility

ELLIOTT RABIN

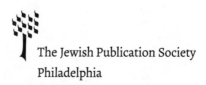

The Jewish Publication Society
Philadelphia

All rights reserved. Published by the University of
Nebraska Press as a Jewish Publication Society book.

Manufactured in the United States of America. ♾

Library of Congress Cataloging-in-Publication Data
Names: Rabin, Elliott, author.
Title: The biblical hero: portraits in
nobility and fallibility / Elliott Rabin.
Description: Lincoln: University of Nebraska Press,
2020. | Includes bibliographical references and index.
Identifiers: LCCN 2019031037
ISBN 9780827613249 (paperback: alk. paper)
ISBN 9780827618343 (epub)
ISBN 9780827618350 (mobi)
ISBN 9780827618367 (pdf)
Subjects: LCSH: Heroes in the Bible—Biography. | Bible.
Old Testament—Biography. | Heroes in literature.
Classification: LCC BS579.H4 R33 2020
DDC 221.9/22—dc23
LC record available at https://lccn.loc.gov/2019031037

Set in Merope by Mikala R. Kolander.

For Batia, חכמת לב, for Bram, אמיץ לב,
and for Adele, לבבי ונפשי

And my parents, Arthur ז״ל
and Rita א״תבלח,

גבורי חיל

GREAT-HEART: Prithee, Mr. Honest, present us with a few particulars.

HONEST: So I will. [Mr. Self-will] said, To have to do with other men's wives, had been practised by David, God's beloved, and therefore he could do it. He said to have more women than one, was a thing that Solomon practised, and therefore he could do it. He said, that Sarah and the godly midwives of Egypt lied, and so did Rahab, and therefore he could do it . . . . He said, That Jacob got the inheritance of his father, in a way of guile and dissimulation, and therefore he could do so too.

—John Bunyan, *Pilgrim's Progress*, Book II

Contents

Preface: *The Need for Heroes*   xi

Acknowledgments   xxi

Author's Note   xxiii

Introduction: *Heroic-Unheroic Heroes, the Biblical Model*   1

1. Moses: *Prototype*   25

2. Samson: *Strongman*   71

3. Esther: *Queen*   97

4. Abraham: *Pilgrim*   121

5. Jacob: *Trickster*   157

6. David: *King*   199

7. God: *Archetype or Antitype?*   245

Conclusion: *The Biblical Hero Today*   269

Notes   273

Bibliography   291

General Index   297

Source Index   301

Preface

The Need for Heroes

Within the groves of academe, the word "hero" has a quaint ring, a musty aroma, like a marble Victorian funerary statue. Most studies of heroism took place more than half a century ago, and since then the topic has fallen precipitously out of favor. The majority of academics today, I suspect, would find the subject distasteful, smacking of elitism, perhaps sexism, and also the eugenics movement, with its search for the perfect human and, in more sinister hands, the master race.[1]

Yet in the wider society, the notion of heroes and heroism remains eternally popular. Americans tend to look up to sports figures and singers, actors in the theater and actors on the political stage. The communal need for heroes especially arises during periods of societal turmoil. Citizens championed as heroes the firemen who lost their lives during 9/11 trying to rescue people trapped in the Twin Towers, and the soldiers who sacrificed life and limb in Iraq and Afghanistan. Tom Brokaw's best seller *The Greatest Generation* characterizes those who fought in World War II as models of "unsung heroes."

Not all of those our (or any other) society upholds as heroes may meet our own definition, but this reality does not negate our larger personal and communal need for heroes. We need heroes to guide us, instruct us, inspire us—to serve as examples of the way to live our lives and to understand who we are. On this matter, the ancient Greek philosopher Protagoras said (in Plato's dialogue of the same name): A student should read great works of literature because "in these are contained many admonitions, and many tales, and praises, and encomia of ancient famous men, which he is required to learn by heart, in order that he may imitate or emulate them and desire to become like them."[2] Hearkening to this advice, the Greek conqueror Alexander the Great kept a copy of Homer's *Iliad* by his bedside so that he might continuously draw inspiration from its main character: his hero Achilles, a warrior like himself.

According to the mid-twentieth-century sociologist Orrin Klapp, all societies rely upon the representation of heroes, along with fools and villains, to mold people's behavior. The kinds of heroes a society projects reveal much about the values within it:

> [Representing types of characters,] then, holds up models for the way people should be and act. Ethically, the hero might be thought of as the bull's-eye of a target, the ideal achievement of right conduct. He gives impetus to rise above the ordinary. Negative types represent deviations and failures important enough to be memorialized by society. An individual feels success to the extent that he lives up to heroes, at least stays comfortably above the folly and wrongdoing represented by the other extremes. . . . It is impossible to speak of ethics, in my opinion, without getting into the realm of these socially produced images of the hero, villain, and fool.[3]

Additionally, philosopher Alasdair MacIntyre observes that the stories a culture tells are essential in enabling people to find meaning in their lives:

> I can only answer the question "What am I to do?" if I can answer the prior question "Of what story or stories do I find myself a part?" . . . It is through hearing stories about wicked stepmothers, lost children, good but misguided kings, wolves that suckle twin boys . . . that children learn or mislearn both what a child and what a parent is, what the cast of characters may be in the drama into which they have been born and what the ways of the world are.[4]

The dramatization of heroes is thus needed because the concretization of these ideals shapes individuals as well as nations. Loyalty, bravery, moral conduct, and conscience can all derive from the kinds of heroes people strive to emulate.

In essence, heroes erect indispensable signposts that orient people toward the adoption of their own identity. What person, character, or superhero we look up to is both one of the most personal aspects of our being, reflecting what we think of as our "true self," and a formative influence on all aspects of our character. For this reason, heroes are most important to the young, during the time of life when identity is fluid and still being shaped. Heroes can energize young people toward particular goals, values, and accomplishments by endowing them with a sense of the kind of person they would like to become, and perhaps suggesting a path to follow to achieve that status. Heroes may inspire them to join the ranks of a certain profession or pursue a specialized course of study. Heroes may also imbue devotees of all ages with something more nebulous and perhaps more intimate—a style, philosophy, or manner of being and acting in the world.

The Purpose of Heroes: Three Models

Three twentieth-century scholars—Otto Rank, Lord Raglan, and Joseph Campbell—have proposed different theories about the purpose of heroes in human development.[5] A disciple of Sigmund Freud, Rank (*The Myth of the Birth of the Hero*) believes the potency of the hero motif originates in childhood fantasies. A male child (the hero in theories, as well as in world literature, tends to be male) longs to restore the infantile impression of his parents as the most powerful and beautiful of people. Upon reaching an age when he discovers they are common and less than perfect, he imagines the parents he knows are not his true parents, and his real parents are nobility. The boy thus justifies his rebellion against his father as an attack against an impostor or usurper. Classic heroes therefore meet a psychological need expressed during a normal process of childhood development: the inner desire to descend from and return to greatness.

Raglan (*The Hero: A Study in Tradition, Myth, and Drama*) holds that heroes represent the human desire to shape our destiny by having dominion over forces beyond our control. An adherent of the early twentieth-century "myth and ritual school," he views heroes as individuals (usually rulers or leaders in the making) given special designation to perform a ritual. As part of the ritual, they typically employ an object endowed with supernatural powers (e.g., King Arthur's sword, a fairy's wand) that empowers the hero or heroine to restore justice, revive nature, bring rain, or otherwise exert a transformative impact upon the hero's world.[6] At the same time, the device enables the hero/heroine to attain his/her rightful place as king/queen.

For Campbell (*The Hero with a Thousand Faces*), the hero embodies our yearning for contact with divine or supernatural forces in order to surmount our natural limitations. The hero dares to leave society, crosses the threshold between the human and divine, and then returns to society, having gained redemptive wisdom for the benefit of humankind.

However divergently these scholars understand the appeal of hero myths, all three essentially regard heroes as human beings who successfully break through the fetters imposed by family, nature, and society. Stories about heroes, therefore, hold such potent appeal because they evoke our universally felt human longings to transcend the boundaries drawn around our lives.

Reclaiming Biblical Heroes

If we take our need for heroes seriously, then it also behooves us to examine the qualities we want to promote as truly heroic. Our quest here is to (1) find the right heroes and (2) cultivate the best ways of admiring them.

In this light, heroes from the Bible are more urgently needed now than ever. Fortunately for us, biblical heroes continue to hold the status in Jewish and Christian cultures that Achilles and Socrates held in ancient Greece. The Bible's preeminent position as the cornerstone of all religious wisdom and instruction in Judaism and Christianity has given it an influence in people's lives well beyond any other book. As such, the Bible profoundly shapes the way that people understand their own identities and place in the world.

Because the Bible covers such a vast range of historical periods and circumstances, describing events that are said to have happened over a range of a thousand plus years, it presents a diverse cast of characters and enables a rich discussion of their heroism. Indeed, millions of people around the world read the "Good Book" precisely with this goal in mind: looking to its protagonists as models for their own ideals of faith, courage, love, self-sacrifice, repentance, service to others, and devotion to a higher purpose.

As you will soon discover (see the introduction), the Bible's definition of heroism is different than that prized in the general culture. Biblical heroes are esteemed not because of a seemingly major accomplishment, such as leading an army to victory, but usually because of a moral accomplishment—such as leading a people to justice. Biblical heroes are also significantly more relatable. They look like all of us: rich and poor, men and women, children and the elderly, and so on. Even more importantly, they act like many of us: they can be heroic *and* deeply flawed.

Welcome on a journey to discover heroes you may have met before and even think you know well, but who appear here in a new light—one that, I hope, will give you the impression that you're encountering them as if for the first time.

About This Book

The book arose from my own experiences as an observant Jew reading the weekly Torah portion in synagogue on Shabbat. I've always loved the kind of close reading practiced by ancient rabbis in their commentaries, but what's often harder to discern is how we are to understand the overall character of people in the Bible. It is assumed that we are supposed to admire them—but for what is much less clear. The more I read their stories, the more I was left with questions rather than answers: What makes these characters great? How are we supposed to emulate them? If they are heroes, why do the stories include so many puzzling and disturbing actions?

When I started working on this book, my perspective was largely shaped by the debates over the literary canon and the question of the

Bible's place in our culture. Should the traditional canon still hold pride of place in our educational system? Has the canon's exclusion of the voices of women and people from minority groups rendered it obsolete, or should we keep the canon and expand it? How does the Bible fit into these debates? After all, the Bible is the cornerstone of the Western canon; in fact, the word "canon" itself was originally applied to the Bible, referring to the measure determining which books would be accepted or excluded when the Bible was given its final form. But if the canon itself is up for grabs, does the Bible lose its privileged position?

By investigating the Bible's portrayal of heroes, I sought to go deep in a scholarly area that rendered the Bible of continued value and cultural relevance. Particularly, I came to believe that in an age in which previous cultural hierarchies are deconstructed and all verities are questioned, the Bible is surprisingly contemporary because it deconstructs its own heroes, both affirming and undermining them.

The Biblical Hero examines biblical stories with an eye to what they have to teach us about the idea of a hero. While the exploration of Bible characters as heroes is hardly new—that examination extends back at least to the writings of Philo (late first century BCE–mid-first century CE) and surely, in unwritten form, centuries earlier—this work is designed to shed novel light on the biblical hero through comparisons to characters from other cultures, authors, eras, and traditions. It investigates the Bible as a major source for conceptions of human stature, agency, and potential for self-transcendence through the ages. It probes how the Bible's depiction of people is shaped in relation to its understanding of God. It also analyzes the challenge presented by monotheism in depicting human greatness in the Bible.

This book is not a work of traditional biblical scholarship, even as it is informed by that scholarship. Instead, *The Biblical Hero* is in the tradition of books (ranging from literary studies to sociology and philosophy) that read the Bible as establishing paradigms reverberating among readers and writers down the centuries.

Here's a brief roadmap. The introduction presents the Bible's view of heroes and compares biblical heroes to ancient and American paradigms. Next is an in-depth portrayal of the Bible's most important hero, Moses—the singularly complex and conflicted founding figure of the Jewish religion. Subsequent chapters examine different types of biblical heroes: Samson, strongman; Esther, queen; Abraham, pilgrim; Jacob, trickster; David, king. Extended comparisons with famous figures from world literature provide insight into their heroic characters. The last chapter asks: Is God the Bible's true hero? Finally, drawing from broad biblical analysis, the conclusion presents five takeaways about heroes designed to help guide how we select and project heroes today.

The British novelist E. M. Forster coined the term "round" (as opposed to "flat") characters: multifaceted individuals whose motivations are revealed as we read—in essence, characters who "jump off the page." To my mind, the six heroes discussed in this book are the roundest, most surprising, and most interesting characters in the Bible, by far. I believe they most fully embody the twin imperatives of biblical characterization: they are both noble and fallible, remarkable and flawed. Eluding simple moral categories, they demand that we as readers recognize their goodness, valor, and/or piety as well as their troublesome characteristics. We are expected to engage with them—or, perhaps better said, to engage our own moral conscience as we work at interpreting and assimilating the different sides of their characters.

Of course, there are far more biblical figures who did not make it into this book, and some readers may question my choices, so let me offer these brief additional explanations. Solomon is noble and fallible, but not at the same time—he's noble at the beginning and corrupted at the end. Joshua's story occupies considerable biblical space—a book with twenty-four chapters—but he comes across as a relatively simple character who lives in Moses' shadow. Joseph's story is often considered one of the most perfect in all of literature, but to my mind, as a hero, Joseph is largely an extension of his father Jacob (as discussed in the Jacob chapter). Ruth's story—casting the bonds of family and community aside to join her mother-in-law Naomi and become a part of the Israelite people—is among the most moving in the Bible, but Ruth lacks the troublesome depths of the characters featured here.

If we define "hero" more typically as "one who takes bold action in leadership," then a great many more women, Yael and Deborah among them, would fit the bill. Deborah, aside from being a prophet and poet, is counted among the chieftains who serve as national leaders in the book of Judges. She instructs her general Barak in military strategy, ascends to the battlefield with her army, and stirs them to a rout of their Canaanite enemy. Yael, the wife of Heber the Kenite, an ally of Israel, then completes the rout. She invites Sisera, the fleeing Canaanite general, into her tent, gives him milk, known for its narcotic properties, to slake his thirst, lulls him to sleep, and drives a tent peg in his temple. But we do not see other sides to these two women. The problem is, almost all of the biblical women, along with the vast majority of men, lack the full range and depth of the most paradigmatic biblical heroes. If we take the standard of a literary hero to mean a fully rounded character, I believe only a few men and one woman qualify.

The selected heroes in this book are not necessarily to be understood as *better* than the other characters in the Bible. In fact, from a standpoint of morality, more than one is highly suspect. But, I contend, these characters are the deepest, bearing the greatest mixture of light and shadow. And as such, they most fully embody the Bible's vision of human heroism.

Some might consider it odd to find a chapter on God as a hero. My intention was not to be irreverent. Indeed, originally I had no plan to write such a chapter. The more I dug into biblical characters, however, the more I found that the Bible portrays its characters as unheroic — and then the more necessary it became to consider whether the Bible's underlying message is that God is the one and only being worthy of heroic stature. Also, I recognized that in most stories, the hero is the one who occupies the most real estate, and in the Bible God alone is present from beginning to end. I became convinced that it was important to reflect on what it might mean to attribute heroism to God.

By the time I finished writing this book, the world had become increasingly chaotic, polarized, and terrifying. In this light, heroism has come to seem much more real, necessary, and important. Worldwide, people who stand up to report the truth and support justice, human rights, and better government policies are often mocked and vilified. They risk their reputations, careers, and sometimes their lives as they pursue their holy work. My prayer is that this book helps you to think more deeply about heroes, to choose them wisely, and to honor the heroes in our midst.

Using This Book

This book is apt for use in a variety of settings.

Clergy and educators engaged in adult as well as youth education, as well as high school teachers in religious or supplemental schools, can use this volume to deepen conversations with students of all ages about biblical heroes. Teachers may wish to begin by framing the concept of a hero and the relation of biblical heroes to other well-known heroes, as discussed in the introduction. It shows how, instead of ignoring, minimizing, or interpreting away biblical characters' uncomfortable actions, we can understand them as part of a larger vision. From there, educators can select characters from the book for in-depth analysis and discussion. I recommend consulting the Study and Discussion Guide to this book, which can be found at jps.org/books/the-biblical-hero/, for guidance on passages to focus on and questions to spark reflection and conversation.

College instructors of religion can use this book to inspire discussions on a range of issues that relate to religion in general, and the particular qualities of the Bible. For example, how do religious texts portray the nature of their founders? What qualities do they possess? Are they divine or human? What relation do they have to God or supernatural forces/ beings? Chapter 1, on Moses, can help sharpen the comparison between Judaism's founder and the founders of other religions and heroes more generally. This book can serve to highlight the Bible's portrayal of the relationship between God and people, which is never straightforwardly positive even with more faithful characters (Moses, Abraham), nor so clearly disapproving of ethically dubious heroes (Samson, Jacob, David). At other times, God is absent, perhaps working behind the scenes (Esther). The question of what makes a text religious, and furthermore how religious texts are similar to as well as differentiated from secular texts, can be approached by exploring the resemblance between biblical and literary characters (see below). The introduction and chapter 7, on God, invite a broad conversation on the biblical depiction of monotheism and humanity's status and role on earth, in comparison with other forms of monotheism, polytheism, and alternate religious traditions.

Professors of English or comparative literature will find here abundant comparisons between biblical protagonists and literary heroes from different cultures. The introduction situates the biblical conception of heroism in relation to portrayals of heroes in both the ancient Mediterranean and American cultures. While chapter 1, on Moses, concentrates on delineating the unique features of a biblical archetype, the remaining characters are illuminated by their resemblances to literary cousins. Samson's resemblance to Heracles renders him a "fish out of water" in the context of biblical storytelling. Like Scheherazade, Esther tells stories to a depraved king in order to save lives. Jacob's saga is elucidated by his similarity to other tricksters, including Odysseus, Coyote, and Reynard the Fox. Abraham's story is read as a pilgrimage, connecting him to Aeneas and Bunyan's Pilgrim. And David, like Julius Caesar, appears as a leader squeezed in the vise of his ambition. Additionally, the chapters feature ways in which biblical characters draw upon earlier characters and shape each other: Esther is a second Joseph, Abraham reprises Adam, David contains an inner Samson, and Jacob's family are all tricksters like him.

For individuals who are committed to reading the Bible, the book will prompt lively conversations with spiritual leaders, friends, and family. To make the most of those conversations, reference the suggested readings and guiding questions in the Study Guide (jps.org/books/the-biblical-hero/).

Acknowledgments

This book started at Makor, a (now defunct) center of the 92nd Street Y, where my colleague Wendy Sabin Lasker encouraged me to present my first ideas on this topic as a talk to her daytime audience. Dr. Ahron Friedberg gave me the opportunity to present my theory of biblical heroes to a working group of psychiatrists at Mt. Sinai Medical Center. The rabbinical team at the Hebrew Institute of Riverdale, Steven Exler and Ari Hart in particular, have inspired me by their intellectual acuity and spiritual audacity, and have generously invited me to teach there over the years. During my time in graduate school at Indiana University, my many extraordinary and devoted teachers provided models for rich literary study of the Bible, biblical interpretation, and Hebrew literature; these include Meir Sternberg, Bernard Levinson, James Ackerman, Sam Preus, and my advisors and friends, Herb Marks and Stephen Katz. I also drank deeply from the wisdom and friendship of my fellow graduate student Jean-Pierre Sonnet, SJ.

I have been blessed to discuss some of my ideas here with like-minded companions, and I want to especially mention Pinny Bulman, poet and biblical exegete extraordinaire, for his incessant willingness to share discoveries, entertain new ideas, and critique mediocre ones. Thanks to Barry Holtz for recommending that I submit my manuscript to The Jewish Publication Society (JPS). JPS director Rabbi Barry Schwartz gave the initial manuscript a prompt and enthusiastic reading, helped me shape it, and ushered me through the publication process. Joy Weinberg, JPS managing editor, is the most dedicated and talented reader I have met, possessing an uncanny ability to grasp the potential in a sentence, paragraph, or chapter that lies beneath a tangled forest of words. My profound thanks as well to the University of Nebraska Press, for giving JPS a home to continue their tradition of excellence.

I am enormously grateful for the support of Gary Rendsburg, who read the book with consummate attention and made numerous corrections, suggestions, and references that have both spared me embarrassments and enhanced my awareness of the scholarship. I take full responsibility for all flaws in reasoning, expression, or scholarship.

Last but first, I thank my wife Adele, who supports my work every day with her love and encouragement; is my devoted, meticulous, and honest reader (complete with architectural renderings); and provides me with the sustenance to find meaning and pursue my eclectic quests.

Author's Note

In this book, the word "Bible" is a shorthand for the Hebrew Bible, known in Hebrew as TANAKH, an acronym for Torah-Prophets-Writings, the three sections in which the Jewish Bible is divided. Among Christians, the Hebrew Bible is known as the Old Testament. Between the TANAKH and the Old Testament, there are differences in the order of biblical books and in the interpretation of their significance. (A framework for grasping these differences can be found in the introduction to Rabin, *Understanding the Hebrew Bible*, 9–16.) All the biblical quotations in the volume are taken from TANAKH: *The Holy Scriptures, The New JPS Translation According to the Traditional Hebrew Text* (The Jewish Publication Society, 1988), except for occasional deviations when relevant to my discussion.

INTRODUCTION

Heroic-Unheroic Heroes, the Biblical Model

We must represent men either as better
than in real life, or as worse, or as they are.
  —Aristotle, *Poetics*

To grasp the way the Bible portrays its heroes, one must start by understanding the place of humanity within the wide canvas of Creation. God has created the world such that people—all people—stand together on a high rung on the ladder of beings:

When I behold Your heavens, the work of Your fingers,
the moon and stars that You set in place,
what is man that You have been mindful of him,
mortal man that You have taken note of him,
that You have made him little less than God,
and adorned him with glory and majesty? (Ps. 8:4–6)

The Psalmist projects astonishment in two directions. When he looks in the heavens, he appreciates the enormousness of the universe—all, in his eyes, the work of God's hands. On this cosmic scale, human existence seems insignificant, a mere pittance. Yet at the same time, on the terrestrial level, people are "adorned in glory and majesty," granted power like a god on earth. Despite the inconceivable difference between God and people, God has nonetheless fashioned humanity with tremendous care, granting people powers above all other creatures on earth. From the first perspective, humankind is impossibly distant from God; from the second perspective, humankind is so close, a "little less than God."

These two perspectives form the warp and woof from which biblical stories are woven.

The Babylonian creation epic the *Enuma Elish* (Tablet VI) presents humanity's mission in far less glorious terms:

> As Marduk hears the words of the gods,
> His heart prompts him to create ingenious things. . . .
> [Marduk says,] "Blood will I form and cause bone to be;
> Then will I set up *lullu*, 'Man' shall be his name! . . .
> Upon him shall the services of the gods be imposed that they may be
>   at rest."[1]

This creation story solely emphasizes the contrast between people and gods. Marduk, the chief god, creates humankind as servants of the gods. People are to do the hard work so that the gods can live a life of leisure.

The Bible's Creation story, by contrast, does not present humanity's role as being in service to God. (This perspective only arises in Genesis 4, in the story of Cain and Abel, well after the Creation account.) Instead, the Bible's opening chapters emphasize the Psalmist's "little less." When God rests on the seventh day, the text does not say that people step in to serve God; rather, God establishes a rhythm of work and rest that (we discover later) is given to people as well: "The Israelite people shall keep the sabbath, observing the sabbath throughout the ages as a covenant for all time. . . . For in six days the Lord made heaven and earth, and on the seventh day He ceased from work and was refreshed" (Exod. 31:16–17). The Bible thus underscores the *resemblance* between humanity and God.

This resemblance is in fact the unmistakable message of Genesis 1: "And God said, 'Let us make man in our image, after our likeness. They shall rule the fish of the sea, the birds of the sky, the cattle, the whole earth, and all the creeping things that creep on earth.'" People resemble God in both their actions and their being. They are called to rule the earth just as God rules the universe. And they are in God's image in the fiber of their existence.

Etymology powerfully reveals the Bible's sense of the resemblance between people and God. The Hebrew word for image, *tzelem*, comes from the Akkadian word *tzalmu*, referring to a physical, man-made object, often a statue or figurine of a king. In some contexts, a *tzalmu* denotes an object in which a divinity chooses to reside.[2] There is something of God within people: people are uniquely god-like, ontologically distinct from other creatures. People are not the image of God, the *tzalmu* itself, but "in" God's image. They are not gods, but similar to God in some fundamental ways. Crucially as well, all people, "male and female," are created in this same condition; no person is created with more or less of God's image.[3] The Bible conceives of human creatureliness in radically democratic terms. This understanding is reinforced by the Covenant between God and the Israelites at Sinai: The body of laws apply equally to all members of the nation.

When we consider the Bible's opening portrait of humanity in this context, we get a glimpse of the challenges that await human heroes. As the Bible has it, a gap extends between God and people. In some ways, at certain times, this gap appears small, the distance merely a "little less"; God seems less a remote, forbidding monarch than a parent speaking to a capable, maturing child. In other ways, at other times, the gulf seems enormous, unbridgeable. Either way, according to the Bible, all people reside together on the other side of this gap. No special individuals—no heroes—can jump over to the far shore, to God's side.

The Bible's emphasis on the essential distance between people and God deeply colors the way it portrays all characters. The biblical narrator ensures that the reader is always cognizant that human heroes are not, and can never become, divine. Compared to heroes that readers encounter from other cultures, then, biblical heroes begin with a profound handicap.

The Problem with Heroes

All the legendary characters in the Bible are marked by flaws, doubts, and ambiguities—just as one would expect to find in real life, but not in an ancient religious document. Often they harbor lust and ambition;

they can also be self-centered, deceitful, and vengeful. Unlike other ancient texts, which tend to wink at their heroes' foibles, the Bible is typically unforgiving. The Bible's God does not judge the characters' failings lightly; these heroes usually reap their comeuppance.

Nor do they improve noticeably with age. The Bible depicts their senescence as a time of physical decay without the compensations of sagacity and honor. As they grow frail and their senses dim, they fall prey to the ambitions of kin and courtiers who compete time and again to inherit their power, wealth, and authority. In short, the closer one examines the biographies of biblical heroes, the more difficult it can be to discern what is heroic about them.

Joseph Campbell, author of *The Hero with a Thousand Faces*, the best-known scholarly tome about heroes, must have registered this disappointment, because his book does not contain any examples drawn directly from the Bible. Only three biblical heroes are mentioned in his volume, and all of their adventures are told in Midrash, a body of Rabbinic teachings that expand upon biblical stories. How startling: of the "thousand faces" of heroes drawn from writings and oral traditions worldwide, Campbell cannot find any faces from the original Bible stories worthy of even a footnote!

Perhaps the source of the oversight derives from Campbell himself. First, he was intent on introducing his readers to unfamiliar examples from non-Western sources. Furthermore, his predilection for myth may have steered him away from the Bible's polemical opposition to myth. Nonetheless, the Bible's absence from Campbell's "bible" on heroes surely reveals something crucial about the Bible itself. Its heroes do not fit comfortably into the mold of "the hero with a thousand faces." As heroes go, biblical heroes are singularly unheroic.

Midrash often restores a mythical or legendary dimension to the spare and unflattering tales found in the Bible. One of Campbell's three midrashic examples drawn from biblical characters imagines the circumstances behind Abraham's birth. For its part, the Bible tells us nothing about the birth of its first great man, only "When Terah had lived seventy years, he begot Abram, Nahor, and Haran" (Gen. 11:26). This sentence concludes a list of "begats" enumerating the generations between Shem and Abraham. A dryer, less romantic account could not exist.

The Rabbis who interpreted this story wanted to know more about Abraham—and assumed there must be more to know. In their eyes, a hero does not enter the world just like everyone else, like Arpachshad, Peleg, and Serug, to pick examples from the list of begats. Here's a summary of the midrash Campbell quotes at length:

> King Nimrod read in the stars that a boy would be born who would rise up against him and show that his religion was false. To defend himself against fate's decree, Nimrod ordered the midwives to kill off all boys born in his kingdom. Seventy thousand boys were killed. At this time, Terah married Abraham's mother. When she was ready to give birth, she hid in a cave to avert the terrible edict. After giving birth, she wrapped up the boy in a garment and left him in the cave, praying for God's help. The angel Gabriel caused milk to flow from the little finger of Abraham's right hand. At ten days old, Abraham left the cave. He saw the stars come out and thought they were gods, but when they descended he realized they were not. He saw the sun rise and thought it was a god, but when the sun set he realized it was not. Then he saw the moon and reckoned it as a god, but when clouds obscured it, Abraham said, "This, too, is no god! There is One who sets them all in motion."[4]

This midrash weaves a legend around Abraham's birth where the Bible is entirely silent. The story's components match many typical features of hero myths. A prophecy, before his birth, heralds that he will overthrow the king (in many myths the king figure is the protagonist's father). The king attempts to kill him, but the boy is spared and exposed, that is, abandoned to the elements (often in water, here in a cave, both images clearly symbolic of the womb). He receives nourishment, often miraculously by animals (here by the angel Gabriel). He grows up to kill or defy the king.

The Rabbis who created this midrash incorporated within this hero myth elements specific to the Bible. Most saliently, Abraham is transformed into a proto-Moses. Abraham rebels against a cruel, oppressive tyrant, just as Moses rises up against Pharaoh. The king decrees the destruction of all male children, just as Pharaoh does. Furthermore, the king employs midwives as the agents of slaughter (in Egypt, though, the midwives refuse to comply).

The midrash finds its proto-Pharaoh in Nimrod. From Genesis 10:8–12, we learn that Nimrod is a "mighty hunter by the grace of the Lord"— hence, a powerful man and monarch—and his kingdom extends from Babylon to the surrounding areas of Mesopotamia (modern-day Iraq). As the only ruler mentioned in these chapters of Genesis to have commanded the region where Abraham is born, Nimrod is the most likely biblical candidate for the king whom Abraham must oppose.

It seems the Rabbis felt they needed this hero myth to comprehend the biblical account of Abraham. After all, the Bible leaves out some crucial information: Why did God choose Abraham to be the founder of the Israelite nation? How did Abraham come to abandon the religion of the surrounding culture and discover monotheism?[5] In other words, the Bible does not explain what made Abraham a great man worthy of God's attention. Through this midrashic story and others, the ancient Rabbis attempt to fill in this rather large gap in the story.

What is more, the Rabbis want to see Abraham, the religion's founder, in far more visibly heroic terms than the biblical account offers.[6] By planting his discovery of God's oneness at the age of ten days, the Rabbis depict Abraham as superhuman. And by rendering all aspects of his birth and survival as miraculous, they elevate Abraham to a heroic status comparable to heroes from other cultures. The tendency to varnish portrayals of biblical heroes is found not only in the legendary tales of Midrash, but even within the Bible itself. The book of Chronicles, for example, among the last biblical books to be written (and the last to appear in the Jewish Bible), scrubs the tarnish off the image of the most famous Israelite kings. Chronicles often repeats verbatim passages from the book of Kings, so the author's choice to omit or change passages is indicative of a conscious editorial decision.[7] Take King Solomon. A cursory comparison between the summations of his life in Kings (the first excerpt to follow) and (then) Chronicles points to a whitewash of Solomon's flaws:

> King Solomon excelled all the kings on earth in wealth and in wisdom. . . . King Solomon loved many foreign women in addition to Pharaoh's daughter—Moabite, Ammonite, Edomite, Phoenician, and Hittite women, from the nations of which the Lord had said to the Israelites, "None of you shall join them and none of them shall join you, lest they turn your heart away to follow their gods." Such Solomon clung to and loved. He had seven hundred royal wives and three hundred concubines; and his wives turned his heart away. In his old age, his wives turned away Solomon's heart after other gods. . . . Solomon slept with his fathers and was buried in the city of his father David; his son Rehoboam succeeded him as king. (1 Kings 10:23, 11:1–4, 11:43)

> King Solomon surpassed all the kings of the earth in wealth and in wisdom. . . . Solomon slept with his fathers and was buried in the city of his father David; his son Rehoboam succeeded him as king. (2 Chron. 9:22, 9:31)

Here, the book of Kings offers a deeply contradictory assessment of one of the Bible's greatest rulers. 1 Kings 10 catalogs Solomon's greatness, albeit largely in materialistic terms: other rulers paid homage to his wisdom—with tributes of precious metals, spices, robes, weapons, and horses; Solomon assembled a massive army of chariots and built numerous cities in which to station them. Yet 1 Kings 11 tells a very different story, at far greater length: Solomon's entanglement with one thousand wives and concubines aroused God's anger and incited the division of the kingdom. In short, the narrator has combined two kinds of material: the first praising the late king, the second condemning him. The second, which overpowers the first in length and impact, seems primarily concerned with historical causality, explaining how the kingdom came to fall apart so soon after the legendary king's reign.

2 Chronicles, written centuries later,[8] neatly excises the long critical insertion, thus restoring Solomon to his original glory as a flawless administrator and paragon of wisdom. Its narrator places the blame for the downfall of the United Monarchy squarely upon the shoulders of Solomon's son Rehoboam.

Classical Model: The Hero as King

Two broad categories of heroes distinct from the biblical model are the classical model and the American model.

Heroes are not born out of thin air; they arise from a society's deeply held values, which in turn reflect the political, social, and economic relations among people at a given time and place. The classical model arose in societies where a single person held complete or nearly total control over the reins of power. Classical heroes are usually considered to have made a significant mark on human history. Outside of founders of new religions or religious movements, such figures have mostly been kings or the equivalent. The king was considered a microcosm of society as a whole; through his domicile and vestments, family and entourage, bureaucracy and army, he symbolized the country in which he ruled. Louis XIV's boast "l'État, c'est moi" ("I am the state") is such an assessment of the king's role in a monarchical state. The king's power represents the state's power; his opulence represents the nation's wealth; his honor represents the collective honor of the people. Hence, the king is naturally the hero of the state he rules, because, at least in theory, his very personage embodies all his subjects' hopes and aspirations.

In the classical model, the hero-king differs from his subjects not merely in status but in his nature. He is "better," or above, ordinary people. Very often the king is a demigod, descended from a deity within a few generations. Even when not, he is endowed with qualities far beyond the capabilities of ordinary mortals. In ancient Egypt, the pharaohs were considered incarnations of gods, and the Japanese emperors are thought to be descendants of the sun goddess. European monarchs claimed authority to rule by the "divine right of kings," while Chinese emperors reigned thanks to the "Mandate of Heaven." Similarly, most of the people surrounding the heroes come from elevated ranks touched by divine status.

This pattern holds equally true in literary portrayals of the classical hero. Homer's epic poem *The Iliad* provides a striking illustration. The poem recounts episodes of the Greek victory over the Trojans during the Trojan War (ca. the thirteenth to twelfth centuries BCE). Of the hundreds of people named, all are generals, princes, or royalty of the numerous islands and potentates in the region. The other soldiers who fill the ranks remain nameless, and indeed they leave scarcely a trace in the narrative. The hierarchy is pitiless: Just as the lesser princes stand no chance in combat against the greater ones, so the ordinary soldiers get no glory in battle because they cannot survive against a semidivine opponent.

One might think that the military subject of *The Iliad* determines its focus on leaders; after all, a modern history of a war would likely also concentrate on the strategies of generals and admirals. Yet Homer's other great epic, *The Odyssey*, which recounts Odysseus's wanderings homeward from the Trojan War, is completely devoid of military scenes and is nonetheless largely confined to the same stratum of society. Odysseus's men do earn a reference, but the portrait is generally brief, tragic, and far from flattering (e.g., "They looked like nine-year-old porkers" in Circe's house[9]). In Homer, heroes resemble the gods much more than they do other humans.[10] Both heroes and gods lie, squabble, fight, even die. Gods often take the appearance of people, and the two can reproduce together. At crucial moments in battle, gods help heroes become temporarily invulnerable, activating their divine genetics, as it were. Heroes are also capable of injuring gods, binding them, holding them prisoner. For example, after Aphrodite complains that Diomedes the warrior stabbed her while she was rescuing her son Aeneas, her mother, Dione, provides perspective with a catalog of similar attacks against the gods:

Have patience, my child, and endure it, though you be saddened.
For many of us who have our homes on Olympos endure things

from men, when ourselves we inflict hard pain on each other.
Ares had to endure it when strong Ephialtes and Otos,
sons of Aloeus, chained him in bonds that were too strong for him,
and three months and ten he lay chained in the brazen cauldron;
and now might Ares, insatiable of fighting, have perished,
had not Eëriboia, their stepmother, the surpassingly lovely,
brought word to Hermes, who stole Ares away out of it
as he was growing faint and the hard bondage was breaking him.[11]

The leading hero of *The Iliad*, Achilles, most noticeably blurs the distinction between human and immortal. On his father's side he is the great-grandson of Zeus; just as Zeus is the most powerful of gods, Zeus's heir and favorite is the most fearsome warrior. When Zeus is on his side, Achilles becomes awe-inspiring, untouchable. Gods who throw their support behind other warriors cannot defend their charges against the favorite of the supreme storm god:

Not powerful Acheloios matches his strength against Zeus,
not the enormous strength of Ocean with his deep-running waters,
Ocean, from whom all rivers are and the entire sea
and all springs and all deep wells have their waters of him, yet
even Ocean is afraid of the lightning of great Zeus
and the dangerous thunderbolt when it breaks from the sky crashing.[12]

The notion that a hero-king erases the boundary between people and the gods can be traced back to the origins of written culture in Mesopotamia (a region extending in an arc from contemporary Iraq to Syria). The Mesopotamian ritual of sacred marriage, dating back to the third millennium BCE, provides a remarkable example of this boundary crossing. By performing this ritual, the king was believed to have guaranteed the success of the crops and herds. After an elaborately prepared ceremony accompanied by poetry, the king would have intercourse with a queen or priestess specifically to stimulate the fecundity of nature. During the act, the king and his consort were considered not merely to represent gods, but to fully become them. The ancient Near East historian Thorkild Jacobsen explains: "As the human king could take on the identity of the god of fertility and yield, so the queen or perhaps a high priestess would probably have assumed in the ritual the identity of [the goddess] Inanna, embodying the numen of the storehouse."[13]

The ambivalent identification of a hero-king with a god is most evident in the cluster of materials that have survived around the greatest Mesopotamian hero, Gilgamesh. Most likely, Gilgamesh was a successful warrior-king from the mid-third millennium BCE. He was the first great popular hero, whose story, chiseled in tablets found throughout Mesopotamia and beyond, appeared in an epic poem as well as separate tales.

His biography establishes the contours of the classical hero. He is mortal, but both of his parents are gods. He is a political ruler, having constructed the walls of his city, Uruk, and a military ruler who leads the people of Uruk in a war of liberation. Proving his more-than-human status, Gilgamesh challenges and defeats the gods. In league with his friend Enkidu, he decapitates the monster Huwawa, insults the goddess Ishtar after she proposes marriage to him, and kills the feared bull of heaven Ishtar sends in revenge. Distraught after Enkidu dies, he seeks the secret of immortality from his ancestor Utnapishtim, who lives forever on an island beyond the waters of death. In the end, though, he fails to capture the secret and returns to Uruk, resigned to his human fate.

The Bible's Objections to Classical Heroes

Biblical protagonists appear to be anything but equivalents of heroes and leaders such as Gilgamesh and Achilles. Specifically, the Bible objects to four aspects of the classical model.

1. Confusion between human heroes and a god. In general, classical heroes appeared closer to gods than to fellow mortals. The boundaries between ancient heroes and gods were tenuous and quite permeable; heroes were usually descended from gods, and even became gods, sometimes by deities inhabiting them for short periods. There are so many examples in Greek literature of people being transformed into gods that the Greeks created a term, "apotheosis," to identify this pattern.

By contrast, the biblical worldview insists on the unbridgeable chasm between divinity and mortal life. The Bible's "a little less," indicating the short distance between people and God, looms enormous in comparison to the proximity between classical heroes and deities. By emphasizing human flaws and limitations, the Bible builds a fence around human aspirations. This is part of God's message in the Garden of Eden story: Don't try to become "one of us."[14]

2. The elevation of an elite portion of society and denigration of the rest of the people. The biblical narrative does not share this aristocratic perspective. The Bible tells many more stories of people far removed from the center of power: servants, lepers, rabble-rousers, resident aliens, disinherited daughters, and more. The repeated censuses of the Israelites in the book of Numbers drive home the point: every member of society "counts." This democratic spirit can be attributed to a relatively young and weak Israelite society, which never had an opportunity to develop an entrenched aristocracy elevated by great power and prosperity.

3. The absence of moral standards. A classical hero is measured only by the glory of victory. Biblical heroes, by contrast, are expected to conform their behavior to God's will as expressed through Divine law. Even kings are held to the same rules and precepts as the rest of society:

> When he [the king] is seated on his royal throne, he shall have a copy of this Teaching [Torah] written for him on a scroll by the levitical priests. Let it remain with him and let him read in it all his life, so that he may learn to revere the Lord his God, to observe faithfully every word of this Teaching as well as these laws. Thus he will not act haughtily toward his fellows or deviate from the Instruction to the right or to the left, to the end that he and his descendants may reign long in the midst of Israel. (Deut. 17:18–20)

For biblical heroes, success is not ultimately dependent on their strength, fate, or even Divine intervention. It comes from their adherence to the terms of the Covenant—their study and internalization of God's commandments. Most biblical heroes are in positions of power, and thereby have more opportunities to transgress. Ultimately, they are judged by how they navigate these considerable challenges.

4. Idealization of power. Whereas for classical heroes, power is tantamount to glory, the Bible repeatedly shows people in authority— rulers, priests, the wealthy—oppressing the poor, flaunting their wealth, engaging in debauchery, and otherwise perverting religion by favoring ritual and ignoring morality. In fact, most of the kings, judges, and other Israelite leaders have their deeds weighed in the scales of unforgiving justice. And, unlike the heroes in most ancient historical documents, their failings, together with their virtues and accomplishments, compose their eternal legacy.

The American Model: Democratic Hero

The classical hero stood at the helm of a world in which distinctions between different classes of people was taken as a fact of nature. The American hero, developed after the American Revolution, took aim at this traditional social structure and flattened it like a toppled wedding cake. Ever since, American heroes—and indeed, heroes from countries throughout the world that have embraced democracy—represent the values of a democratic society. No longer can one person sitting atop the social order embody the entirety of the state.

Unlike their ancient counterparts, American heroes do not inherit their roles at birth, nor get to keep them for life. Take American presidents, who are sometimes deemed heroes. They have to compete to earn power from the hands of the people. Even when that power is secured, it is limited by the Constitution, politicians, and the public. Presidents are largely beholden to the will of the people, and the people's will is embodied in the notion of public opinion. Because public opinion can be fickle, is easily swayed, and is often harshly divided, it's extremely difficult for even the best of presidents to retain the consistent esteem of the people and establish the enduring respect of a hero.[15]

And how the electorate regards them is crucial, for no rituals of power, special thrones, robes, or crowns will ensure their continued popularity and consequent reelection. What is more, even if presidents do preserve their good graces with the public, they can only hold onto power for a short time. The first American president, George Washington, set the tone: In the words of historian Garry Wills, he "gained power from his readiness to give it up."[16]

American Literary Heroes

American heroes are by no means limited to the people on top. In the nineteenth century, Walt Whitman's poetry gave voice to a hero celebrated for being ordinary, anonymous, a part of the new urban masses. To Whitman, the greatness of modern democracy lay in the culture of movement, encounter, change, a vast engine churning people back and forth, colliding and embracing in their daily rounds. Princes and serfs no longer occupied fixed, separate quarters of the social universe, with an elite perched above the rest of humanity. In the burgeoning democratic culture of the United States, it became possible for every person to become a hero.

In his poem "Song of Myself," Whitman presents himself as a representative of the new democratic citizen:

> Divine am I inside and out, and I make holy whatever I touch or am touch'd from,
> The scent of these arm-pits aroma finer than prayer,
> This head more than churches, bibles, and all the creeds.[17]

In Whitman's view, every person is "divine," a mini-god. Whitman especially finds heroism in people who were not previously reckoned heroic. Aiming his lens on individuals at or near the bottom of society, he exuberantly and capaciously touts sailors and farmers, current and escaped slaves, even "those who have fail'd" as heroes:

> Vivas to those who have fail'd!
> And to those whose war-vessels sank in the sea!
> And to those themselves who sank in the sea!

And to all generals that lost engagements, and all overcome heroes!
And the numberless unknown heroes equal to the greatest heroes
known![18]

Whitman built the keyboard on which American writers would play the song of the new heroism. Other heroes summoned by American writers (Willa Cather, John Steinbeck, Erskine Caldwell, Edgar Lee Masters, Thornton Wilder, James Agee) could be characterized as "salt of the earth": common, decent, hardworking, poor, sometimes immigrant men and women. Examples include the 1930s subsistence farmers in Steinbeck's *Grapes of Wrath*, driven from their homes by poverty and dust storms; or the more than two hundred small-town characters in Masters's *Spoon River Anthology*, who reveal their secrets, woes, and jealousies as they recite their lives in poems uttered from beyond the grave. In Masters's collection, no one person rises in heroism above another; the town itself, in its aggregation, is in effect the protagonist.

Still other writers (Theodore Dreiser, Nelson Algren, Damon Runyon, Flannery O'Connor, Raymond Carver, Charles Bukowski, and Jim Thompson, among others) trawled for and raised up heroes on the seedy side of American life: hard-luck cases ("grotesques" in the language of Sherwood Anderson), pimps and prostitutes, drug addicts, bohemians, gangsters, assorted miscreants, even murderers. Often they portrayed their protagonists as "antiheroes," characters who transgressed socially acceptable norms and morals, sometimes in the name of a higher good or philosophy. Runyon's short stories from the 1920s and 1930s (the basis for *Guys and Dolls*) romanticized the life of petty criminals and bookies; Thompson's 1940s and 1950s dime-store thrillers such as *The Killer inside Me* brought readers into the mind of killers who engage in sexual violence. Still another variation of American heroes (by authors such as Richard Wright, Malcolm X, Eldridge Cleaver, William Styron, Alice Walker, and Toni Morrison) can be found in depictions of African American rebels. Toni Morrison's *Beloved* portrays the pain and courage of an escaped slave who kills her child rather than have her captured by bounty hunters, and Malcolm X's *Autobiography* recounts his change from a criminal to a black nationalist.

Perhaps the most popular and quintessential model of American hero is the outsider. Just like immigrants the world over have come to America's shores to escape restrictions and persecutions, start afresh, and make their fortune, this new hero is what literary critic R. W. B. Lewis calls the "American Adam": a person with no ties to the past who ruptures social formalities and is continually self-inventing.

> The Adamic hero is the equivalent, in American fiction, of the prince or king in the long tradition of classical drama. The telling distinction is one of strategic distance: the distance at the outset between the hero and the world he must cope with. For the traditional hero is at the center of that world, the glass of its fashion, the symbol of its power, the legatee of its history. But the American hero as Adam takes his start outside the world, remote or on the verges; its power, its fashions, and its history are precisely the forces he must learn, must master or be mastered by. Oedipus, approaching the strange city-world of Thebes, was in fact coming home; the hero of the new world has no home to begin with, but he seeks one to come.[19]

In this formulation, society is a compromising web of artifice and deceit, hence requiring the hero to consciously step outside it in order to preserve the integrity and purity of his self.[20] Such diverse writers as Herman Melville, Henry David Thoreau, Mark Twain, Ernest Hemingway, Raymond Chandler, Jack Kerouac, and J. D. Salinger cultivated the Adamic outsider as hero. Melville's mid-nineteenth-century nautical protagonists create their own society off of the mainland, while in *Walden*, Melville's contemporary Thoreau lives amidst the pastoral serenity of nature, in opposition to a clamorous and corrupt human civilization.

A prime example of this American hero in popular culture is the Western gunslinger. He is a mythical creature born yesterday. No one knows where he comes from; he seems to be without parents or family, friends, or hometown. No teacher is known to have trained him. He is wholly self-made, in such a manner that we never get to see the making. No matter how long he stays in one place, he will never plant roots there; nor will the locals ever fully accept him, no matter how vital he is to the town's survival. Once his job is done and the banditos are routed, the hero must move on.

Perhaps no actual figure personified this American ideal of the hero as outsider with greater popular appeal than Charles Lindbergh. With one thirty-three-and-a-half hour flight, Lindbergh went from being an unknown midwestern stunt aviator and mail flier to the first modern celebrity.[21] He was not the first pilot to fly across the Atlantic; in fact, eighty-one people had made the trip before him. But because his was the first solo flight, and the flight was accompanied by a $25,000 prize, spurring intense competition and media interest, Lindbergh's flight caught the American imagination and drew attention in a way few other events have, before or since. This latter-day Daedalus, a lone adventurer who defied and conquered the elements by himself ahead of competitors throughout the world, embodied the collective dream that, as cultural historian Leo Braudy put it, "the will is finally free, untrammeled by social forms, the expectations of others, or the pressure of the past—bounded if at all only by the confines of nature."[22]

Comparing Biblical and American Heroes

In many ways, the biblical model is closer to the American model than the classical model. This truth is not altogether surprising, given the Bible's enormous influence on American culture.

For starters, in neither model can the hero be reduced to a single person who sits atop the social pyramid. Just like American presidents, biblical leaders such as Moses and David are depicted with suspicion and subject to judgment (as we see in chapters 1 and 6). Even as presidents are prone to attacks from opposing parties, politicians, and pundits, so too biblical kings (such as David) wither under the criticism of prophets endowed with God's judgment against them and suffer the scheming of power-hungry opponents (such as David's son Absalom's quest to supplant him).

Similarly, the Bible shares the American faith that everyone, regardless of gender, profession, wealth, or position in the social order, has the potential to become a hero. The character Rahab in Joshua 2 provides a textbook example: A prostitute in the city of Jericho, she saves the lives of two Israelite spies by hiding them, lying about their whereabouts, and abetting their escape by lowering a rope down the city walls.

A third resemblance between biblical and American heroes lies in the prevalence of characters who are outsiders to differing degrees. Far from the embodiment of the Israelites' will, Moses is often portrayed as estranged from them. The question posed by an Israelite slave in Exodus 2—"Who made you chief and ruler over us?"—hovers over his entire career as a leader. He is frustrated by the people's incessant complaints about the hardships of desert life and requires God's help to suppress an internal rebellion against his authority. As for Samson, the text calls him a "judge"—in effect, he is a chieftain of Israel—but he spends most of his life among the Philistines instead of his own people, chasing women and massacring his personal enemies.

The biblical prophets established the paradigm of the outsider with justice on his or her side. Like the American cowboy and gunslinger, the biblical prophet is often portrayed as acting alone against overwhelming odds to restore justice, truth, and compassion in a society corrupted by the rich and powerful. When Elijah first encounters Ahab, the Israelite king, he greets him with contempt: "Is that you, you troubler of Israel?" (1 Kings 18:17). With no one but God on his side, Elijah triumphs over four hundred false prophets, Ahab's lackeys, to convey God's harsh judgment on the despotic ruler and predict his downfall at God's decree.

However, the American model goes beyond the biblical one in reversing the traditional values of hero worship. Often, in the American narrative, the outcasts can do no wrong, while the leaders and powerful can do no right. For Whitman, quoted above, the "fail'd" are heroes precisely *because* they failed, because no one had ever thought to make them heroes. In a similar vein, some American novels justify all the actions of underdog heroes precisely because of their powerlessness. Bigger Thomas, the hero of Richard Wright's controversial novel *Native*

Son, for example, commits rape and murders two women, yet Wright judges him with considerable sympathy, as a victim of society.

Although the Bible is emphatically sympathetic to the plight of the poor, orphan, and widow, it also insists that all members of society share an equal obligation of moral responsibility: "You shall neither side with the mighty [or multitude] to do wrong—you shall not give perverse testimony in a dispute so as to pervert it in favor of the mighty—nor shall you show deference to a poor man in his dispute" (Exod. 23:2–3).

Furthermore, the Bible teaches that the pretense or fantasy of freedom outside of community, like that of the American Adam, is far from salutary—it is dangerous. The solution to an unjust society is not to escape from it but to restore its principles of justice and equity: "Justice, justice shall you pursue, that you may thrive and occupy the land that the Lord your God is giving you" (Deut. 16:20). Again, take the biblical prophets as an example. The prophets depicted as biblical heroes (many "court prophets," fulfilling a function in the royal entourage, are not considered heroes) regard their outsider status as a temporary phase conditioned by corrupt leadership and widespread immorality. The stench of sin compels them to proclaim their, and God's, denunciation. Once those blights are atoned for, however, the prophets presumably can cease from inveighing and reintegrate with their society. By contrast, after the Western cowboy restores order, he rides his horse into the sunset. He retains the mystique of the outsider forever.

Judaism Is Not Mosesism

The diminished stature of heroes in the Bible can also be seen by contrasting Moses' place in Judaism with that of leading exemplars in other religions. Unlike most other religions, Judaism is not based on hero worship.

For Christianity, Islam (Muhammadism), Confucianism, Buddhism, and Zoroastrianism, the religion's message is inseparable from the adoration of the message's original bearer. The religion's founder is considered to be perfect, a model for all adherents to emulate throughout the generations. Judaism, by contrast, is not "Mosesism." Despite Moses' centrality in the Torah, Moses is too flawed in character, too physically weak, and too limited in his role to be venerated. He is mentioned surprisingly little in the rest of the Bible, mostly in the expression the "Torah of Moses." In the Bible he is not the paragon of wisdom—Solomon is; nor is he the greatest leader—that is David.

The same holds true for Moses' place in Jewish tradition. Consider that in the Passover Haggadah (the text read at the seder table containing a collection of ancient Rabbinic teachings about the Exodus), Moses is mentioned only once—and even there he is not acknowledged as a hero, but called "My [God's] servant." In fact, the Haggadah greatly minimizes Moses' role in Israel's salvation, thereby increasing God's credit in the process.

A well-known midrash (Talmud Menahot 29b) envisions Moses visiting the academy of Rabbi Akiva, who lived some thirteen centuries later. Moses does not understand Akiva, yet "his mind [is] set at ease" when Akiva attributes his teaching to "Moses, given at Sinai." The Rabbis recognize Moses as the supreme receiver of the law, but not the supreme interpreter.

Judaism does not invest in one central role model because it does not propose that one human being can so greatly exceed all others in the quest for perfection. One cannot imagine Jews asking, as Christians do of Jesus: What would Moses do? Likewise, Jesus's biography is an essential message of Christianity, and the same can be said of Muhammad for Islam or Buddha for Buddhism; their lives embodied their messages. By contrast, even without Moses' presence, the religious messages in the Torah largely endure.

Put plainly, Moses is the transmitter, not the originator, of God's laws. The Torah makes it clear that Moses is not to be mistaken for an object of worship. Perhaps most telling in this regard is that the Torah is not given first to Moses, as God's appointed vessel, to then be conveyed to the people. Rather, God gives the Torah to all the people standing at Mount Sinai. Since the people grow fearful of God's presence, Moses steps in to receive God's word, but the fact remains that God's intended communication was to all the people at once. God effectively conveys the message: Do not confuse any human intermediary with Me.

At the end of Deuteronomy, the Torah calls Moses the greatest Israelite prophet who ever lived, because he saw God "face to face." Yet even this praise appears somewhat mixed. A prophet is not the primary role associated with Moses' career, and his close relationship with God derives as much from God's special care for him as from any of Moses' particular qualities. Also, Jacob makes the identical claim to have seen God "face to face" after wrestling with the angel (Gen. 32:31).

Moses thus serves a most ambiguous role: as a hero to emulate, and as an object lesson against turning people into heroes.

The Unexpected Patterns of Biblical Heroes

Just as, in history, a general may win a battle one day and die by the sword the next, so too the stories of biblical heroes generally do not conform to a familiar or expected pattern. The life of Jacob provides an apt illustration. God appears to him in a dream to reassure him of God's protection; in the next sequence, his uncle Laban fools him into marrying the sister he does not love and to working on Laban's farm for twenty years to marry the other. No sooner does he reconcile with his long-lost brother Esau and establish his new home in the land of Canaan than his daughter Dinah is raped and his sons massacre the entire village. God grants him a magnificent blessing (like Abraham's): He will father not only one nation but many. The next moment, his favorite wife, Rachel, dies in childbirth.

In the Bible, a heady distance also lies between the narrator and the characters. Narrators do not identify with biblical characters; biblical heroes are depicted to be judged as much as celebrated. Literary scholar Meir Sternberg notes that the biblical narrator brings an arsenal of narrative resources to sharpen the reader's attentiveness to the multiple layers of these stories and characters: a range of viewpoints among diverse characters, the narrator, and God; a variety of artfully planted gaps in the story; and the use of repetitions, often with subtle discrepancies.[23]

Such techniques thwart the likelihood of the reader's straightforward identification with the biblical hero.

Even when heinous acts ensue, the Bible's objective narrator sometimes refrains from voicing judgment. In the story of the rape of Dinah (see chapter 5), for example, whom the narrator holds responsible remains unclear. Is blame to be cast on Shechem, who commits the rape but then attempts to rectify the situation by marrying Dinah and undergoing circumcision? Or does the true villainy rest with Dinah's brothers Simon and Levi, who avenge the deed through a massacre? The narrator's reticence leaves the Bible's judgment ultimately in doubt. By highlighting the complexity of human character and motivation, the Bible renders its heroes as both recognizable and troubling in the reader's eyes.

Occasionally, the narrator's judgment does emerge, but well after the original transgression and in the voice of a character. For instance, after King David sleeps with Bathsheba and arranges for her husband's death so he can marry her, the narrator refrains from condemning David's actions. Later in the story, however, David's prophet Nathan accuses David of abusing his power to commit adultery and murder, and conveys God's anger and punishment: "[God said,] Therefore the sword shall never depart from your House—because you spurned Me by taking the wife of Uriah the Hittite and making her your wife" (2 Sam. 12:10). David's crimes are now clearly condemned, but by putting the censure in the mouth of God, through Nathan, the narrator preserves the objectivity of his own voice. The storyteller tells the facts and leaves judgment to God. And, in most stories, even God does not weigh in.

What is more, the Bible presents dozens of heroes or potential heroes rather than one single, flawless hero. This abundance serves to provide us with a spectrum of models of both people and actions that can be considered heroic and worthy of admiration—men and women, young and old, fighting and counseling, leaders and loners. To return to Moses, he may be the greatest prophet ever, but Abraham (who argues with God over the fate of entire cities), Isaiah (who has a vision of God seated upon the Divine throne), Elijah (who castigates King Ahab and reveals his four hundred prophets of Baal to be imposters), and Jeremiah (who conveys God's message of hope and comfort after the destruction of Jerusalem) are surely not too far behind. Each fulfills the prophetic role in a completely different way.

The Bible teaches us both to have high expectations of our leaders *and* to tolerate their imperfections. It teaches us that it is worthy to have heroes—exemplars who can help us climb higher as individuals and as a society—*and* to view them as they are, not as we wish them to be.

Biblical heroes are role models precisely because of the difficulties they encounter, both out in the world and inside themselves. Readers are not meant to remove the parts they don't admire like bones from a fish, because then one misses the message of the Bible's portrait of heroism: Biblical heroes are like us, so that we may be like them.

Because the Bible is much richer than it is often portrayed, it can speak to a great many of us, whether we happen to be religious or secular, believing or agnostic. Its complex heroes hold our attention and fascination, as they did for people thousands of years ago.

1

MOSES

Prototype

In Jewish tradition, Moses is deemed *Moshe rabbeinu,* "our teacher Moses." His character, behavior, and actions exemplify lessons that Jews are to study in the Bible every week throughout the year, in the attempt to parse their meaning and integrate the moral guidance into their lives.

Moses' greatness is certainly apparent in the Bible's portrayal. We see it in his bold actions, taken both alone and in obedience to God's instructions. We see it in his ability to persevere despite rebellions against both his and God's authority and to preserve the cohesion of the people during their long suffering in the desert. We also see it in his implanting in his followers an understanding of God's laws, and in his creation of the social and political structures that enable them to fulfill God's will. In the words of the first-century Jewish philosopher Philo, "Having brought himself and his own life into the middle, as an excellently wrought picture, [Moses] established himself as a most beautiful and Godlike work, to be a model for all those who were inclined to imitate him."[1] As the person who leads the Israelites during the crucial period of their formation, Moses is portrayed as the prototype of the biblical hero.

Perhaps the most powerful teaching embedded in Moses' leadership lies in the paradox of his humility: "Now the man Moses was very humble, more than any other person on the face of the earth" (Num. 12:3). The terms "leadership" and "humility," which on the surface appear to be opposites, according to the Bible are inherently related—to wit, greatness in leaders is proportional to their humility. Moses' greatness resides in the consciousness he always bears of living together with all of his fellows on the far side of the gap from God. Being selected by God does not make him into a god.

At certain times Moses does grow frustrated with the people—he is not a paragon of patience—but he nonetheless chooses to throw in his lot with them rather than set himself apart. After the sin of the Golden Calf, God proposes to destroy the people and create a new line directly from Moses; Moses, however, insists that he would rather be erased from God's book than for God to erase the Israelites. In the Bible there is no finer example of leadership, independence, and strength of character, exercised humbly in devotion to and identification with the people.[2]

Since Moses is the Bible's preeminent leader and prophet, the founding legislator of Israelite religion and the ruler who shaped a population of slaves into a unified nation that rebelled against its mighty oppressors, a reader might expect to find Moses portrayed as larger than life at every turn. Such a reader, if well versed in heroic writings from other cultures, would surely be perplexed by the conflicted portrait of Moses encountered here. The biblical Moses defends his followers one moment and then disparages them the next. He vigorously and repeatedly asserts his inability to lead, but then leads the people with vigor. He is supposed to be their model of proper behavior, but marries a non-Israelite, a union forbidden repeatedly in the Bible, before seeming to abandon her and their children. As a magistrate he judges the cases people bring before him with equanimity, but at the end of his life, his caustic bitterness, ignited by his own short fuse, colors his judgment of all the people. Ultimately, he never entirely wins over the flock he reluctantly leads. He is a leader charged with giving the people hope, who, when stuck in the middle of the desert, himself loses hope of ever arriving at the Promised Land.

Although Moses frequently speaks with God, divinity does not rub off on Moses. (For the sole exception, see "Moses as Leader: Playing God" below.) Instead of buffing the hero's image by portraying Moses at a reverential distance, the Bible gets close to Moses, finding faults and complications in his relationships with his family, the Israelites, and even with God. The biblical stories seem to invite us to learn from Moses' flaws as much as from his virtues; in the words of Aaron Wildavsky in *Moses as Political Leader*, "Moses' mistakes are almost his most important legacy."[3] Precisely as a multifaceted, imperfect leader whose greatness is annealed with his all-too-human character, Moses offers the quintessential model of a biblical hero against which other biblical figures are to be measured.

Heroic Frame

In birth and death, Moses' life is framed in classic heroic terms. In between, the course is far more serpentine and problematic.

The story of Moses' heroism begins with his birth (Exod. 2:1–10). Notably, the tale bears marked similarities to the nativity scenes introducing many other heroes, including what is known as the "exposed-infant motif."[4] One rather close parallel is seen in this account of the birth of Sargon, the great Mesopotamian king who reigned from 2333 to 2279 BCE:

> I am Sargon the great king, king of Agade. . . .
> My mother, the high priestess, conceived me, she bore me in secret.
> She placed me in a reed basket, she sealed my hatch with pitch.
> She left me to the river, whence I could not come up.
> The river carried me off, it brought me to Aqqi, drawer of water.
> Aqqi, drawer of water, brought me up as he dipped his bucket.
> Aqqi, drawer of water, raised me as his adopted son.[5]

Like Sargon, Moses was born in secret to a family of priests, hidden by his mother for three months. Both heroes were placed, like a message in a bottle, in a river; both of their mothers laid them in wicker baskets made waterproof with sealant of pitch. The two heroes were discovered and raised by strangers. Subsequently, both become rulers of their people.

These similarities help bring to focus some important differences between the two accounts. We do not learn why Sargon's mother hid her son and exposed him to the elements; we might conjecture that, by Sargon's time, these plot elements were clichés expected of any hero-king. By contrast, the Bible contextualizes the actions of Moses' mother: The Egyptians have decreed the death of all Israelite boys. Notably, here the target is not Moses in particular, but Moses as a member of the Israelites. Meanwhile, Pharaoh is anxious—not that Moses will kill him and usurp his throne, but that the Hebrew inhabitants will grow too numerous and support an enemy army. Thus, even in describing Moses' birth, the Bible withdraws some glory from Moses, apportioning it instead to the people whom he will serve. The focus shifts from the hero-king to the nation, in accord with the transition from a narrative based on myth to one trained on history.

In the stories of their rescue, Sargon and Moses also take opposite social trajectories. Sargon is saved by Aqqi, a lowly water carrier, after which he must wend his way back up to the throne. The story empha-sizes his obstacles; his heroism lies in overcoming them. Moses, starting out life as a slave, though of the preeminent Levite tribe, is rescued by Pharaoh's daughter and raised in Pharaoh's court. Moses' heroism lies in rejecting the comforts of the court and the trappings of royal power; he accepts his identification with the enslaved Israelites and chafes at their oppression. Moses' youth in Pharaoh's court renders him worthy of leadership as the only Israelite not ground down by slavery.

Another crucial difference between the stories lies in the narrative voice. Sargon recounts his own legend: "I am Sargon the great king, king of Agade." The use of the first-person voice renders his account as a boast narrative—the hero gloating of his great deeds and claiming credit for society's accomplishments under his reign:

> I became lord over and ruled the black-headed folk,
> I . . . [ ] hard mountains with picks of copper,
> I was wont to ascend high mountains,
> I was wont to cross over low mountains.[6]

Contrastingly, the Bible's third-person narrative adds distance and a certain objectivity to Moses' account. Not only is there no braggadocio, there is no discernible distinction between this story, these characters, and all the stories that come before and after in the Bible's epic history. After all, as opposed to Sargon's chest-thumping (admittedly not without justification, considering the extent of his conquests), the opening lines of Moses' birth could not be more unassuming: "A certain man of the house of Levi went and married a Levite woman. The woman conceived and bore a son." No grand annunciations, on heaven or earth, accompany the birth of this unnamed child to unnamed parents. He does not even receive a name until verse 10, a long delay by biblical standards.

Moreover, in between, the story emphasizes the care and cleverness of the people who rescue and raise Moses: his mother and Pharaoh's daughter. The Bible has removed the spotlight from its hero to cast it upon the secondary characters. In essence, by its depiction of its central hero, the Bible makes clear that Moses' heroism is of a different order than the heroism of characters in other cultures. Instead of overshadowing others, Moses shares attention with the figures around him.

As with his entrance, Moses' departure too recalls the exeunt of classical heroes (at least at first glance): "So Moses the servant of the Lord died there, in the land of Moab, at the command of the Lord. He buried him in the valley in the land of Moab, near Beth-peor; and no one knows his burial place to this day" (Deut. 34:5-6). His death more or less conforms to the criteria and pattern that Lord Raglan describes for the expiration of a hero: "18) He meets with a mysterious death, 19) Often at the top of a hill. . . . 21) His body is not buried."[7] Certainly, Moses' death is enigmatic. He dies standing atop Mount Nebo, "the summit of Pisgah" (Deut. 34:1), where God has just granted him a panoramic vision of the land into which he shall not enter. The special attention God affords Moses in his final minutes signifies the unique, personal relationship between Israel's human and Divine leaders.

Then, mysteriously, from a literal reading of the text, God commands Moses' death and buries him in an unknown grave in the Moab valley. When it comes to the third criteria, contra Raglan, Moses *is* buried, but the location is hidden.[8] By our not knowing the site of the hero's tomb, it is as if he is everywhere among us.

Yet even this seemingly straightforward framing of Moses' heroic status is not entirely waterproof. Consider the description of Moses in his final scene. What does death "at the command of God" (Deut. 34:5) mean? The expression *'al pi*, literally translating as "at the mouth" of God, is a common idiom conveying "at God's behest." The verse appears to be a continuation of God's description of Moses' death two chapters earlier: "[The Lord spoke to Moses: . . .] Die on the mountain that you are about to ascend, and be gathered to your kin, as your brother Aaron died on Mount Hor and was gathered to his kin; for you both broke faith with Me among the Israelite people, at the waters of Meribath-kadesh in the wilderness of Zin, by failing to uphold My sanctity among the Israelite people" (Deut. 32:50–51). In this passage, Moses' death appears brutally unheroic—a punishment for his failure to faithfully execute God's instructions. God had commanded him (in Numbers 20) to speak to a rock to obtain water for the Israelites; instead he struck a rock. Note that God's command in Deuteronomy 32:50 is the imperative verb "Die!" The prettier account in Deuteronomy 34, in which God personally buries Moses, cannot obscure the fact that the relationship between the two is laced with conflict to the very end. Only in the closing verses of the Torah does the narrator step in to buff Moses' reputation as a flawless paradigm of Israelite heroism: "Never again did there arise in Israel a prophet like Moses—whom the Lord knew face-to-face."

The Rabbinic tradition develops these conflicting currents in the Bible's depiction of Moses' end. Rashi, representing the majority of commentators, prefers his hero to go out in style. Instead of taking the expression *'al pi* at face value, to mean "at the command of," Rashi understands the idiom literally: "at the mouth of" means "with a kiss"!⁹ Rashi further comments that "And he buried him" in the next sentence means, "The Holy One, Blessed Be He, by Himself." God cared so much for Moses that God chose to make all the arrangements for the burial, unlike all other people who are buried by human hands.

However, some other interpreters cling to the more negative judgment of Moses found in Deuteronomy 32:50–51. Onkelos, a translator of the Torah into the Aramaic language, renders *'al pi* as "according to the word" of God—that is, God's command. Rabbi Ishmael (quoted by Rashi, from Sifrei Bamidbar 32) conceives of Moses as actually carrying out God's final order: "And he buried him" (Deut. 34:6; note ambiguity of pronouns) means "he buried himself"! In Rabbi Ishmael's vision, the unheroic spectacle of Moses' death as punishment is transformed into a paradoxical sort of apotheosis in which Moses obeys God to the unimaginable end. In atoning for his infidelity in Numbers 20, Moses carries fidelity to the extreme, performing his own form of self-immolation. Notably, Rabbi Ishmael lived during the Roman era. Perhaps he had in mind Jewish martyrdom during that time, for in essence he defines a hero as one who obeys God in the face of excruciating circumstances.

As with his birth, Moses' death encapsulates both heroic and unheroic elements. Some aspects are reminiscent of other literary heroes; others diverge markedly from standard heroic depictions. This mixture characterizes Moses' life from cradle to grave.

Heroic Résumé

The traditional hero is measured first and foremost by his actions, and not by interior qualities. What kind of a hero would Sir Lancelot have been, for example, if he wasn't the strongest and bravest knight of his day, triumphing in countless armed encounters and rescuing a myriad of damsels in distress? Moses likewise performs his share of courageous and heroic deeds. The deeds we hear of come mostly from the beginning of his life, as a means of establishing his bona fides as the supreme Israelite hero.

Moses' very first actions, killing an Egyptian taskmaster and breaking up a fight between two Hebrews (Exod. 2:11–15),[10] telescope a cluster of his enduring heroic qualities:

> When Moses had grown up, he went out to his kinsfolk and witnessed their labors. He saw an Egyptian beating a Hebrew, one of his kinsmen. He turned this way and that and, seeing no one about, he struck down the Egyptian and hid him in the sand. When he went out the next day, he found two Hebrews fighting; so he said to the offender, "Why do you strike your fellow?" He retorted, "Who made you chief and judge over us?[11] Do you mean to kill me as you killed the Egyptian?" Moses was frightened, and thought: Then the

matter is known! When Pharaoh learned of the matter, he sought to kill Moses; but Moses fled from Pharaoh.

Moses immediately evinces the characteristics that will justify God's choice of him as leader in chapter 3. Despite his royal Egyptian upbringing, he knows he is an Israelite, a relative of the slaves. As he observes their oppression, he sympathizes with them and ventures out to be near them. And once he witnesses the cruelty of slavery firsthand, he takes prompt, decisive action to alleviate the slave's suffering, even at the cost of killing the oppressor.

Note that just one day later, when Moses attempts to break up a contest between two Israelites, he has a considerably more difficult time asserting his leadership. Not only do both men reject his authority, they use their knowledge that he killed the Egyptian against him. The passage foreshadows Moses' future success in striking the Egyptians, and future difficulties in directing his own charges.

At this early point, Moses stands before us as both a conventional and an unconventional hero. Similar to characterizations of other heroes, Moses' decisiveness, strength of body and mind, and fearless ability to act in ways no one else would dare demonstrate he is destined for extraordinary achievement. However, unlike other heroes, who take actions first and foremost to elevate themselves, Moses acts entirely for others: his Hebrew kinsmen. Other heroes are driven by desires for adventure, revenge, or glory; Moses is driven by sympathy for the slaves.

Furthermore, the Bible's depiction of the act of killing is also unheroic. In traditional heroic tales, killing adds to or even defines the glory of the hero, but here it is drawn in far darker shades. Before Moses acts, he looks both ways, fearing he will be discovered and his reputation among the Egyptians compromised. What other ancient hero would think twice before lopping off his opponent's head? Furthermore, the method of killing lends him no honor. There is no struggle from which our hero emerges victorious; in fact, the story gives the impression that Moses struck the Egyptian from behind. What is more, the Hebrew slaves, whom we might expect would laud Moses for his bold deed, do anything but. They explicitly deny that the killing affords Moses any right to be considered a hero. Moses will have to find other ways to prove his mettle and earn the people's respect.

In addition, Moses acts as a leader before God assigns him that role, and the people undermine his authority even before he has authority! Whereas other heroic sagas cast their leaders as near flawless paragons holding a divine right to govern that no one (excepting scamps and renegades) is allowed to question, Moses learns from the outset that he cannot rely on the trust and reverence of his followers. His judgments will not go unquestioned; his rule will not abide unshaken.

Last, in contrast with traditional heroes who plunge into action with little forethought and few cares, Moses acts with calculating deliberation. He surveys the situation, then proceeds. He remains cautiously aware that action can bring unwanted consequences.

When on the subsequent day the Hebrew slaves taunt him about his killing, Moses does not react in anger to their provocation. Instead, he instantly gleans the relevant information—his life is threatened—and flees the kingdom rather than submit to Egyptian henchmen. For all his bursts of rage later in life, here Moses proceeds with cold calculation, weighing the evidence and determining the necessary course of action. He lacks the supernatural strength of most other heroes; instead, he must survive by the same means—insight, planning, alacrity, decisiveness, willingness to move forward or retreat, and some luck—required by most human beings.

The next scene, in which Moses meets his wife, Zipporah, clinches the early portrayal of his heroic qualities. "Now the priest of Midian had seven daughters. They came to draw water, and filled the troughs to water their father's flock; but shepherds came and drove them off. Moses rose to their defense, and he watered their flock" (Exod. 2:16–17). This episode repeats certain formulaic events earlier in the Bible's narrative that together make up a "type-scene," in the words of literary critic Robert Alter.[12] Readers are likely to catch the parallels between this scene ("betrothal at a well") and similar ones matching Isaac with Rebecca (Gen. 24:10–61) and Jacob with Rachel (Gen. 29:1–20).

The variation with Moses here is distinguished primarily by its concision and its emphasis on Moses' actions. Whereas previous versions of this type-scene require fifty-two and twenty lines, respectively, this time the story occupies only six and a half lines (Exod. 2:15b–21). Perhaps the biblical narrator determined that by this time, readers would know the crux of the story, and so a less elaborate narrative would suffice. Regardless, there is a more crucial distinction between the Patriarchal narratives in Genesis and Moses' actions in Exodus: In the earlier stories, there is no nation apart from the individuals whose stories are being told. Abraham, Isaac, Jacob, Joseph, and their wives and siblings *are* the people of Israel; their stories, therefore, constitute the history of Israel. Moses, by contrast, is only one person among a large and growing community. Apparently, the narrator no longer desires to luxuriate upon an episode involving Moses that will have little to do with the history of the people he is about to lead.

Unlike previous versions of the betrothal scene, the story in Exodus seems to have one sole purpose: to boost Moses' profile as a hero. Strikingly, the woman he will marry, Zipporah, is absent from the scene until the very end. At the well, she is merely one of seven nameless daughters. Contrast this with the portraits of Rebecca, who shows hospitality to a stranger (Abraham's servant) by giving him and his camels water (Gen. 24), and Rachel, a beautiful shepherdess whom Jacob approaches and kisses after watering her flock (Gen. 29). The as-yet-still-unidentified Zipporah does not learn Moses' name at the well—and in fact, all she hears of Moses is misleading, as the sisters call him "an Egyptian man." She is not invested either with the romance of Rachel or the reader's admiration of Rebecca. In fact, all the Midianite sisters come across as helpless damsels in distress who never remember to show courtesy and invite their hero Moses in for a bite. Zipporah's diminished role portends the lack of affection and the broken relations between the two.

Moses gets the spotlight—he saves the day: "Moses rose to their defense, and he watered their flock." His act in response to conflict with an oppressor (here, nasty shepherds), and the verb "save" (*hoshi'a*), foreshadow the much greater act of salvation he will help orchestrate in the chapters to follow. Here, however, his heroic action is told in only one short line! Nothing illustrates more clearly how little the biblical narrator adheres to standard measures of heroism.

Rather than dwelling on Moses the individual, the narrator wants to hurry back to the main events of national importance. While he must establish Moses' credentials, he does so as swiftly as possible, lest the reader think the book is about Moses and not about Israel. And when the biblical account takes stock of Moses, it zeroes in solely on those characteristics that will define him, and render him worthy, as a leader.

Self-Doubts and Reluctance

When Moses encounters the Burning Bush, his internal conflicts burst forth in dizzying abundance. This scene, which contains one of the longest exchanges between God and a human being in the Bible, offers us the best opportunity we have to understand Moses, because here he reveals his personal feelings to a far greater degree than in any other encounter. One might think that this should be Moses' crowning moment: his selection for leadership by none other than God. Instead, it becomes an increasingly barbed exchange between characters acting at cross-purposes:

> But Moses said to the Lord, "Please, O Lord, I have never been a man of words, either in times past or now that You have spoken to Your servant; I am slow of speech and slow of tongue." And the Lord said to him, "Who gives man speech? Who makes him dumb or deaf, seeing or blind? Is it not I, the Lord? Now go, and I will be with you as you speak and will instruct you what to say." But he said, "Please, O Lord, make someone else Your agent." The Lord became angry with Moses. (Exod. 4:10–14)

Moses' reluctance to don the mantle of authority stems in great measure from a sense of his own unworthiness. Unlike other heroes, he is not the product of a divine bloodline—some adulterous dalliances between a god and a person that would have affirmed his privileged status. Rather, he is just a man born of man and woman whose royal aura faded as soon as he abandoned his position in Pharaoh's court. Now he appears as a lowly stuttering shepherd attached to the Midianites after having fled his home and country. At this point in Moses' career, God's promises to "send [Moses] to Pharaoh, and [Moses] will free My people, the Israelites, from Egypt" (Exod. 3:10) sound as absurd as God's promise of a son sounded to ninety-year-old Sarah.

Moses' reluctance derives as well from his uncertainty about the task demanded of him: Is this a people he wants to lead, or who want him to lead them? The Hebrew slaves have questioned his authority, rejecting his spontaneous bid to judge the dispute between two slaves and intimating that he is not a hero but a cold-blooded killer. How can he possibly be fit to lead an entire nation of such people?

A paradoxical dialectic is at work in their exchange. God's speech to Moses is a demonstration of God's omniscience and omnipotence. When Moses raises objections regarding his ability to serve as leader, God swats them away time and again with reassurances of God's support. With God's backing, no problem can stand in Moses' way, no dangers lie unforeseen. Yet for all God's power on the plane of history, God cannot even convince Moses to act the part of God's spokesman and messenger. No blandishments, perks, or promised assistants seem able to convince Moses to accept the role God proposes for him. Instead, Moses keeps prodding God for more signs of Divine providential guidance. While at first Moses' requests seem aimed at bolstering his shaken confidence, at a certain point Moses' persistent demurrals accumulate into a provocation to God's authority:

Who am I that I should go to Pharaoh and free the Israelites from
    Egypt? (Exod. 3:11)
When I come to the Israelites and say to them "The God of your
    fathers has sent me to you," and they ask me, "What is His name?"
    what shall I say to them? (3:13)
What if they do not believe me and do not listen to me, but say: "The
    Lord did not appear to you?" (4:1)

Moses seeks to account for every eventuality in advance; he needs to know how he can conquer Egyptian might and Israelite skepticism. His questions start large—*Why me?*, *Who are You?*—and get smaller, more detailed: *What if they don't believe me?*, *How can I, a stutterer, speak before Pharaoh?* God's answers seek to allay Moses' anxiety by affording him a unique revelation into God's secrets. God reveals a Divine Name not granted to the Hebrew Patriarchs (3:14), as if to say to Moses: "You can trust in Me, because you know Me with an intimacy that even your great ancestors did not enjoy." God reveals to Moses an outline of the plan of history about to commence: the people's liberation from slavery and entry into their homeland. God stoops to lend Moses magical instruments with which he can impress the people, and concedes, against God's will, to allow Moses' brother Aaron to become Moses' spokesman. Yet even after all this, Moses still does not wish to accept God's assignment.

In the end, because God is more persistent and powerful than Moses, God's will overcomes Moses' resistance. Still, Moses never says "I agree" to God's demands; he merely abandons the field of argument.

Precisely herein lies a further paradox central to the biblical conception: Moses' reluctance to play the role of hero is what elevates him to true heroic status. In the eyes of the biblical narrator, he is a hero because of, not despite, the fact that he does not want to play one. (We will see this same paradox fleshed out in David.)

If Moses' complaining and self-doubts render him an authentic hero, then why did "The Lord [become] angry with Moses" (Exod. 4:14) when he asked God to appoint another leader? Perhaps it is because the Bible's hero problem creates a problem as well for its depiction of God. In classical mythology, the gods demonstrate their power by supporting their heroic half-divine, half-human progeny. With the Bible etching such an indelible portrait of its heroes' humanity, stripping them of all pretensions to deification while ennobling all mankind as "children of God," it is not so apparent how God can utilize heroes as instruments for Divine glorification and achievement of God's designs in history. God's flash of anger toward Moses, God's greatest agent, seems to express God's frustrated recognition that Moses will not serve as the simple channel of Divine will. God cannot inhabit Moses like Zeus lends his spirit to Achilles in *The Iliad* or Athena takes human form to support Odysseus in *The Odyssey*. And not only hasn't Moses offered God temporary residence; he has let God know that he will be a singularly unpliant, insecure conveyor of God's intentions.

In short, the scene at the Burning Bush provides an epiphany not just to Moses but also to God: God will be challenged to influence the course of human events without a steady supply of reliable heroes to draw upon.

Partial Visions

In many hero stories, one of the key gifts that deities often shower on their heroes is the privilege of visions.[13] The hero enters into supernal realms forbidden to ordinary mortals. There he (for the hero is usually male) comes into contact with the godhead and sees an image filled with dread and power. He usually cannot make sense of this image but yearns to penetrate its mysteries. The divinity allows him to obtain partial understanding, and the hero takes the knowledge he has been given back to human society. This new, revealed knowledge becomes widespread among the people, affording humanity as a whole some access to the gods through the thick gauze separating the earthly from the cosmic spheres.

The visions God shows to Moses put him squarely in the same category as other religious and cultural heroes. Although many other heroic Bible figures—especially the prophets—receive visions, God grants Moses more visions, more iconic visions, and more crucial visions concerning the course of Israel's history. If visions constitute an index of a hero's greatness, then Moses is surely the Bible's greatest hero.

Yet God's visions for Moses do not represent pure access to Divine secrets. Instead, these visions afford and deny access simultaneously. God does not give Moses a key for understanding these visions (as some of the later prophets receive). Rather, Moses' visions are like the backward glance of Adam and Eve after their expulsion: They can peer inside, but the angels and their flashing swords obstruct their view. Insofar as Moses' visions convey a message, part of that message is that there are things that people should not know, cannot know, and will not be allowed to know. People can go beyond their mortal estate, can perceive beyond their physical senses, only to a point. Even Moses, the Bible's archetypal hero, cannot see God in any simple, straightforward sense. Moses' visions of God reveal his human blinkers.

God's initial appearance to Moses at the Burning Bush is tantalizingly unexplained. Unlike God's initial approach to Abraham, God first reaches out to Moses not through words but with an enigmatic image:

> Now Moses, tending the flock of his father-in-law Jethro, the priest of Midian, drove the flock into the wilderness, and came to Horeb, the mountain of God. An angel of the Lord appeared to him in a blazing fire out of a bush. He gazed, and there was a bush all aflame, yet the bush was not consumed. Moses said, "I must turn aside to look at this marvelous sight; why doesn't the bush burn up?" When the Lord saw that he had turned aside to look, God called to him out of the bush: "Moses, Moses!" He answered, "Here I am." And He said, "Do not come closer. Remove your sandals from your feet, for the place on which you stand is holy ground. I am," He said, "the God of your father, the God of Abraham, the God of Isaac, and the God of Jacob." And Moses hid his face, for he was afraid to look at God. (Exod. 3:1–6)

Why the indirection? Why the need to entice Moses to approach the bush, and to puzzle over its significance, before God speaks to him?

Perhaps the answer lies in a crucial difference between the Patriarchs and Moses. One of the most striking characteristics about Moses at the beginning of this scene is his utter incomprehension that he is in the presence of something supernatural. He acts like a scientist encountering an unfamiliar species of flora: "I must turn aside to look at this marvelous sight; why doesn't the bush burn up?" It is as if a magnifying glass and a sketch pad might help him explain this phenomenon. When he discovers that God is calling him from the bush, Moses is overwhelmed with surprise and hides his face. In this scene, Moses is acting like most people would if they stumbled on God's presence; he is thoroughly unprepared, filled with dread, and convinced that "there must be some mistake," for he is altogether unworthy of such a visitation.

Moses' attitude in God's presence distinguishes him from the three Patriarchs, who always seem ready for—and, sometimes, even expecting—God's call. When God first speaks to Abraham in Genesis 12, instructing him to go forth from his land "to the land that I will show you," Abraham immediately "went forth as the Lord had commanded him." No doubts, no hesitation, no dialogue! We know not how—by temperament or biography—Abraham was prepared to receive the voice of God, but this is certainly not so of Moses. Perhaps because of his Egyptian upbringing, Moses appears completely unfamiliar with the God of the Israelites. The Burning Bush thus serves as a transitional device, a means of training Moses to the presence of the supernatural as a step toward speaking to God. Had God spoken to him directly at first, Moses might well have fled (as he did from Pharaoh).

Moses' next vision is perhaps the strangest:

> Then Moses and Aaron, Nadab and Abihu, and seventy elders of Israel ascended; and they saw the God of Israel: under His feet there was the likeness of a pavement of sapphire, like the very sky for purity. Yet He did not raise His hand against the leaders of the Israelites; they beheld God, and they ate and drank. (Exod. 24:9-11)

The first striking thing about this apparition is its democracy: A vision of God is revealed not just to Moses but to the entire hierarchy of Israelite leaders—Moses (chief), Aaron (high priest), Nadab and Abihu (Aaron's sons), and the seventy elders (legislative/judicial body).

This scene recalls the even more democratic revelation at Mount Sinai, and the commandment that all Israelite males shall appear three times a year in the Lord's presence.[14] This vision takes place as the capstone to the Sinai revelation, after the Ten Commandments and subsidiary laws. In effect, it represents a sealing of the Covenant. After all, a covenant cannot be made by proxy; both sides need to be present—for if one does not see the other party, how can one know that the party exists, let alone agree to the terms? At Sinai, that other party shows the Divine Presence, thereby guaranteeing God's side of the bargain.

With its talk of God's feet and hand,[15] this passage affirms the anthropomorphic vision of God found throughout the Bible. Ordinarily, though, human beings are not granted permission to see God's body—even a glimpse of which risks death. Thus the narrator underlines how unusual this particular vision is: "Yet He did not raise His hand against the leaders of the Israelites." The forbidden is here permitted, not just to Moses and Aaron but to the assembly of Israelite leaders, to complete this central Covenant between God and humanity.

What is the meaning of the object seen under God's feet—literally, "like a brickwork of sapphire"?[16] According to Rashi (borrowing from the Talmud Sotah 12), the people are shown an image of a brick that God has kept as a reminder of the Israelites' hard labors with brick when they were slaves in Egypt. In this view, God is certifying that the brick of slavery is now transformed into the brick of freedom—alternatively, from slavery to the Egyptians into service of God.

Rashbam, Rashi's grandson, offers another interpretation, based on a different understanding of the word *livnat*, which appears only this once in the Bible: "in appearance like the *whiteness* of the sapphire." The people did not witness a celestial pavement but an intense, glowing light.

In either case, the object is something that stands between them and God's presence above, partly blocking their view, like the sun blocking our view of the sky at noon. A kind of membrane that normally enshrouds the Divine Presence is temporarily rolled back or made transparent so as to confirm the validity of an eternal Covenant between God and the people.

A subsequent passage in Exodus offers additional insight regarding human limitations on knowing God:

[Moses] said, "Oh, let me behold Your Presence!" And He answered, "I will make all My goodness pass before you, and I will proclaim before you the name Lord, and the grace that I grant and the compassion that I show. But," He said, "you cannot see My face, for man may not see Me and live." And the Lord said, "See, there is a place near Me. Station yourself on the rock and, as My Presence passes by, I will put you in a cleft of the rock and shield you with My hand until I have passed by. Then I will take My hand away and you will see My back; but My face must not be seen." (Exod. 33:18–23)

From a narrative perspective, what is most unusual here is the three-fold introduction of God's speech without intervening dialogue from Moses: "And He answered," "He said," "And the Lord said." Between each utterance, God pauses to weigh Moses' response, to absorb his wishes. The lack of reply is pregnant with suggestion. Moses' desire to encounter God more closely is so palpable that he no longer needs to mention it verbally.

Meanwhile, God appears to be balancing the Divine desire for intimate contact with Moses against God's need to show Moses the boundaries of human-Divine interaction. It is as if, with each new statement, God is thinking, "Perhaps this will satisfy Moses," and then, realizing that it does not, God tries again.

What God offers Moses in the first sentence is unclear; the accumulation of abstract terms — "goodness," "grace," "compassion" — obscures the uncertainty of what is actually revealed. Certainly, Moses is not seeing God's self or body (see chapter 7 for a discussion of God's physicality). Anticipating Moses' disappointment, God confirms that Moses, as a human being, is incapable of seeing God's face and remaining alive.[17] Yet such a brush-off provides thin satisfaction to Moses — and God wants to give him more.

Then comes another highly mysterious moment of revelation, this time a very private one between Moses and God. Stationing Moses in the cleft of a rock, God sends him a message: This event is for him alone. It is the opposite of Sinai, where the message resounds in a wide-open setting, before the eyes of all. When God covers Moses' eyes, God shows him the kind of parental love we see again only at Moses' death, when God buries him. Right now, in a place unknown, God seems to be saying to Moses, *This is the most that a human being can see of Me.* Even in this most intimate moment with God, Moses cannot transcend the limitations of his physical body. Moses is, however, granted a view of God's back—a privileged view he keeps to himself (leaving the rest of us in ignorance).

How, then, are we to understand the text at the close of Deuteronomy, appearing in conjunction with Moses' death, that states that Moses was the only prophet whom "the Lord knew face to face" (Deut. 34:10)? After all, God's warning in Exodus 33:20 is clear: No person can live after seeing God's face. Deuteronomy seems to be making the kind of qualitative distinction between Moses and other mortals that the Exodus narrative was meticulous to avoid.

The declaration also draws two rings of separation between Moses and other people. He is a prophet—a term not used for him in Exodus, Leviticus, or Numbers—indicating he belongs to an elite group with a privileged relationship to God. And he is exclusive among prophets: the only one to see God's face.

Jewish commentators also struggled with this assertion, particularly its anthropomorphism. The Targum Yonatan, an Aramaic translation from around the eighth century CE, translates metaphorically that there arose no prophet like Moses "who understood God's teaching," while Rashi glosses that God "would speak to Moses at any time that he wished." The Ramban, who frequently disagrees with Rashi, takes Moses' "seeing" literally but essentially understands the "seeing" to mean what God does rather than what God is: No other prophet saw God's signs and wonders—manna, Mount Sinai, the pillar of fire, the cloud of glory, and so on—as plentifully as Moses did (along with the Israelites).

Such allegorical interpretations accord with the standard medieval theological view that God is invisible, but in doing so they skirt the plain meaning of the biblical text. Is there another way to reconcile Moses' seeing God's face, according to Deuteronomy, and earlier, in Exodus, being forbidden to do so at the cost of his life?

Perhaps a clue comes from the talmudic interpretation (Bava Batra 15a) that Joshua, not Moses, wrote the final verses of the Torah. While Moses is alive, he wears the garments of human mortality. Only after his passing does he don the splendid new raiments of legend. Other people may turn Moses into a classical hero, a figure who exceeded the limits of the human condition to encounter God "face to face." But the truth is that he is a hero because of those limits, because his accomplishments take place within them or despite them.

Moses as Leader: Playing God

Toward the beginning of the Exodus from Egypt, God seems to break the biblical ground rules firmly separating the human and the Divine. In preparing Moses for his showdown with the Egyptian ruler, God casts Moses in the role of God, with Aaron playing Moses: "The Lord replied to Moses, 'See, I place you in the role of God to Pharaoh, with your brother Aaron as your prophet'" (Exod. 7:1). Perhaps God is setting Moses up for success. After all, since the Egyptians considered their pharaoh to be a god, hypothetically Moses would also need to be a deity in order to constitute a weighty adversary.

This verse suggests a two-sided portrait of Moses as leader. On the one hand, Moses is exalted. Like other heroes, he inspires dread, appearing invincible in combat, certain of the justness and ultimate victory of his side. Like Achilles and his ilk, Moses has no fear that he will lose; nor has he any reason to. All heroes have a god on their side, making them believe in their own indomitability as they appear as gods themselves to their enemies.

On the other hand, the Bible emphasizes that Moses is not in charge. God is the dramatist and director, calling all the shots in the showdown with Pharaoh. At most, Moses gets to plead with God to remove one of the plagues, given Pharaoh's urging and how much the Egyptians have suffered. Almost never do we hear Moses' own voice—not even "Moses spoke to Pharaoh," only "The Lord spoke to Moses." Nor do we hear Moses' own words; rather, Moses as prophet repeats God's instructed speeches. As with the revelation of the Torah at Mount Sinai to come, God gives dictation to Moses, who as God's faithful servant can be trusted to repeat his lines correctly. Moses, the humble stutterer, plays and only plays the exalted leader.

God's instructions here showcase the paradoxical situation in which Moses finds himself as a new sort of hero. The Egyptians can comprehend a hero only in their own mold: the pharaoh as god. The hero must be a leader of a nation, and by definition, being the incarnation of a deity, he contains immortal powers. In the person of Moses, God delivers.[17]

In effect, Exodus 7:1 renders the protracted drama between Moses and Pharaoh, the Israelites and the Egyptians, as a divine comedy. Pharaoh thinks he is confronting Moses as a lesser but comparable god, not realizing that there is another God above Moses. The flashes of comedy injected into an epic narrative of the fate of nations accentuate the contrast between the biblical and non-Israelite conceptions of heroism: Pharaoh believes he is a hero because he is a god, while Moses is a hero because he knows that he is not God.

The dramatic conflict between Moses and Aaron, who are play-acting as God and prophet, and Pharaoh and his men, who are deluded that they really are a god and prophets, gets carried out in a magic contest between the two sides (Exod. 7:8–8:15). God scripts the entire scene: "The Lord said to Moses and Aaron, 'When Pharaoh speaks to you and says, "Produce your marvel," you shall say to Aaron, "Take your rod and cast it down before Pharaoh." It shall turn into a serpent.' So Moses and Aaron came before Pharaoh and did just as the Lord had commanded" (7:8–10). Pharaoh has his magicians perform the same trick, but Aaron's serpent swallows the magicians', demonstrating the superiority of his god's power. Upon God's direction, Aaron produces the plagues of blood, frogs, and lice; the magicians attempt to produce lice and fail. They tell Pharaoh that hope is lost: "This is the finger of God!" (8:15). Nonetheless, Pharaoh hardens his heart against the Israelites.

The fact that Moses has only one "prophet" and still triumphs over Pharaoh's retinue dramatizes the contrast between true and false heroism. (Compare the contest between Elijah and the 450 prophets of Baal, also played with elements of farce, in 1 Kings 18, as discussed in chapter 5.) There's a touch of silent-screen melodrama here: Pharaoh's henchmen hover like a claque of mustachioed villains, ineffectually colluding to try to stump their upright, unflappable opponent. Eventually they come to recognize that the truth resides with their enemies, but they cannot convince their evil lord. Pharaoh's hardness of heart represents the contradiction between his external opposition to the Israelites' claims for justice and his unspoken internal awareness that God and the truth dwell with them. (This kind of conflicted character, an opponent of Israel who nonetheless recognizes the power of its God, recurs in the prophet Balaam, Numbers 22–24.) A heart that is hardened must at one time have been soft, open, receptive. Moses' heroism resides not in making himself into a divinity but in acknowledging the power of the true God and heeding that God's instructions.

Pharaoh: Nemesis or Foil?

A narrative principle as sure as a rule of chemistry holds that every great hero must have an antihero, and Moses is no exception. Like Lancelot and Arthur, Moriarty and Sherlock Holmes, or Darth Vader and Luke Skywalker, the menacing Pharaoh elicits the heroic features of his noble opponent. From this perspective, Pharaoh is Moses' nemesis, the two archenemies clenched in a perpetual struggle.

But one may legitimately take a different view of Pharaoh. Sometimes, instead of appearing the powerful yet worthy opponent, Pharaoh comes across as the buffoon. As he rants and raves, commands and dismisses, his bluster comes at the price of a vast ignorance of himself and a cosmic overestimation of his own powers.

From this view, Pharaoh serves as Moses' foil rather than his nemesis. A foil refers to the gold or silver leaf upon which a ring is placed; it sets off the ring and makes it shine. A character who is a foil is of a different order than the protagonist. He is a lightweight, a diversion whose sole purpose is to help us see an aspect or aspects of the main character more clearly. Whereas a nemesis is the opponent one can't ignore, a foil is a reflection that serves only to make the protagonist appear brighter.

Pharaoh may be the opposite of Moses, a fool or madman who makes Moses' wisdom and sanity more evident. Or he may be an equal of Moses, a figure who possesses something of Moses inside himself and perhaps reveals a side of Moses through their resemblance.

Which is the real Pharaoh? Is he a buffoon who doesn't listen or learn, a fool who can't change or acknowledge the truth? If so, he is akin to the character of Malvolio in Shakespeare's *Twelfth Night*, who embarrasses himself by believing he has powers and charms far above his actual capacities. Or is his self-delusion the kind of a raging lunatic who believes he is God's gift to the world, the destined heir of a universal empire? Like Christopher Marlowe's Tamburlaine, a world conqueror who starts out calling himself the "scourge of God" and ends in the belief that he is greater than God, perhaps Pharaoh is a figure whose conceitedness is so vast that the reader has no handle for sympathy, only horror and amazement.

Or, is there something more worthy in Pharaoh, a touch of the heroic in him? Is he the victim of a more powerful enemy (God), who attacks both his physical and mental powers? Is there in fact a deeper side to Pharaoh? Might he, like Moses, wrestle with himself, but nonetheless act impetuously and commit mistakes with dire consequences? Might some part of him know what's right but can't openly acknowledge it because it is too much of a threat? Or might he desire but ultimately prove unable to entirely control his acts or emotions? In other words, is there a tragic, even sympathetic side to Pharaoh, which might be compared to a tragic side of Moses—a side that leads Pharaoh to descend into madness in the face of the inescapable, overwhelming arm of justice bearing down on him? Is Pharaoh an Egyptian version of King Saul, flailing about with desperation and helplessness once God severs him and his offspring from the seat of power?

Another narrative principle is that the nemesis is at the same time a mirror; the evil enemy is a repressed twin or a spurned, long-lost father (Darth Vader to Luke Skywalker). Growing up in Pharaoh's house, Moses could not have avoided regarding the paterfamilias as his own father figure. Pharaoh thus may provide the model of a powerful national ruler whom Moses can struggle against but find impossible to cast aside. Pharaoh is to Moses as Claudius is to Hamlet: the spurned, spurious paternal substitute alternately fled and opposed by his troubled, insecure stepson.

The ambivalence of Pharaoh's true role vis-à-vis Moses parallels the Bible's ambivalent depiction of the relationship between God and other gods.[19] In ancient mythology, a supreme god demonstrates his preeminence through the conquest of another god, especially one who has previously held sway: Marduk slays Apsu and Tiamat, Zeus triumphs over Chronos. According to biblical scholars, this military cosmology is hinted at in several places throughout the Bible. In the Creation story, for example, the word for chaos in Genesis 1:2, *tohu*, recalls the Babylonian god Tiamat, whose destruction and dismemberment enabled the Creation of the universe; the sea monsters in 1:21 likewise recall mythological beings. God's dominance over the creature Leviathan in Job and Psalm 104 similarly invokes God's mastery over Creation as a matter of subduing mythical beasts. A fuller monotheistic perspective, found elsewhere in the Bible, invariably denies the reality of alternate divinities: "Their idols are silver and gold, the work of men's hands" (Ps. 115:4). Foreign gods are mere idols, gilded figments of human imagination that hold no reality and are no contest against God.

Similarly, the contest between Moses and Pharaoh portrays the narrator's ambivalence about the need for an antagonist to reveal a character's heroism. Moses' overwhelming victory against the world's mightiest ruler demonstrates his greatness and, by extension, God's. For the triumph to be praiseworthy and miraculous, Pharaoh must appear as a worthy foe—the implication being, the worthier the foe, the more wondrous the victory. However, if Moses acts as God's agent, the representative of God's people, then from the beginning there can be no contest. Pharaoh has no true deity on his side, so his men and chariots are merely multiple toy pieces for God to topple.

In sum, Pharaoh is a figure who must be *both* foil and nemesis, because for him to be only one would diminish either God or Moses. In historical terms, he represents the pinnacle of human power, as the mighty ruler of a vast empire; in Israelite theological terms, he represents the pinnacle of human arrogance and self-delusion, the chimerical idea that people can attain divine control and invincibility. A passage in Ezekiel inveighing against a later pharaoh conflates the two sides of the Egyptian king as both a human and divine antagonist:

> O great beast among the nations, you are doomed!
> You are like the dragon in the seas,
> Thrusting through their streams,
> Stirring up the water with your feet
> And muddying their streams!
> Thus said the Lord God:
> I will cast My net over you
> In an assembly of many peoples,
> And you shall be hauled up in My toils. (32:2–3)

Moses' Arm

The contest pitting Moses and Aaron against Pharaoh's magicians gives Moses the opportunity to try out his newfound powers as a hero, God's agent, on a small scale. When the struggle becomes a direct, personal confrontation between Moses and Pharaoh, Moses' powers correspondingly magnify.

Moses effects dramatic, instantaneous change throughout nature and the Egyptian empire. Having surpassed his early period of self-doubt, he now understands in his own skin the meaning of God's promises to him. By harnessing the forces of life and death, light and darkness, water and earth, Moses reenacts God's cosmic display of might at the Creation. When he channels God's awesome force, Moses appears godlike to the people of Egypt, and even to the Children of Israel: "When Israel saw the wondrous power which the Lord had wielded against the Egyptians, the people feared the Lord; they had faith in the Lord and His servant Moses" (Exod. 14:31).

All during the plagues, Moses not only conveys God's warnings to Pharaoh; he and his brother Aaron also frequently initiate the threatened actions themselves. When Aaron instigates a plague, he stretches out his rod over the designated area. The first two plagues afflict the Nile, revered as a god in Egypt, as if to refute the pagan belief in theomachy, the battle between gods that befalls whenever two armies clash. Egypt's god will be no match in this contest. Aaron again extends his rod over the dust of the earth, causing lice to spring up and attack man and beast.

The intermediate plagues take place with minimal human agency. God tells Moses (and sometimes Aaron) to warn Pharaoh of an impending pestilence should he fail to release the Israelites to worship God. Pharaoh hardens his heart, and God carries out the threat. The charade between Aaron and the Egyptian astrologers is over; now there is no doubt in the Egyptians' minds who is causing their destruction. Even Pharaoh cannot help but acknowledge the truth: "I will let you go to sacrifice to the Lord your God in the wilderness; but do not go very far. Plead, then, for me" (Exod. 8:24).

For the seventh, eighth, and ninth plagues, of hail, locusts, and darkness, the extension of Moses' arm sets off the promised punishment. There is a clear progression from rod to arm—the rod serving as a magical device (compare the flowering of Aaron's staff in Num. 17:16–26), whereas the arm is metonymic of God's power, exercised "with a mighty hand and an outstretched arm" (Deut. 26:8). God commands Aaron to take the rod and Moses to extend his arm, yet Moses does not immediately accede. For hail and locusts, Moses instead holds out his rod. God doesn't comment on Moses' change or adaptation of the command, let alone punish him, as God will with a later transgression involving a rod; nonetheless, the change is striking. Perhaps Moses did not yet believe that his arm alone could be effective. Having seen the wonders his brother wrought by a rod, perhaps he assumed that he too required the magical powers the rod possessed. Or perhaps he thought his audience would not understand what he was doing without a rod, since the rod was in fact serving to reinforce the Egyptians' comprehension of his power. Only with the plague of darkness are we told that Moses stretched out his arm alone.

The climax of the Exodus story is, of course, the passing of the Israelites through the Sea of Reeds. Here, too, Moses' arm is a definitive character in the cosmic drama. When the Israelites reach the sea, Moses' arm parts the waves before them: "Then Moses held out his arm over the sea and the Lord drove back the sea with a strong east wind all that night, and turned the sea into dry ground" (Exod. 14:21). God commands Moses to raise both his rod and his arm (14:16), which Moses takes as a choice. God displays an awareness of Moses' uncertainty in his own power, and so the Divine covers both bases, as it were, in case Moses is not yet secure enough to rely on his arm alone. Now, finally, Moses' rejection of the rod at this pivotal moment in Israel's history signals his complete confidence in his ability to play the role of God's agent. No trickery is required to rouse the Almighty to action; God indeed works in harmony with God's faithful shepherd.

This verse describes Moses at the peak of his strength, and, simultaneously, at the limits of his strength. Moses holds out his arm, yet God drives back the sea: What, then, precisely is Moses' arm doing? The Torah gives us three explanations for the splitting of the sea: human, Divine, and natural (east wind); what are the relations between the three? All three appear necessary to carry out the miracle. Moses' arm signifies his and his people's faith in the saving power of God. Imagine if Moses had stretched out his arm and nothing happened! Moses' extended arm expresses his leap of faith.

From God's perspective, then, Moses' arm is a sign that God has a human partner. Without someone to receive the miracle, to recognize the miracle and give thanks for it, the splitting of the sea would be nothing more than a tree falling in the forest. God needs Moses to demonstrate and proclaim God's power; without Moses, God is alone. Moses has finally become the human agent God was hoping to have found at the Burning Bush.

Furthermore, by using nature—the wind—to cause the waters to split, God is also signifying that miracles take place within, not beyond, nature. People must "read" nature to discover the miraculous. If miracles were instead obvious interventions from above, they would require no effort or discernment on our human part. They would constitute Divine spectacles, to be absorbed passively, rather than acts of Divine partnership, to be experienced and contemplated. Perception is half the miracle.

Moses stretches out his arm again for the second part of the miracle: "Moses held out his arm over the sea, and at daybreak the sea returned to its normal state, and the Egyptians fled at its approach. But the Lord hurled the Egyptians into the sea. The waters turned back and covered the chariots and the horsemen—Pharaoh's entire army that followed them into the sea; not one of them remained" (Exod. 14:27–28). Here, the relationship between Moses' arm and the miracle is even more perplexing than in the previous cases. At first it appears that Moses' arm is actually the causative agent—it does not trigger God's intervention upon the water, but itself brings on the pivotal change. Could God be extending Moses' powers as a miracle maker? The next phrase, "At daybreak the sea returned to its normal state," puts that possibility in question. Now, it appears that Moses caused nothing: Nature resumed its course. The third clause clears the confusion: not Moses, not nature, but God caused the miracle. Moses plays the hero for a moment, and the next moment recedes to his proper place.

These ambiguities are crucial to the contradictory ways in which the Bible conceives of a human hero. Moses' depiction is the culmination of a process by which these contradictions have been thoughtfully integrated into the biblical art of characterization. Moses is chosen by God, instructed by God, chastised by God, directed to play God, but never becomes God.

The limitations on Moses' power of action—the strength of his arm— become clear in the Song of the Sea, a poem that summarizes the preceding action:

Your right hand, O Lord, glorious in power,
Your right hand, O Lord, shatters the foe! . . .
You put out Your right hand,
The earth swallowed them. (Exod. 15:6, 12)

According to the poem, God, not Moses, stretched out God's arm. Moses is never mentioned; his outstretched arm vanishes in God's saving activity. God is Israel's true hero.

What, then, did Moses accomplish when he himself stretched out his arm? As the poem explains, Moses' arm is perhaps a cue, or at most a conduit, for God's arm. The power Moses directs comes not from himself but from God. His limb hangs clearly on the sublunary side of cosmic forces.

The Weak Arm Prevails

A scene that takes place shortly after the Exodus encapsulates the mixture of weakness and strength, enterprise and dependency, that characterizes Moses as a model of Israelite heroism. The people of Amalek attack Israel; Joshua leads the Israelite troops in combat. Though he is no longer fit for battle, lacking the muscle he possessed when he killed the Egyptian slave driver, Moses nonetheless calls on his experience with the plagues to play a determinative role in the battle: "Then, whenever Moses held up his hand, Israel prevailed; but whenever he let down his hand, Amalek prevailed. But Moses' hands grew heavy; so they took a stone and put it under him and he sat on it, while Aaron and Hur, one on each side, supported his hands; thus his hands remained steady until the sun set. And Joshua overwhelmed the people of Amalek with the sword" (Exod. 17:11–13).

More succinctly and poignantly than in any other passage, the Bible here bodies forth in the figure of Moses its own struggle with the status of the hero. Moses is the great intercessor. He raises his hand upward from humanity toward God, and he channels Divine power into the service of the Hebrew army by holding his rod once again as a sign beckoning God's action (Exod. 17:9). At the same time, Moses appears old, tired, pitiful: Like an ordinary mortal, he cannot sustain his arms in the air for a long time.

To my mind, no image better epitomizes the Bible's profound ambivalence concerning heroes. Not Moses' power but God's upholds the Israelite minions; not Moses but Joshua defeats the Amalekites in battle. Moses' hands would not even have remained pointing heavenward without his two helpers, Aaron and Hur, holding them up. And yet, for all his weakness, Moses in the final tally makes the difference.[20] For without

Moses, without his intimacy with God that empowers him to call on God's assistance, the Hebrews would have been swept off the stage of history long before they had a chance of glimpsing the Promised Land.

Unlike the previous episodes in Egypt, in the battle with Amalek there is no question that Moses' arm *does* bring salvation. Israel's army thrives when his arms are raised upward and falters when his arms grow slack. Here, the narrator does not choose to downplay Moses' power by pointing to God's arm, God's saving intervention. Is the Bible changing its message about Moses' ability to work wonders? Or, instead, has it etched the causal relation between Moses' and God's arms so indelibly that mention of God at this moment would be superfluous? Regardless, the emphasis in this scene is entirely different than previous appearances of Moses' arm. In Egypt, the extension of Moses' strong arm brought to mind the actions of God's stronger arm; here in the desert, Moses' weak arms are stronger than the armaments and armies contending below. The Torah zooms in on Moses' frail arms to draw attention away from any human achievement on the battlefield. "They call on chariots, they call on horses, but we call on the name of the Lord our God. They collapse and lie fallen, but we rally and gather strength" (Ps. 20:8–9). Moses calling on God's assistance, not Joshua mobilizing his troops, wins the day. God does not need to be mentioned; no other power could explain the events described.

Contrast this biblical image with a version of this account as it would plausibly appear in *The Iliad* or an Icelandic edda (a medieval narrative of heroic bands of warriors). The epic writer would glorify the hero by recounting tales of his strength and derring-do. He might sing of the power of Moses' limbs soaring heavenward while his minions triumphed below on the battlefield. Even more likely, an epic would plunge Moses in the thick of battle, showing him slaying three valiant warriors with a single javelin throw and pitilessly slicing through other worthy opponents with his colossal sword. An epic hero would not be an old man raising his arms at a distance from the clash of armies; nor would his army win by virtue of his doing so. Do the Achaeans thrive when Achilles abandons the field of battle and sulks in his tent? From the perspective of an epic bard, the sentence dwelling upon Moses' frailty would be more than unnecessary; it would appear to contradict the very premise on which storytelling and heroism is based.

To the biblical author, however, that detail captures the entire point. It portrays a heroism that is entirely human, that has smudged over with frailty and emotion the older portrait of a man-god. In Moses' prayers and old age, the classical hero gives way to a new archetype: a hero in the image of man. Moses prays, God responds: "In distress I called on the Lord; the Lord answered me and brought me relief" (Ps. 118:5). With a pure heart and God's favor, we can all be such a hero.

Sinai: Peaks and Lows

If the depiction of the battle against Amalek edges Moses ever-so-slightly closer toward a classical hero, as someone with access to Divine powers that exceed ordinary human capacity, the revelation of the Torah at Mount Sinai surely displays the culmination of his heroic forces. One of the central definitions of a hero is a person who goes where others cannot, who through personal daring or Divine permission crosses boundaries and territories of mortal peril.

In this regard, Moses' ascent of Mount Sinai is akin to Sir Edmund Hillary's ascent of Mount Everest. The Torah describes Sinai as a terrain of terror: enveloped in a dense cloud, shielded by thunder and lightning, emitting the piercing sound of a horn's blast that makes the people tremble (Exod. 19:18–19). Then the Lord descends upon the mountain in fire, causing it to smoke like a kiln. Now it is the mountain itself that trembles. The blasts of the horn grow louder and louder, and God speaks in thunder. Yet when God calls Moses to ascend, Moses "went up," full stop (19:20). He seems impervious to the terror pervading the people and omnipresent within the natural world. By now, his character, experience, and relationship with God have girded him to confront the supernatural with sangfroid.

Sinai contains elements that do and do not fit the classical pattern of the hero. Moses is clearly in charge; he ascends and descends the mountain several times, bearing messages between the people and God. The passage introduces a hierarchy—Moses relays God's instructions to the elders, who represent the people and convey information to them—that elevates him further above his followers. God tells Moses to set bounds around the mountain lest the people come too close and die. At first only Moses is permitted to enter this holy space (later, Aaron is welcomed too). How Moses has matured since he encountered God at the Burning Bush! Now, in public, before the entire nation, he shows no twinge of reluctance to follow God's commands and fulfill his heroic mission.

Yet unlike stories of classical heroes, the defining revelation in the history of Israel is for all the people, not for Moses alone. A simple contrast with Jesus, Buddha, or Muhammad is striking in this context. God casts Moses as the shepherd of his people, not as the lone wolf who teaches his people to howl. He brings them to the mountain, but God speaks in thunder to everyone. True, Moses does dwell alone with God on the mountain for forty days—twice; but at the initial encounter, all Israel sees God descend and hears God speak the Ten Commandments.

Heroic visions, like the ones examined above, tend to be intensely private affairs—intimate, transformative moments of encounter between a person and a deity. The Bible's staging of its central vision as a collective experience, therefore, is extremely telling. From a certain perspective, the people are the protagonist of the Torah, which, in the words of biblical scholar Ilana Pardes, constitutes the "biography of ancient Israel."[21] Perhaps uniquely, the Bible presents a "foundational myth" in which an entire people, together and at once, receives a Divine revelation.[22] As we've come to expect, Moses hovers slightly above the people at Sinai—more than an average mortal, less than a divinity.

The text clearly depicts the people as seeing and hearing the awesome effects around the mountain: the smoke, the cloud of God's presence, the blast of the ram's horn, and the Lord speaking in thunder. Less clear is whether they hear and understand God's words. "And the Lord said to Moses, 'I will come to you in a thick cloud, in order that the people may hear when I speak with you and so trust you ever after'" (Exod. 19:9)— hear when, not what.[23] By this time, Moses has developed his spiritual muscles to be able to withstand God's presence; only he can listen to

God directly for a sustained period. The Israelites are cast in a position like Moses at the Burning Bush: overwhelmed by awe and fright. Moses stands apart through greater experience and a closer relationship to God, but at Sinai, all the people get a taste of being Moses.

The Crisis: Breaking the Tablets

Joseph Campbell describes the classic scenario of the hero as follows:

> When the hero-quest has been accomplished, through penetration to the source, or through the grace of some male or female, human or animal, personification, the adventurer still must return with his life-transmuting trophy. The full round . . . requires that the hero shall now begin the labor of bringing the runes of wisdom, the Golden Fleece, or his sleeping princess, back into the kingdom of humanity, where the boon may redound to the renewing of the community, the nation, the planet, or the ten thousand worlds.[24]

The Torah sets the reader up perfectly for this script to play out: Moses ascends the forbidden mountain, is quarantined with God for forty days, and returns to the people with God's message—laws and principles for running society. But the story does not play out as smoothly as expected. Instead of a grateful public welcoming their prophet-hero, Moses finds a camp aflame with anxiety and betrayal.

The people could not wait for their hero. In his absence, they sense the absence as well of the new God whose existence they have only recently discovered. For this people unused to freedom, lacking faith in God or themselves, and having nowhere to go and nothing to do in the heart of the wilderness, forty days proves a long time to wait. They ask for Aaron's help in constructing a molten calf from their golden jewelry, a representation to endow them with the feeling of security and Divine presence amidst their barren desolation. Do they see themselves as building an idol of a foreign god to worship—thereby completely abandoning the God of the Exodus and Sinai—or do they merely and misguidedly seek to give concrete expression to the God of Israel? Opinions differ.

Nonetheless, Moses clearly interprets their act as a deep betrayal of God and his own mission. The people have shattered their trust in God; now Moses shatters the tablets, the sign of God's trust in them.

The breaking of the tablets represents the Torah's shattering of the model of the ancient hero. All in all, the tablets themselves embody everything a hero strives for. They are the fruit of the hero's journey from ordinary mortal, through tests and trials, to personal encounter with God. They are proof to humankind that the hero is indeed who he claims to be: the one who has rekindled the people's relationship with their Divine guardian. And they are the boon that every hero delivers, an astonishing gift (akin to the fire of Prometheus) that transforms the way people live and understand their role on earth. Moses returns with a contract between Divine and human parties stipulating instructions for individual behavior and social values. Thus, when he shatters the tablets, everything Moses has accomplished crumbles to naught.

It is hard for us to fully register how shocking Moses' gesture is. The biblical history of God's actions in the world builds up to the giving of the law at Sinai. God creates the world based on a series of separations: light-darkness, water-ground, sun-moon-stars, and so on. The course of human development reveals further divisions between peoples, some benign, others violent. Separate languages form; territories are staked. Finally, one person is singled out for a life devoted to a relationship with God. This relationship grows with his descendants until the family forms a tribe, then a nation. A nation cannot maintain the same intimate relationship with God among all its members; it needs a contract, at once social and Divine, spelling out the means for the new society to preserve its favor in God's eyes. Moses ascends the mountain to receive this contract—one that will be binding on all Jews forever. The marriage between God and the people is consummated; God writes the law on the tablets and Moses brings them down. Here to come is the climax of the story, the happiest moment in the whole saga . . . the people will receive the law, they will learn what to do, they will carry out God's will. How could it end so badly? How could the Torah depict the pinnacle of Israel's history as so utterly botched?

Our incomprehension shows how deeply our expectations as readers derive from the classical legends of heroes. But a story like the shattering of the tablets—indeed, like most of the stories associated with Moses—reveals how powerfully the Bible opposes those legends and the worldview that sustains them. Biblical monotheism presents a vision of God detached from nature and distant from humanity.[25] The Golden Calf expresses a longing for an "enchanted" world where the people feel divinity resides near at hand, within the contours of nature: tree, animal, mountain, field, rain. The hero of both legend and fairy tale emerges from this enchanted universe where gods can impersonate people, take over and then leave their bodies at will, as well as sleep and reproduce with them; meanwhile, the people themselves can be semidivine. When Moses abandons his people to commune with God for forty days, the people revert to the comfort of this old sense of divinity immanent in nature. The new sense of distance from God is hard enough, but separation from their guide as well leaves them wholly bereft. The psychological, theological, and emotional vacuums need to be filled.

Smashing the tablets is Moses' way of emphasizing the rupture between the new religion of Israel and the ways of the people's ancient Near Eastern neighbors. *This God is not like the old ones*, Moses is saying, *and I am not like the heroes you are used to. You must break the idols of the mind along with the idols in form.* Breaking the tablets conveys Moses' disapproval in the strongest terms, but it also communicates his sense that the people are not yet ready for God and the Divine message. They must prepare themselves again, and God must deliver a second set of tablets. The biblical take on the hero story comes filled with such letdowns and remakes; it tells a history strewn with second acts.[26]

Chaos and Conflict in the Desert

The book of Numbers portrays Moses as the leader of society, a political and judicial authority attempting to establish order and harmony among his impatient, disgruntled ranks. At times, Numbers paints an idealized picture of stability among the Israelite masses as they wander through the wilderness. Tribal pennants, tribe positions arranged by geographical coordinates, censuses, numbers according to tribes, tribal heads, warriors, the components and vessels of the Tabernacle, the factions and specialized assignments of the Levites—what current system of government could be any more organized than this elaborate assembly of fleeing slaves arrayed in the vast waste?

Ultimately, though, the stories recounted in Numbers convey exactly the opposite impression. The society is rotting away, stateless, consigned to wait for decades in the middle of nowhere. Upstarts are snarling and scheming to replace their leaders. The people are impatient to be settled permanently, somewhere; by this time, whether that's the Land of Israel or back in Egypt matters little.

The conflict between these two opposing portraits—Numbers' superego and id, as it were—breaks out in the transition from chapter 10, where Israel's army is arrayed in serried ranks that would make the U.S. army proud, and chapter 11:1: "The people took to complaining bitterly before the Lord."

Smack in the middle, between the classical facade of a well-ordered structure and the seething cauldron of popular discontent, sits Moses. In episode after episode he seems as lost as his flock, repeatedly seeking Divine guidance to handle situations for which he is surprisingly and woefully unprepared. He struggles yeomanly and ultimately unsuccessfully to rectify his and God's ideals of social harmony with the messy reality of human desire, impatience, and shortsightedness. In the end, he does manage to achieve some level of social order, establishing a chain of authority and delegation of responsibilities that enable the growing society to function with a degree of bureaucratic efficiency. But if he has left his permanent mark upon society, the reverse is also true, as years of frustration over his ungovernable minions leave Moses the old man riven by pain and anger.

A basic pattern repeats itself throughout Moses' dealings with the Israelites. The people complain about their situation and Moses' leadership; Moses complains to God about the people and the burden God has placed upon him; God solves the problem, at times after presenting God's own complaints. This recurring plot reinforces Moses' ambiguous status as hero. The people expect him to behave like a hero-king and are continually disappointed at his inability to take charge. Moses, overwhelmed, does not know what to do except to turn to God. Imagine Moses' anxiety, then, when his one trusted advisor, his father-in-law, asserts his desire to leave the Israelites and return home to Midian. Moses pleads, flatters, and tries to bribe him: "Please do not leave us, inasmuch as you know where we should camp in the wilderness and can be our eyes. So if you come with us, we will extend to you the same bounty that the Lord grants us" (Num. 10:31–32). Moses himself feels lost in the wilderness.

On several occasions, his followers try to wrest control from him and steer their own destiny: the episode of the spies (Num. 13–14), the subsequent fatal march into the hill country (14:39–45), Korach's rebellion (16) and the proceeding Israelite insurrection (17), and the illicit sexual union with Moabite women (25). In reaction, God alternates between systemic improvements and harsh punishment—none harsher than in the last episode: "The Lord said to Moses, 'Take the heads of the people and have them publicly impaled before the Lord, so that the Lord's wrath may turn away from Israel'" (25:4). The relationships between God, Moses (and Aaron), and the People of Israel—the triangle that forms the basis for Israel's existence and history—progressively unravel throughout the book of Numbers. Only in the final section, as the tribes prepare to enter the land, do the rifts start to heal and does unity reassert itself in the face of national challenge.

Moses is also involved in a continuous series of spats and contentions. Besides his major confrontations with Korach, the people, and, later, foreign kings who refuse to permit the Israelites to walk past their lands in peace (Num. 20:14–21:35), Moses experiences arguments, conflicts, and jealousies as part and parcel of relating to those closest to him. Moses' siblings, Aaron and Miriam, gossip slanderously about their brother: "Miriam and Aaron spoke against Moses because of the Cushite woman he had married: 'He married a Cushite woman!' They said, 'Has the Lord spoken only through Moses? Has He not spoken through us as well?'" (12:1–2). In this highly enigmatic passage—Who is the Cushite woman? Is Cushite an ethnic or racial designation? When did Moses marry a second woman?—Moses' siblings question their brother's rule. Strikingly, the only intimate conversation among the siblings in the entire Torah is an occasion for talebearing and betrayal. Furthermore, Aaron and Miriam's defamatory sentiments evince parallels to those of Korach and his followers.

In short, this passage shows the extent to which Moses' rule lacks traction among the Israelites. Rebellion comes not only from a band of malcontents; the whole society is against him (except for Joshua and Caleb, the two spies who will bring back a positive report about the land). Moses is the archetypal lonely ruler, abandoned even by those closest to him. He is not even surrounded by duplicitous sycophants (as are the Israelite kings later on). Instead, there is a rampant impulse to undermine his human authority and legitimation from God. God must intervene time and again to shore up Moses' ever-flagging popularity.

Even Moses' relationship with God progressively frays. After the "riff-raff" (Num. 11:4) complain about their diet of manna and long to return to Egypt, Moses utters this astonishing cry to God:

> "Why have You dealt ill with Your servant, and why have I not enjoyed Your favor, that You have laid the burden of all this people upon me? Did I conceive all this people, did I bear them, that You should say to me, 'Carry them in your bosom as a nurse carries an infant,' to the land that You have promised on oath to their fathers? Where am I to get meat to give to all this people, when they whine before me and say, 'Give us meat to eat!' I cannot carry all this people by myself, for it is too much for me. If You would deal thus with me, kill me rather, I beg You, and let me see no more of my wretchedness!" (11:11–15)

Nowhere more powerfully do we witness Moses' emotions on full display. His loneliness as a leader, his pain at his people's stubbornness, his deep reluctance to carry out his assigned role, and his resentment against God for the casting decision—all these explode with the force of pent-up fury toward the only being Moses can turn to. *The people are as rash and demanding as children — am I supposed to be their mother? They are wasting all these years in the wilderness, losing faith in the land they have repeatedly been told they will inherit. Compared to their current uncertainty, they are starting to feel nostalgic about Egypt!* Ironically, even while he is embittered over his followers, feeling powerless and cut off from them, Moses demonstrates his resemblance to them: his own impatience and need to complain. Unable to exert his authority and restore calm, he faults God for his struggles and asks God to take charge. God gives Moses bureaucratic support in the form of seventy elders who will share some of the decision making.

Like Moses, God grows angry at the people and punishes them with too much meat, "until it comes out of [their] nostrils and becomes loathesome to [them]" (Num. 11:20). But a small part of God's anger may be reserved for Moses himself. Moses displays histrionics, comparing himself to a nursing mother and begging to be killed. (God ignores him.) Contrast Moses' gushing outburst here with Aaron's conspicuous silence following the mysterious death of his two eldest sons (Lev. 10:3). Is there something unseemly about Moses' behavior? Does God disapprove?

The bond between Moses and God comes to an unexpected breaking point at the Waters of Meribah:

> Moses took the rod from before the Lord, as He had commanded him. Moses and Aaron assembled the congregation in front of the rock; and he said to them, "Listen, you rebels, shall we get water for you out of this rock?" And Moses raised his hand and struck the rock twice with his rod. Out came copious water, and the community and their beasts drank. But the Lord said to Moses and Aaron, "Because you did not trust Me enough to affirm My sanctity in the sight of the Israelite people, therefore you shall not lead this congregation into the land that I have given them." (Num. 20:9–12)

As we've seen, the rod is not something to be waved lightly. In Exodus, Moses dares stretch out his arm holding a rod only at God's command. The rod may be a vehicle of miracles, but it is not a magic wand to be wielded at the will of a human magician. It is, rather, a token that emblematizes that its holder's power derives from a more-than-mortal power beyond him.

Momentarily, Moses forgets what he learned in Exodus. His frustration with men and even with God leads him to channel Divine forces without partnership with God or acknowledgment of God as the source. His *I'll show you!* reaction to the Israelites drives him to undermine the basis on which his rule was established—as an agent of the Lord.[27]

At this point Moses appears at his most angry and arrogant. Whereas earlier, when he poured out his heart to God, he was careful to conceal his emotions from the people, now he can no longer bridle his feelings. Perhaps this is why God decides on the spot to announce the end of Moses' career. God has tried unceasingly to bolster Moses' leadership, giving him the political, structural, and emotional support to eradicate enemies, direct the spy mission, appoint judges, and much more. Moses' outburst reveals that he is no longer capable of exercising the restraint and judgment needed to lead his flock. He is "burned out"; through years of solitude and antagonism, he has lost his empathetic tie with the people he rules. He is certainly not the right person to command them in the battles to come when they cross the Jordan.

Bitter Ending

> When the Lord heard your loud complaint, He was angry. He vowed: Not one of these men, this evil generation, shall see the good land that I swore to give to your fathers. . . . Because of you the Lord was incensed with me too, and He said: You shall not enter it either.
>
> —Deut. 1:34–35, 37

Even at the end of his life, long after his time for heroic action, Moses offers up a speech that is in notable contrast to the parting words fit for a hero. In the book of Deuteronomy, which contains nothing but Moses' own words, one might expect his heroic valedictory, a grand farewell to his people summarizing the main events and lessons of his life, in the tone and style of aged wisdom. He would survey the landscape of his days from the detachment of a great height that would be wont to yield harmonious insight. He would luxuriate in a sense of accomplishment for himself and his people. He would inspire fondness, perhaps nostalgia, pride, and courage. Above all, atop his wise perch, already distant himself from the conflicts of communal life, he would lace his words with the threads of affection and love.

Not so the unheroic biblical hero. Moses complains about the people's complaining, and his complaint is equally vehement and distorting of the truth.

Deuteronomy might be titled "Moses' Version." As Moses narrates the events recorded earlier in the Torah, we see his perspective on the formative period of ancient Israel. As we might expect from the flashes of Moses' character that emerge throughout the story, his memory is thickly colored and mottled by the emotional toll of the journey. In the jarring passage above, Moses' ire leads him to interpret the plot of Numbers in a far different way than the previously narrated events. Casting all the blame for being barred from entering the Land of Israel upon his followers, he entirely ignores the scene at Meribah where God gives him this very punishment! In effect, Moses is telling the people, *I am blameless; I am punished because you sinned against God; God decided to punish the entire generation, and as a member of your generation I am made to suffer with you.*

Moses' resentment against the people and God rages to the end. Most remarkably, the Bible does not permit its greatest hero to depart with a glow of saintliness. In his going, as in his coming, Moses is a complicated, difficult, conflicted man.

Moses' Greatness

Despite all the limitations, ambiguities, and qualifications, the Torah leaves no doubt of Moses' stature as a hero. Moses *did* lead the people. Moses *did* overcome his initial resistance to leadership, even if that disinclination never entirely left him. Even as a reluctant leader leading a reluctant people, Moses *did* follow God's will. He knew when to encourage the people and when to reprove them. Sometimes he nurtured them;

at other times he punished them. He came to their defense when God considered destroying them. He maintained a faithful assessment of his own powers, knowing that his strength and authority derived first from God, and second from the people's will. Most tellingly, he had the advantage of timing. He led the people successfully at the three greatest moments of their history: the Exodus, Revelation, and approach to the Promised Land. In this light, he was George Washington, Abraham Lincoln, and Franklin Roosevelt rolled into one.

Giving weight to the hero's journey, Campbell points out that the hero sets out alone on a quest where no one else has been and no one else can follow. He wins permission to cross forbidden boundaries to the world of immortal divinities. Following in this universal tradition, Moses, alone among the Israelites, gains access to God, first at the Burning Bush and later at Sinai: "The Lord came down upon Mount Sinai, on the top of the mountain, and the Lord called Moses to the top of the mountain and Moses went up. . . . So the Lord said to him, 'Go down, and come back together with Aaron; but let not the priests or the people break through to come up to the Lord, lest He break out against them'" (Exod. 19:20, 24). Like other heroes, Moses returns from the Divine encounter with a gift for his people. In the Bible, the treasure is God's law.

From birth to grave, this biblical hero is the great outsider. At birth Moses is a Hebrew among Egyptians, not belonging to the latter but not entirely comfortable among the former. Nor does his subsequent elevated role as leader transform him into the perfect "man of the people." Time and again his followers question his rule. Sometimes they seem unable to tell the difference between Pharaoh's tyranny and his own just command! Despite the fact that he becomes their savior, the distance between him and the Children of Israel is much greater than the distance between him and the Land of Israel at the close of his life.

And, as we've seen, unlike other classical heroes, Moses attains authority not as the culmination of his aspirations, but despite his efforts to the contrary. He rules solely because God has assigned him to lead. The reluctant, outsider leader, then, evidences a very different kind of perseverance than seen in the typical hero motif. Even as, time and again, Moses chafes at the leadership role, he persists in upholding it. His abiding commitment testifies not just to God's continuing influence but also to the call to responsibility within his own conscience, to a significant and emulation-worthy component of his character.

Ultimately, Moses' quest is a search for the proper means to lead the people, and the proper form their society should take. We don't hear about his family because Moses is devoted to his work 24/7. In this he is like Aeneas, the hero of Virgil's epic poem *The Aeneid*, and indeed the most human and least godlike of ancient epic protagonists. Fleeing pain and tragedy, Aeneas leads his people to a new land, a new destiny, from Troy to Rome. At the end of his journey, though, Aeneas questions the costs of victory, just as Moses doubts whether the people he has led are worthy of God's providence.

The most striking resemblance between the two heroes can be found in their relationships with women. In book 4 of *The Aeneid*, Aeneas enjoys a brief, passionate romance with Queen Dido, and then—forced to choose between personal domestic fulfillment and his destiny as the founder of the future state of Rome—he abandons her. Similarly, Moses seems to part from his wife Zipporah and their family early in his passage as leader of the future Israelites, but if their parting is similarly dramatic and somehow tragic, we readers do not know; the text never mentions it. The closest we get to a parting scene is the confrontation in Exodus 4:24–26, in which Zipporah throws their child's foreskin at Moses' feet and calls him a "bridegroom of blood." Perhaps this enigmatic exchange is meant to convey a message similar to Dido and Aeneas: Moses is not capable of being simultaneously a father to the nation and to his own children. Zipporah may be telling him, *You have failed the most basic responsibility toward your son. You have chosen a different path, or God has chosen a different path for you. Do not return.*

It is not surprising, therefore, that Moses, unlike Aaron, does not groom his son to walk in his footsteps. He is very far from being a "family man." Besides, he is not happy enough in the role he is playing to wish to pass down the mantle through his generations. Let another hero suffer that inheritance.[28]

In many ways, Moses emerges as a new kind of hero on the ancient stage. As portrayed in the Bible, he is the leader of a sizable nation, not just a band of soldiers or marauders of a small island or fiefdom. He is not free to pursue his own destiny, to endeavor to achieve whatever is in his mind and heart; he is responsible for other people. His narrative consists primarily of acts and choices that determine the destiny of his nation. In spirit and story, he is closer to Lincoln than Odysseus or King Arthur.

Moses' Difference

Many writers have regarded Moses as one more example of the ancient hero, fitting the mold of characters from Oedipus to Siegfried. In the words of the Austrian psychoanalyst Otto Rank, "Summarizing the essentials of the hero myth, we find the descent from noble parents, the exposure in the river, and in a box, and the raising of lowly parents; followed in the further evolution of the story by the hero's return to his first parents, with or without punishment meted out to them."[29] The basic plot of Moses' story is the opposite of this classic hero template. Moses passes from low-born parents (Hebrew slaves) to dwell in the house of the king, where he is raised. Moses does not return to his first parents; he does not set out on a quest for his royal origins, for revenge against his parents, for regaining a throne wrongfully denied him. Instead, he flees his royal stepfather and strikes out on his own, returning to challenge Pharaoh—not in order to capture his throne but to liberate his people from Pharaoh's land.

There is also a completely different relationship emphasized in the Moses story. His chief relationship is not with his parents, but with his people. At Moses' birth, his father is called simply *ish*, a man. His specific identity is of no importance; what matters is that he is a Hebrew. When Moses goes out of Pharaoh's house for the first time, he is not seeking his father but his brothers—namely, the Israelites. The Bible replaces the familial setting of the typical hero's actions with the national dimension of Israelite history.

In classic hero stories, the national dimension is suppressed entirely or subordinated to the glory of the king. The Bible's account of Moses conveys exactly the opposite values. Moses is described as "the most humble" man. His extreme reluctance to assume leadership directly challenges the mythological narrative of what constitutes a heroic ideal. For Moses, what matters are the people and God's mission for them; he is merely God's agent and, in his own eyes, thoroughly replaceable. Rebuked once already by the Israelites, he sees no reason to assert his own dominance over them. Hence, he asks God to choose a more suitable instrument for Divine purposes. Only after God's lengthy cajoling and even irritation toward the adverse Moses does Moses consent to shepherd his people.

Is Moses a hero because of or despite his flaws? *Both*. His flaws—stubbornness, impatience, anger, reluctance to lead, frequent lack of sympathy for the Israelites—are real and problematic. But he could not be a hero without flaws, because he would not be human. Moses' heroic status derives not in overcoming his flaws but in achieving greatness while at the same time being a flawed, nondivine person. Unlike Greek heroes, Moses is not a semidivine being with one fatal flaw (such as Achilles' heel). As with most people, his flaws and virtues are inextricably bound together into the fiber of the man.

The Bible's portrayal of its chief hero and role model as flawed carries profound implications for our understanding of the hero. In the biblical view, a hero is not someone whose followers should place him on a pedestal, nor a figure whose feet of clay cause the whole statue to collapse. Instead, heroes should be emulated for their fine qualities, while their flaws are acknowledged and open to reproach. They can be admired without being idolized, criticized without being demonized. As full human beings, heroes are to be granted the same balance of consideration and sensitivity, along with critical engagement, we accord people in our own circles whom we know and respect. There are no biblical superheroes, only ordinary souls writ large through their place in history and relationship with God.

In sharing plotlines with his predecessors, the Patriarchs, Moses demonstrates his worth as their successor and achieves the culmination of the historical efforts they set in motion. Like Abraham, he leaves the land of his birth for a new one promised by God, and merits God's intimacy and access to arguing with the Almighty. Like Jacob, he flees from a close relative and his native land, then returns home. Like Joseph, he holds a high position in the Egyptian court and marries a foreign wife.[30]

Moreover, Moses exemplifies the model of a proper hero for those who come after him in the Bible. Often these protagonists repeat his actions, step in his footsteps, and are measured by his standard. Furthermore, we as readers uphold Moses' example as the pinnacle of the biblical hero, thus judging the political and religious leaders who follow him in his light. The best they can be is a "second Moses."[31]

2

SAMSON

Strongman

Samson is a biblical hero who serves largely as an antihero: a protagonist whose behaviors, values, and characteristics markedly differ from those of typical heroes in the same society. Samson the antihero rubs against the grain of the audience's expectations.

Antiheroes became especially popular in the twentieth century. Famous antiheroes include the charming narrator of Agatha Christie's first mystery, *The Murder of Roger Ackroyd*, who, as the reader discovers at the end, himself committed the murder; and Yossarian, protagonist of Joseph Heller's *Catch-22*, who exerts all his antic, mind-bending effort to escape combat during World War II.

Whereas Ackroyd is an antihero simply because at the end he is shown to be a negative character (a murderer), Yossarian is a far more complicated example. Despite his paranoia and cowardice, Yossarian emerges as partly a hero by achieving his goal of saving his skin through the combat and chaos of war. Clearly, the author views him as one. At the same time, Yossarian is a highly problematic hero because he displays peacetime qualities—evasion of life-threatening dangers, yearning for luxuries—that are considered inappropriate during wartime, when soldiers are called upon to sacrifice their desires and well-being. He is an antihero not by being a bad person but rather by being antithetical to the traditional mold of a military hero.

Samson is an antihero in the Yossarian mold: His very character traits that might render him an unadulterated hero in other environments appear far less glorious within the Bible. To his misfortune, however, he finds himself right there in the Bible, confronting a set of expectations he can scarcely meet. He is a Greek warrior washed up on the wrong side of the Mediterranean, a Heracles or Achilles adrift in the society of Abraham and Moses. How are we to situate a muscleman who can single-handedly outmaul a lion or rout an enemy army? We would call him a freak of nature if an angel in the story didn't tell us his strength comes from God.

The point is, physical strength is not widely prized in the Bible. When Israel does battle with the Amalekites, the victory is attributed to Moses' weak hands, propped up high to God in prayer (Exod. 17:11–12). Joshua and his troops arrayed on the field have no power of their own to secure the triumph. As Gideon prepares to engage the Midianite camp in combat with twenty-two thousand men, God tells him to whittle down his troops to a mere three hundred to show that "the glory [is] due to Me" (Judg. 7:2).

This is not to say that there are no strong biblical heroes. Rather, those who are strong are not great because of their strength. Joshua conquers the Land of Israel because he listens to God and follows in the path of his mentor, Moses; David defeats Goliath by means of his cleverness and skill with a slingshot. By and large throughout the Bible, it is not the characters' ability to dazzle with their might or looks but their inner qualities as projected outward in their behavior that render them admirable or despicable.

For his part, Samson acts more like a hero from a foreign legend. Even Samson's name aligns him with foreign heroes: Shimshon comes from the Hebrew word *shemesh*, meaning "sun." Unlike other biblical characters whose theomorphic names indicate their indebtedness to the Israelite God—for example, Elijah, "My God is the Lord," or Saul, "borrowed" or "requested of God"—Samson's name suggests the pagan view of the sun as a supreme deity, and associates him with a well-known transcultural pattern of sun heroes. And, like Achilles, Samson has one point of physical weakness: his "Achilles' heel," his hair.

Samson: Lion in a China Shop

No character in the Bible fits the classical, nonbiblical profile of a hero nearly so perfectly as Samson. His birth is miraculous, heralded in his mother's womb by God's angel, who declares that he shall be a nazirite, possessing a special status apart from other mortals. His superhuman strength is matched by superhuman passions; he conquers anything in his path with equal disregard and disdain: man, beast, woman. For the majority of his life he serves as a national leader, although, like the depictions of most classical heroes, we don't see him acting in that capacity. (By and large, descriptions of everyday leadership were of little interest to epic poets.)

However, precisely because the arc of Samson's life fits the universal pattern of the hero, his inadequacies in fulfilling his mission become glaringly apparent. Samson is the Bible's travesty of an ancient hero, the Bible's protest against this ancient ideal of heroism. He represents all that is wrong with that ancient ideal. "Not by might, nor by power, but by My spirit—said the Lord of Hosts" (Zech. 4:6). By relying entirely on his own strength, Samson forgets that God is the source of his strength. Aware of his mission to redeem the Jewish people, Samson confuses the means—his strength—with the goal. As we will see, the hero he resembles most closely is not Moses but the Greek strongman Heracles. The negative portrayal of Samson's Heracles-like qualities confirms the Bible's rejection of the classical model of the hero. The French poet Charles Baudelaire captured this sense of a hero who is out of place in his description of an albatross that lands on the deck of a ship: "Exiled on the ground, surrounded by hoots, / His giant wings prevent him from walking."[1]

Over time, Samson's strength becomes the basis of his weakness. He is so intoxicated by the effects of his power that he forgets that he is human, mortal, housed in a vulnerable body. In other words, he makes the mistake of conceiving of himself as a semidivine hero. Paradoxically, only after his hair is shorn, his eyes gouged out, his strength depleted to that of an ordinary man, and his existence reduced to slavery—after he is made to fully feel his own mortality and fragility—can he succeed in calling out to God to restore his strength and defeat his enemies. But by this time, Samson is no longer the same hero he once was.

In short, Samson is the Bible's foremost antihero. He embodies a polemic staged as a story: This is what we think of your kind of heroes, the Israelite authors are telling their ancient Near Eastern neighbors. Whereas modern antiheroes are often characters you wouldn't expect to turn into heroes (cannibals, murderers, bunglers, and so on), this biblical antihero is precisely the person you would expect to be a hero. His failure to act as a hero is all the more glaring for the fact that he is born with all the right machinery. He is like the child prodigy who loses his touch in adolescence. What great promise was unfulfilled! His story demonstrates that it is never the machinery that counts. The hero is made of different stuff.[2]

Annunciation

Samson's introduction in Judges 13 presents an example of an annunciation scene, made famous by the birth of Jesus in the New Testament and its hundreds of medieval and Renaissance depictions. A messenger of the Lord ("angel" and "messenger" are the same word in Hebrew) appears to a barren woman, identified as the wife of Manoah, to inform her that she will have a son. He instructs her to be meticulous with her son's food and not give him any alcohol to drink, nor cut his hair, for he will be a nazirite (compare with Num. 6:1–21). Manoah pleads to God that the messenger return; he does so and repeats his message. Manoah then tries to feed his guest, for he "did not know that he was an angel of the Lord," but the angel refuses to eat the food and to tell his name. Subsequently, Manoah makes a burnt offering to God; he and his wife see the angel ascend upon the flames.

Strikingly, Samson's scene far exceeds other annunciations found in the Hebrew Bible in its length and grandeur. In fact, only a few characters in the Hebrew Bible have their arrival foretold. An angel visits and consoles Hagar (who has run away from her mistress Sarai's harsh treatment) with news of Ishmael's forthcoming birth (Gen. 16). Three men or angels tell Abraham and Sarah that they will have a son, Isaac, one year hence (Gen. 18:9–15). The Lord speaks to Rebecca before she gives birth to Jacob, but only to tell her the import of her twins wrestling in her womb, not to cast glory on Jacob (Gen. 25:23). Eli, the high priest, blesses Hannah, a barren woman, that God should grant her wish for a son, after which she conceives that son, Samuel (1 Sam. 1:17–20). And, in Jeremiah's first prophecy, a kind of annunciation after the fact, he sees that God appointed him as a prophet before he was born (Jer. 1:5).

Note that the greatest biblical figures — Moses, Aaron, Abraham, Joseph, David, Solomon — are never heralded in utero by Divine voice. In general, the annunciation is a minor type-scene in the Bible, a short episode — taking at most a verse or two — that emphasizes God's power to intervene in human affairs. Conversely, Samson's impending arrival, foretold by an angel to his parents, occupies a full chapter. As such, there is no real precedent for the aura of Samson's birth.

It is hard to understand why, of all the biblical heroes, Samson merits such an entrance. As we shall see, the Bible scarcely depicts him as praiseworthy; he is far from the paradigm of a hero. Rather, Samson's annunciation in Judges 13 appears to establish a pattern of irony through the striking contrast between the exterior features of the narrative and the interior qualities of the character. The more elaborate the annunciation scene, the less worthy Samson proves to be.

The relationship between his parents is particularly telling with regard to Samson's future, highly troubled liaisons with the opposite sex.[3] His mother, the unnamed "wife of Manoah," is repeatedly shown to be more perceptive than her cloddish husband. Both times the angel delivers his message, he comes to her, not to Manoah. Even though Manoah pleads for the angel to speak to him, even as he tries to detain him, feed him, find out his name as if the angel were human, the angel will not address him. For all that Manoah hears his wife's account and speaks at last with the angel, he still "did not know that he was an angel of the Lord." Finally, even after Manoah witnesses the angel ascend the flame of the offering, he believes that he and his wife will be punished with death for an illicit glimpse.[4]

His wife, the level-headed, clear-sighted member of the family, points out the multiple reasons why her husband's reasoning is fallacious: "Had the Lord meant to take our lives, He would not have accepted a burnt offering and meal offering from us, nor let us see all these things; and He would not have made such an announcement to us" (Judg. 13:23).

Manoah's repeated errors of judgment and understanding render him almost a comic target, a figure out of Italian farce. However, far from serving as mere comic relief and a foil for his wife, Manoah sets the stage for his son's own poor judgment and defeat by smarter, cleverer women. He provides a bad model that Samson will utterly and unwittingly follow.

Samson as Nazirite

Notably, Samson is the only character in the entire TANAKH to be explicitly identified as a nazirite.[5] According to Numbers 6, a nazirite is an Israelite consecrated to the service of God, under vows to abstain from alcohol, to let the hair grow, and to avoid defilement by contact with corpses: "If anyone, man or woman, explicitly utters a nazirite's vow, to set himself apart for the Lord, he shall abstain from wine and any other intoxicant. . . . No razor shall touch his head. . . . He shall not go in where there is a dead person" (6:2–6). Ostensibly, a nazirite possesses an inner desire to serve God with greater intensity than the normal array of religious practices enable him or her to accomplish. After adopting additional restrictions for a strictly defined period of time, the nazirite is assumed to have achieved a sort of catharsis or emotional purification, after which he or she must now return to a normal regimen of behaviors within society.

With Samson, we find an entirely different motivation, purpose, and duration behind the same set of rules. The adult Samson does not choose this special status because of his personal longings; it is assigned to him from birth. God appoints Samson to be a nazirite in utero. And God's intentions for Samson become clear in the next sentence: "He shall be the first to deliver Israel from the Philistines" (Judg. 13:5). In other words, Samson's nazirite status symbolizes his role as a national savior.

In certain ways, the two accounts diverge in their depictions of the nazirite. Numbers establishes the institution of the nazirite to enable religious seekers to physically and mentally withdraw from societal distractions and thereby experience a kind of spiritual cleansing. In the Judges story, however, being a nazirite propels Samson not inward but outward, toward physical encounters and entanglements of all sorts. At no time do we witness his special status inducing him to retreat from the world or to achieve spiritual states.[6] We also experience the physicality of Samson's ringlets; they are erotic, irresistible. Except for the formality of not cutting his locks, he appears to be nothing like the pious acolyte of Numbers 6.

Still, Samson's responsibilities as a nazirite and the general institution do share crucial similarities. In the Samson story, as in the book of Numbers, a nazirite is someone consecrated for a special relationship with God—and in both cases, someone who otherwise would not have been likely to be so designated (not a king, not a Kohen, not a Levite). In both cases as well, the nazirite must perform or refrain from certain actions in order to preserve his position. If he drinks wine, cuts his hair, or has contact with the dead, he loses his status. The nazirite's responsibility to preserve his status differentiates him from, say, a prophet whom God chooses for a mission. As the book of Jonah comically illustrates, however Jonah tries, nothing he can do will nullify his prophetic mission. Samson's role can be shorn as easily as a strand of hair.

Surprisingly, the annunciation scene makes no reference to Samson's chief physical characteristic: his strength. Why? Dwelling on a character's strength gives the impression that the character is in control: in charge of his or her own destiny and able to subdue others to his or her will. The impression in Judges 13 is precisely the opposite: Samson is not even in charge of himself. His role, his duties, his limitations are scripted before he's even born. This opening scene conveys to the reader, *Don't let his strength fool you. Samson is no Superman—because there is no Superman.* Samson is worthy of leadership not because he is strong but only to the extent that he is faithful to his appointed mission.

The final and most critical detail for Samson the nazirite is, of course, his hair. In Numbers 6, growing the hair is not merely one of several ritual observances; because it is mentioned repeatedly throughout the chapter, it seems to be the determining element of the role. Unshorn, long hair was the public sign of the nazirite's mission, betokening to all who saw him or her that this person was set apart for a holy function: "No razor shall touch his head; it shall remain consecrated until the completion of his term as nazirite of the Lord" (Num. 6:5). Imagine a white-collar male employee in the 1950s allowing his hair to grow long for months; apparently a nazirite in biblical times stood out likewise. If a nazirite did something forbidden — for example, being in the presence of a corpse — he was considered to have defiled his "consecrated hair." Once he brought an offering for atonement, however, he was considered to have "reconsecrate[d] his head."

The new element in Judges is Samson's dependence on his hair for strength. The representation of strong warriors as long-haired was common in ancient epics (compare Gilgamesh and *The Iliad*).[7] In Samson's case, however, his dependence appears to extend the connection between the nazirite's hair and mission, to wit: hair — mission — national leader — strength. An ordinary nazirite's mission is to serve God more closely; if his hair is shorn, he cannot carry out this mission. Samson's mission is to lead Israel with his strength; should his hair be shorn, he will lose his strength and hence no longer be able to lead the people.

By making Samson's superhuman strength reliant on his maintaining intact hair, the biblical narrator jarringly combines in Samson's hair the nazirite's symbol of piety with the Greek motif of an Achilles' heel. The seductive quality of Samson's hair is likewise more Greek than biblical. Except for the formality of not cutting his locks, his behavior shares nothing with the pious acolyte described in Numbers 6. The rather shocking alteration of this symbol powerfully marks Samson's identity as out of place, a Greek hero caught in a web of biblical expectations.

In his poem "Samson Agonistes," John Milton portrays Samson as a Greek-style hero, albeit a much more pious one than the biblical character. Drawing a connection between Samson's hair and his dependence on God, Milton/Samson muses:

God, when he gave me strength, to show withal
How slight the gift was, hung it in my Hair. (58–59)

Milton recognizes the Bible's message: physical strength is far from a quality of heroism. Might is bestowed by God and removed by God. It shines no radiance on its possessor.

The Jewish Heracles

The middle sequence of the Samson saga consists of a series of demonstrations of the hero's might. The reader attends, as it were, the performance of a circus strongman. Samson kills a lion with his bare hands! He taunts the men of Ashkelon, then kills thirty all at once! Later, he catches three hundred foxes, ties burning torches to their tails, and sets them loose among the Philistine grain, destroying their crop! When the Philistines confront him, Samson grabs the jawbone of an ass and slays another thousand Philistines! Fearless of his enemy, he goes down yet again to Gaza, the Philistine heartland; while the Philistines wait to ambush him, he rises in the middle of the night, grabs the massive doors to the town gates, and carries them on his shoulders miles away! After each feat, one can imagine an emcee calling, "And for his next act . . ."

In this section, Samson appears to resemble Heracles (also called Hercules) much more closely than he approximates other biblical heroes. (This comparison has been noted since Eusebius in the fourth century CE.) For their first displays, both heroes kill a lion, showcasing their supreme strength and courage. Heracles' exploit emphasizes the supernatural basis of his strength; just as the Nemean lion he kills is itself half a monster, so Heracles himself is more than human:

> Eurystheus ordered him to bring the skin of the Nemean lion; now that was an invulnerable beast begotten by Typhon. . . . And having come to Nemea and tracked the lion, he first shot an arrow at him, but when he perceived that the beast was invulnerable, he heaved up his club and made after him. And when the lion took refuge in a cave with two mouths, Hercules built up the one entrance and came in upon the beast through the other, and putting his arm round its neck held it tight till he had choked it.[8]

By contrast, under the sway of monotheism, the biblical passage does not portray the lion or Samson as supernatural. Instead, the description of Samson's exploit emphasizes the raw brutality of his strength:

When he came to the vineyards of Timnah, a full-grown lion came roaring at him. The spirit of the Lord gripped him,[9] and he tore him asunder with his bare hands as one might tear a kid asunder; but he did not tell his father and mother what he had done. (Judg. 14:5–6).

If Samson is not part deity like his Greek counterpart, he is at least a temporary deity, a vehicle for God's will ("the spirit of the Lord gripped him") at crucial moments in his story. The way in which Samson destroys nature's most feared and vicious killer makes him appear like a lion himself.[10]

This comparison aligns Samson not only with Heracles but more broadly with the ancient pagan hero, for whom the lion provided the model of bravery, strength, and nobility in military action. Dozens of heroic similes in *The Iliad* compare warriors to lions.

Yet the fact that Samson hides this deed from his parents indicates that, within the biblical context, there is something unseemly about his evisceration of the lion. The exercise of his strength, instead of aligning Samson with his people's destiny, as suggested in chapter 13, now serves exactly the opposite function: It severs him from them.

Thus, the passage establishes a conflicted view toward Samson's strength that will come to characterize the entire Samson saga. On the one hand, Samson's ability to taunt (without fear) and then defeat the Philistines, Israel's more powerful enemy, demonstrates a level of both inner and outer strength that his fellow Israelites admire and envy. Contrast Samson's single-handed mastery over the Philistines with the Israelite nation's fear of them starting at the Exodus: "Now when Pharaoh let the people go, God did not lead them by way of the land of the Philistines although it was nearer; for God said, 'The people may have a change of heart when they see war, and return to Egypt'" (Exod. 13:17). In a positive sense, Samson negates the feeling of powerlessness that induces the Israelites to cower before the region's dominant military leaders.

At the same time, however, Samson's exercise of his strength is so unbounded, it respects none of the limits defining Israelite identity and behavior. Specifically, it goes against the Israelite expectation of leaders (established by Moses) as humble, tireless servants of their people, reliant on God for wisdom and military success. Samson longs for a people who understand his passion and power; the Israelites spurn such displays of pride and ferocity. Thus, instead of marking him to become their leader and savior, Samson's strength mutually alienates him from his kin and people.

Even within the context of Greek heroes, Samson does not shine. In both the Samson and Heracles stories, for example, a series of episodes reveal the heroes' physical prowess. With Heracles, these episodes are tests imposed from without: According to legend, Heracles' twelve labors are exacted as penance after the goddess Hera drives him mad enough to kill his own children. Samson's challenges, by contrast, are largely self-generated. He is not acting with the consciousness of a revolutionary leader of the oppressed. Instead, like a Western outlaw, he picks fights because someone had it coming, or just because he felt like it.

The contrast is crucial: Heracles seems noble by surviving superhuman demands that he appears to have no choice but to execute; Samson's "heroics" seem at best unnecessary and at worst gratuitous bloodbaths. The only aspect that makes his actions seem remotely heroic is their effect on an enemy recurrently depicted as genuinely tyrannical.

Both heroes display insatiable sexual appetites. Heracles is said to have impregnated fifty sisters in one day. By this standard, Samson seems rather chaste, but he is not virtuous by biblical norms. While some men of the Bible have more than one wife—Abraham has two, Jacob, four; and Solomon has "seven hundred royal wives and three hundred concubines"—the concern with Samson is not the number but the quality of his relationships with women. His relations are raw, illicit, oozing lust and sex; he acts like a character in a modern French movie. The interactions are not based on love but on mutual exploitation. After some time, the lust is exhausted, the instability of the match comes to the fore, the relationship flames out in bitterness and violence, and the characters progress to the next *amour fou*.

In the final striking resemblance, both Heracles and Samson are undone through their love. Here, again, Heracles comes off as more heroic. Heracles kills the centaur, Nessus, for attempting to rape his wife, Deianira, but he too is killed, by a trick of the centaur:

> Being at the point of death, Nessus called Deianira to him and said that if she would have a love charm to operate on Hercules she should mix the seed he had dropped on the ground with the blood that flowed from the wound inflicted by the barb. . . . Deianira learned about Iole, and fearing that Hercules might love that damsel more than herself, she supposed that the spilt blood of Nessus was in truth a love-charm, and with it she smeared the tunic. So Hercules put it on and proceeded to offer sacrifice. But no sooner was the tunic warmed than the poison of the hydra began to corrode his skin.[11]

Heracles saves his wife, Deianira, from the advances of the concupiscent centaur by shooting him with a poisoned arrow—but in trying to rein in her husband, Deianira inadvertently kills him with the centaur's blood that Heracles has poisoned. Indirectly, Heracles' strength causes his downfall; the poison he inflicts becomes the poison that afflicts him. Both husband and wife act to preserve the other's sexual allegiance.

The parallels with Samson are evident. Samson's fall is likewise caused by a woman he loves. He too assumes that his strength renders him invulnerable—a form of vanity that induces him to lower his guard and leave him exposed.[12]

Yet Delilah, unlike Deianira, is intent upon harming her romantic counterpart. Perhaps this is not surprising. As we shall see, Samson's amorous relationship with Delilah is far more murky, and his actions far less noble, than those of his Greek counterpart Heracles.

Samson among the Philistines

Unlike other muscular literary characters, such as Melville's Billy Budd and Steinbeck's Lennie Small, who by circumstance are forced to kill and then are destroyed by society, Samson is no innocent. He is ever defiant, aware of his enemies; he taunts them, mocks them, tries to play their game and outsmart them, grows angry and kills them. In effect, he spends his entire life in relation to them—thinking about them when not being in their presence. The disturbing aspect of his story is the degree to which he becomes absorbed by them. He relishes the struggle against them, which he treats like a children's game.[13] He needs his Philistine enemies, for without them all his strength and strategizing are worthless.

For Samson, the act of killing is not accidental and tragic. It is a necessary activity in a society that values violence, as well as a triumphal assertion of his own supremacy over others who threaten and would destroy him. The Philistines, like the lions, seem to live by the law of kill-or-be-killed. By accepting this law, Samson comes to resemble them more than the people he supposedly leads.

Samson's choice in women, and his manner of relating to them, expresses his alien characteristics:

> Once Samson went down to Timnah; and while in Timnah, he noticed a girl among the Philistine women. On his return, he told his father and mother, "I noticed one of the Philistine women in Timnah; please get her for me as a wife." His father and mother said to him, "Is there no one among the daughters of your own kinsmen and among all our people, that you must go and take a wife from the uncircumcised Philistines?" But Samson answered his father, "Get me that one, for she is the one that pleases me." (Judg. 14:1–3)

Contrast Samson's brute attraction, his lust for foreign women, his insistence on taking a wife of his own choosing and his ordering his parents to do his bidding, with the classic tale describing the pattern of Israelite matchmaking: the story of Isaac and Rebecca. Isaac's parents arrange his marriage; he neither chooses his spouse nor has any say in the matter. The match is socially sanctioned, predicated upon family relations (endogamy). Rebecca's worthiness emerges from the way she takes initiative to welcome a stranger (Abraham's servant) into her village, and feed and water his camels. Abraham's trusted, mature servant recognizes her qualities; his seasoned judgment certifies that Rebecca will make a fitting wife for Isaac.

With Samson, this entire process is turned on its head; the Bible's marriage manual, as it were, is disregarded point by point. Samson, who possesses no experience in such matters, no judgment really in any sense heretofore—indeed, this is his first action narrated since his birth—selects a wife solely out of lust for her. He does not abide by his family and community's values; rather, he even enforces his choice on his parents, making them arrange his desired marriage against their judgment. However dismayed they are by his selection, because of Samson's physical might, it seems they are powerless to sway him. Samson's choice, and his manner of choosing, immediately reveals his identification with the Philistines.

In this marriage scene Samson resembles not Isaac but Isaac's wayward son, Esau: "And when Esau was forty years old, he took to wife Judith the daughter of Beeri the Hittite, and Basemath the daughter of Elon the Hittite; and they were a source of bitterness to Isaac and Rebecca" (Gen. 26:34–35). In the self-selected taking of foreign wives, the indifference to or defiance of parents' wishes, and the consequences of the taking—assimilating into a foreign tribe and abandoning one's native people—in all these ways, Samson's gestures reveal his unworthy model.

Samson's killing of the lion in the biblical episode that follows shows a similar pattern of behavior. In both cases he appears brutal and unstoppable, powered by urges that not even he, and certainly no one else, can contain. The ease with which he obtains what he desires serves to feed his arrogant self-assuredness. Like many a classical hero, he forgets his mortality, his limitations. He becomes increasingly certain that no person can defeat him, and no circumstance can withstand his godlike resistance.

In the few chapters about Samson after he kills the lion, he repeats a cycle of self-destructive behavior: foreign girlfriend, courting danger, taunting the enemy, lashing out. The stories' repetitiveness lends them the appearance of fate: Like the heroes of Greek tragedy, Samson the strongman is overpowered by narrative forces beyond his control.

As we will see, in all ways—characterization, plot elements, overall structure—the narrator reinforces the pervasive impression of Samson's incongruity in the biblical corpus.

Round One: Wedding Feast

The pattern is set when Samson throws a weeklong wedding feast for the first bride he "took" (Judg. 14:10–19). Thirty Philistine men join the festivities, and the revelry quickly grows tense when Samson challenges them with a riddle. If they guess the right answer, they each win a set of clothes; if they fail, they each owe him an outfit. The contest further darkens when Samson's wife pleads to receive the answer. What started as a test of wits descends into a test of his wife's loyalty. Samson cannot withstand his wife's pleading (as recurs with Delilah): He reveals the answer to her, she tells the young men, and they report the solution to Samson. Enraged, Samson kills thirty Philistine men of Ashkelon, strips them, and hands their clothes to the wedding crashers.

The episode raises many troubling questions concerning this enigmatic character: Are the Philistine men his friends or his enemies? Why does he provoke them? What lies behind the riddle/challenge? How come he accedes to his wife? What motivates her to side with the revelers against her husband? And, most glaringly, how does their answering the riddle explain or justify the murder of thirty men of Ashkelon?

Nonetheless, Samson's behavior is established: capitulation to women, provocation of the Philistines, eruptions of violence.

Round Two: Fox Tails

The wedding episode creates a rift between Samson and his wife, to the extent that she marries one of his wedding guests. (The Philistines' permissive views on marriage and divorce—if they even know of divorce—is yet another token of the alien culture in which Samson has chosen to immerse himself.) Instead of moving on, Samson returns to the house of his (ex? still?) wife and her family. The motive, as usual, is not given and not clear: Does he seek to reclaim her, or to avenge her betrayal? Does Samson himself know his motive, or is he acting again on brute impulse? Her father tells Samson, "I was sure that you had taken a dislike to her, so I gave her to your wedding companion. But her younger sister is more beautiful than she; let her become your wife instead" (Judg. 15:2).

Samson takes this as not just a personal betrayal by his wife and father-in-law but a treachery justifying his revenge against all the Philistines. The revenge, although conveyed in but one sentence, is intricate, deviously planned: He catches three hundred foxes, ties their tails together in pairs, burns a torch between each pair of tails, and sets them loose in the Philistines' grain fields, thus ruining their crop.

In response, the Philistines act as brutally and impulsively as their enemy: They burn Samson's wife and father-in-law (in revenge for their loss? to appease Samson?). For his part, Samson promises—and then exerts—revenge again: He butchers a thousand Philistines with the jaw of an ass. Never does Samson demonstrate his affinity for the Philistines more than when he slaughters them.

Round Three: The Prostitute

The next time Samson meets a woman, he gives the impression that he is toying with his enemies. Worse, he thinks he can toy with them—outsmart them and outfight them—at will. In truth, he is setting himself up for eventual downfall.

Samson goes to Gaza and sleeps with a prostitute. The townspeople discover his presence and plan an ambush at daybreak; but he finds out that they found out, and hence escapes at midnight. As expected, he leaves his mark—a gaping hole where the city gates once stood. With his bare hands he has stripped the gates off the posts and carried them many miles away.

At this point in the story, Samson appears as unhinged as the gates he removes. While his behavior with his wife was unseemly, at least he sought a wife; here he has "hooked up" with a prostitute, displaying a kind of sexual immorality altogether removed from biblical norms—much closer to Sodom than Abraham. In the ease and insouciance with which he plays with the city inhabitants—daring them to catch him, certain they are incapable of it—Samson has moved callously beyond the previous episodes, where he at least seemed to show some emotional vulnerability, a desire for connection and relationship. By now, the game is all. Moreover, his feat of strength here so far exceeds what is humanly possible, the reader can no longer identify with him. At this point he is pure self-parody. He is infinitely remote from the humble, all-too-human Moses, whose weak hands could not even stay aloft, let alone drag city gates the width of the country.

Round Four: Delilah

With Delilah, all of Samson's flaws—summed up by the term "hubris," a confidence that blinds him to his vulnerabilities—overpower him more than his enemies. The same pattern recurs, but this time the result is altogether different.

Once again, Samson sleeps with and falls for a Philistine woman. Unlike the previous episodes with Philistine women, however, the narrator now uses the word "love" in the first sentence (Judg. 16:4), clueing the reader in to Samson's heightened vulnerability. Sensing their opportunity, the Philistine lords offer Delilah eleven hundred shekels of silver if she can discover the secret of Samson's strength.

Much more openly than his first wife, Delilah colludes with Samson's antagonists. Three times, she asks him to reveal the source of his strength; each time, Samson deceives her, tricking her into trying different methods of overpowering him. She attempts to bind him down with fresh tendons, ropes, and a peg in his hair (getting closer to the truth), and each time a posse of Philistines awaits in the next room to help her overwhelm him. Three times she cries out "The Philistines are upon you!" only to find that he can easily remove her means of entrapment.

Not only is Samson unperturbed by her betrayals, he keeps returning to her and toying with the Philistines. With every lie he tells Delilah, each time he facilely extricates himself from the trap, the reader can imagine his arrogant laugh. He seems to be tempting fate. Perhaps he believes that God or his strength will always protect him.

But then Delilah asks Samson to divulge the source of his strength for the fourth time. And, finally, she comes upon a way to overpower his will: "How can you say you love me, when you don't confide in me?" (Judg. 16:15; literally, "when your heart is not with me"). Delilah's words penetrate Samson's armor. Suddenly he tells her "his whole heart," the true story behind his strength. Immediately, Delilah lulls Samson to sleep and calls in the assailants, who cut his hair, gouge his eyes, bind him in bronze shackles, and drag him to prison. For the first time he is completely powerless, emptied out like the lion in whose bones the bees made honey (14:8–9). As with his wife, Delilah's persistence overcomes him, costing him much more than thirty outfits. He loses his sight, his strength, his hair, and with it, his *nezirut*: his special status and mission to accomplish the Divine will in human affairs. Because Samson recklessly keeps returning to Delilah and seems to believe he is invulnerable, he becomes complicit in his own betrayal and downfall. Samson loses the relationship with God that was promised before his birth.

As we've seen, comparisons with other biblical characters tend to cast Samson in a poor light. In his downfall, Samson bears resemblance to Zimri ben-Salu, an Israelite prince impaled along with his Midianite lover by the zealous, heroic Pinchas (Num. 25:14). Like Zimri, Samson is seduced and felled by a woman used as tool of enemies. A Philistine Mata Hari, Delilah employs her wiles to procure secrets and stage-manage targeted attacks. Similarly, Zimri's lover, Cozbi, a princess of the Midianites, leads a campaign of mass seduction to lure the Israelite men away from their God and Protector, instigating a plague that abates only when Pinchas the priest kills Zimri and Cozbi.

In this light, Samson's repeated returns to Delilah, reckless belief in his invulnerability, and ultimate complicity in his downfall speak not only to personal weakness but national betrayal. Even Samson's earlier inability to withstand Delilah's appeals, his taking her as a lover, can be seen as demonstrating his abdication of his national role—the pursuit of personal pleasure at the expense of collective responsibility. And Samson's ultimate betrayal of his people is a betrayal of his God, an act of apostasy for which he must pay dearly.

Delilah's name—which, like Samson's, is freighted with symbolism—may also hint at this Divine betrayal. The root of the name, *d-l-l*, means poor, weak; indeed, Delilah (pronounced de-lee-lah in Hebrew[14]) exerts all her power to weaken Samson. A more remarkable meaning of this root emerges in Song of Songs 7:6: "The head upon you is like crimson wool, and the locks of your head [*dallat rosheikh*] are like royal purple." Here, *d-l-l* means hair! Specifically, it refers to a full growth of dark, glorious ringlets on a woman's head—or, perhaps, on the head of a young male nazirite. Delilah's name may suggest she had a mane to rival Samson's. More so, her name and mane may also symbolize the profanation of his hair: a sign of holiness and devotion to God transmuted into an object of erotic desirability.

Among the Israelites

The overwhelming majority of Samson's stories take place among the enemy Philistines. Yet the biblical account never intimates that Samson would feel more at home among his own people.

The one time Samson finds himself in the company of Israelites is a disaster that underscores his alienation from them (Judg. 15:9–13). After an escapade of slaughtering Philistines, Samson hides out in the "rock of Etam," presumably located near an Israelite habitation in Judah. The Philistines raid the Israelites to find him; the people of Judah send three thousand men to retrieve Samson and hand him over. When the Judahites finally locate Samson, they accuse him of recklessly endangering their lives before their much more powerful foe: "You know that the Philistines rule over us; why have you done this to us?" Samson makes them swear not to kill him; they bind him with ropes and escort him back to the Philistines.

The Israelites treat Samson not as a leader but as an erratic vigilante whose acts of lone violence imperil their lives. The actions that Samson regards as heroic the Israelites consider foolish and dangerous. The Israelites, like Jews throughout much of history, have chosen to acknowledge their position of weakness and accommodate themselves to being ruled by others. They see no point in courting certain annihilation for the cause of sovereignty.

Interestingly, Samson puts himself at their mercy. He is unwilling to attack the Israelite mob. Although they don't physically harm him, they do bind him and hand him over to the enemy. Thus, in his confrontation with the Israelites, Samson's physical vulnerability surfaces for the first time. The scene foreshadows his downfall at the hands of Delilah.

Is Samson Remade into a True Israelite Hero?

The concluding biblical episode about Samson presents a mirror image of the episode between Samson and Delilah: The Philistines are waxing arrogant while Samson probes for his opportunity to turn the tables. The Philistines' celebration of victory over their great enemy Samson is complete with songs and sacrifices to their god Dagon in his temple. They also toy with Samson, fetching him from prison and forcing him to dance before them. However, their belief that now, finally, he is powerless to harm them proves deadly wrong. Samson leans against two middle pillars, prays for God to restore his strength, and then tears down the pillars while crying "Let me die with the Philistines!" Samson perishes along with three thousand Philistines, his intimate enemies among whom he chose to live.

There are different ways to explain God's restoration of Samson's strength at the end of the story. Each explanation offers vastly different motivations for the characters and hence divergent ways for the reader to understand the story's meaning.[15]

Scenario 1: Samson Repents

Does Samson somehow merit the second chance allotted him? Does the story indicate, explicitly or implicitly, that he experiences genuine repentance? In other words, during his period of suffering, does Samson molt his Greek form and transmogrify into an Israelite hero?

A comparison between two prayers that Samson utters at different moments of vulnerability does indicate a degree of transformation. After the Israelites deliver Samson to the Philistines, Samson kills a thousand of them and then feels thirsty. He calls out to God, "You Yourself have granted this great victory through Your servant; and must I now die of thirst and fall into the hands of the uncircumcised?" (Judg. 15:18). Even in prayer, Samson cannot hide his brazenness. Apparently annoyed at God, he laces his plea with sarcasm and incredulity: *After I single-handedly vanquished the enemy, You're going to let me die of thirst?*

Samson's tone is altogether changed when he's standing by the pillars of the Philistine temple: "O Lord God! Please remember me, and give me strength just this once, O God, to take revenge of the Philistines, if only for one of my two eyes" (Judg. 16:28). When he now pleads with God, he seems to admit that his past actions do not merit God's mercy. Whereas in the earlier prayer he does not mention God once, here he uses three different names of God (in the Hebrew). In this mix of humility and boldness, as he pulls out all the stops in hopes of moving God to action, Samson starts to sound like the great biblical figures pleading intimately for Divine compassion. One might argue that Samson's desperate situation has forced him into a posture of humility. Yet, nonetheless, for the first time in his life, he is starting to resemble a biblical hero and not a biblical villain.

The problem with this theory, though, is that this one prayer is the only thread of evidence the story supplies to support Samson's repentance. Between the time of his blinding and his final revenge, no other verse offers a clue into his thoughts or feelings, his suffering, or his reflections on his life.

By contrast, Milton's "Samson Agonistes" spends nearly all of its 1,758 verses at this very point in time, imaginatively reconstructing the great lacuna of Samson's thought processes:

[Chorus:] But he though blind of sight,
Despis'd and thought extinguish't quite,
With inward eyes illuminated
His fiery virtue rous'd
From under ashes into sudden flame. (1687–91)

Milton, who identified with Samson in part owing to his own blindness, regards him as one whose outer darkness engenders a powerful inner illumination, as if only after the destruction of his body could his true self emerge. Milton compares Samson to the Phoenix: The form of death he endures is followed by rebirth into a purer form of heroism nourished by a newfound clarity of vision and formerly unattainable moral virtue. Still, Milton's version of Samson has only this one line of prayer as proof text of the hero's transformation.

Scenario 2: Samson Does Not Genuinely Repent

Samson's final act is in fact the culmination of his lifelong quest for vengeance and domination. Samson annihilates the Philistines not in battle, but during their revelries, when they can hardly fight back. And, once again, unlike other biblical heroes triumphant in battle whose victory is usually attributed (directly or indirectly) to God, here Samson's strength is the sole source of his salvation. After Samson prays for strength, God's support and Samson's humility disappear from the story.

Even worse, Samson himself dies in his final act—a consummation that never happens to any other biblical hero. And Samson begs for death—"Let me die with the Philistines!" (Judg. 16:30)—suggesting that his destruction is also self-slaughter. Like a Greek warrior, he seeks glory through death in battle. And unlike Joseph, who makes his sons swear to take his bones out of Egypt to be buried with his people in the Promised Land, Samson chooses to be buried alive with his people's enemies. Only after his death do Samson's brothers rectify the situation by burying him in the tomb of his father, Manoah. Just as his life was like that of a Greek hero, his death too belongs more in *The Iliad* than in the Torah.

A contrast with Moses reveals how, even at the end of Samson's life, he still does not live up to the standards of a biblical hero. The hero Moses ascends to the scenic height of Mount Nevo, taking in a panoramic view of the Land of Israel and dying gently by the word of God. Samson's end comes in an orgy of violence: He descends to a prison, then is buried beneath an enormous building. Before Moses dies, he offers all the assembled Israelites an extensive oration that summarizes his wisdom born of experience and guides them on their journey forward with new leadership. Samson's death, like his life, takes place among the Israelites' chief enemy. In short, after a brief hint of repentance, Samson in death seems to return to his old ways.

Scenario 3: God Takes Pity and Recalls Samson's Mission

Or: Does God remember Samson's mission and restore it to him after a needed chastisement? As Milton sees it, Samson reminds God of the special assignment God had allotted him from birth — akin to the way Moses recalls Israel's special mission when God threatens to destroy the people after their backsliding (e.g., Num. 14:11–19). Samson never appears as more of an Israelite than during his suffering. Shorn of God's protection, he calls out for God's mercy, for the restoration of God's special relationship:

> Why was my breeding order'd and prescrib'd
> As of a person separate to God,
> Design'd for great exploits; if I must die
> Betray'd Captiv'd, and both my Eyes put out,
> Made of my Enemies the scorn and gaze;
> To grind in Brazen Fetters under task
> With this Heav'n-gifted strength?
> . . . Promise was that I
> Should Israel from Philistian yoke deliver;
> Ask for this great Deliverer now, and find him
> Eyeless in Gaza at the Mill with slaves,
> Himself in bonds under Philistian yoke. ("Samson Agonistes" 30–42)

In this view, Samson's revival owes less to his own merit and internal change than to the overriding vision of God's plan. Once God has decided upon Samson's role, Samson himself is powerless to reverse his assignment. Samson's blinding is merely a temporary punishment for his arrogance; it does not cancel his role as Israel's savior.

Scenario 4: God Is Angry at the Philistines

Or, instead, do the Philistines' provocations finally invoke God's wrath? The Philistines celebrate their victory over their mighty enemy with feasts and dances to their pagan gods. Clearly, the Philistines view their defeat of Samson as the triumph of their divinity over the Israelites': "Now the lords of the Philistines gathered to offer a great sacrifice to their god Dagon and to make merry. They chanted, 'Our god has delivered into our hands / Our enemy Samson'" (Judg. 16:23). Does God return Samson's strength because God cannot bear to witness the hero's punishment interpreted as a theological defeat?

This scenario would explain why Samson's final victory ends with his own immolation: God is not so much forgiving Samson as refuting the claim of God's defeat at the hands of the Philistine deity Dagon.

Samson's prayer suggests another motive for God's vengeance: "Give me strength just this once, O God, to take revenge of the Philistines, if only for one of my two eyes" (Judg. 16:28). According to Samson, God is also avenging Samson's brutal defeat at Philistine hands. Had the Philistines merely killed Samson when he lay sleeping in Delilah's lap, it might have been understandable, but to take out his eyes and, pointedly, parade him in their temple—this is more than God can accept for God's chosen leader, even for one so deserving of his self-inflicted disgrace.

By this interpretation, the Samson saga is not really about Samson. He is merely a weapon in a "battle of the gods" (theomachy) between God and Dagon, similar to the theological war between God and the Egyptian deities in Exodus.[16]

Final Verdict

What does the narrator mean to tell us in the last line: "He [Samson] had led Israel for twenty years" (Judg. 16:31)? The story, of course, shows no such thing, so it is hard to take this statement as an objective summation of his life. Samson may have seen himself as Israel's leader, but here the narrator seems to be presenting his own perspective.

Perhaps the author is simply inserting a stock phrase that connected Samson's story to the larger premonarchical period of Israelite history. By this view, the phrase doesn't have to be taken too literally. Samson, the narrator may have been saying, was the dominant figure of his time, whose greatness lies in being "the first to deliver Israel from the Philistines" (Judg. 13:5). In other words, Samson is the first of a series of warriors (including Saul and David) who lead Israel in battle against the Philistines.

Or, perhaps instead, the narrator is making a moral evaluation: Despite appearances to the contrary, Samson was a true ruler of Israel—the only true ruler at a time when Israel lacked genuine authority. Perhaps Samson was like Noah, whom Genesis 6:9 describes as "a righteous man, blameless in his age," suggesting, according to Rashi, that in another age he would have been seen as less than righteous.

Along these lines, perhaps the story's conclusion affirms Samson's version of history—the people need to arise and shake off their shackles— and thus implicitly condemns the Israelites' acceptance of their inferior status. In this reading, the ending is like the glowing inscription on the tombstone of a deeply flawed man, telling the visitor to forget the ugly episodes and remember him in his moment of glory—or, in the famous line from the movie *The Man Who Shot Liberty Valence*, "When the legend becomes fact, print the legend."

The alternative is to regard the narrator as ironic. For those twenty years, as throughout the period of Judges, Israel was leaderless and rudderless, a weak agglomeration of disunited tribes. Samson "ruled" Israel the same way most of the other figures in Judges did—blindly, recklessly, venally. At such a time, when there was no "Israel" to speak of, the only leaders who arose were, like Samson, warlords, brigands, and vigilantes. Samson's deathbed conversion cannot undo a lifetime of wantonness and indiscriminate destruction. He was a leader *in* Israel for twenty years, but hardly a leader *of* Israel.

3

ESTHER

Queen

Anywhere else but the Bible, Esther—along with Samson (see chapter 2)—would be considered an unadulterated hero. Within the matrix of biblical values in the culture of ancient Israel, however, the two do not fit. A definition of a weed is a "plant out of place"; Esther and Samson are "heroes out of place."

After all, the noble qualities of biblical heroes conform to a typical pattern: They are the underdog/younger child, have a concern for guests and take haste to serve them, use caution and shrewdness in dealing with real and potential enemies, exhibit honesty and caring about people in general, and have a close relationship with God marked by both deference and daring. Other qualities—modesty, reliance on God, selflessness in defense of other people and the nation—are embodied by Moses and the greatest Israelite heroes, to different degrees.

Esther and Samson, by contrast, resemble heroes from foreign legend more than biblical characters. Samson's name evokes the sun as deity; the name Esther derives from Ishtar, the chief Babylonian goddess. Both socialize in foreign circles: Samson mostly with a low class of Philistines, including violent youths and prostitutes; Esther with the highest echelon of the Persian court. Both become enmeshed in a tangle of foreign plots quite alien in ethos and atmosphere to Israelite narratives. Both act alone within a more powerful society, confronting threats to the Jewish people at great personal danger. In both cases, their loyalty to the Jewish people is questioned and tested. In both, women and men oscillate between a "fatal attraction" across cultures and a "battle of the sexes" that can become frighteningly literal. And, ultimately, both their stories center upon the question of whether they can extricate themselves from the foreign cocoon and emerge, butterfly-like, as true Israelite heroes.

Esther as Scheherazade

The opening chapter of the book of Esther immediately transports the reader worlds away from Israelite history in both location and ethos. King Ahasuerus's palace in the Persian capital of Shushan operates with a set of norms, values, and institutions utterly alien to ancient Israel. Instead, this setting seems right at home in the universe of Persian epic, such as in the following famous frame story to *The Thousand and One Nights* (also known as *The Arabian Nights*) that introduces Scheherazade, the storyteller who recites all of the subsequent tales:[1]

There was, in ancient times, a King of the countries of India and China, possessing numerous troops, and guards, and servants, and domestic dependents; and he had two sons; one of whom was a man of mature age; and the other, a youth. Both of these princes were brave horsemen; but especially the elder, who inherited the kingdom of his father, and governed his subjects with such justice that the inhabitants of his country and whole empire loved him. He was called King Shahriyar: his younger brother was named Shah-Zeman, and was King of Samarkand. . . .

Now there were some windows in the King's palace commanding a view of his garden; and while his brother was looking out from one of these, a door of the palace was opened, and there came forth from it twenty females and twenty male black slaves; and the King's wife, who was distinguished by extraordinary beauty and elegance, accompanied them to a fountain, where they all disrobed themselves, and sat down together. The King's wife then called out, O Mes'ud! and immediately a black slave came to her, and embraced her; she doing the like. So also did the other slaves and the women; and all of them continued reveling together until the close of the day. . . .

As soon as they had entered the palace, Shahriyar caused his wife to be beheaded, and in like manner the women and black slaves; and thenceforth he made it his regular custom, every time that he took a virgin to his bed, to kill her at the expiration of the night. Thus he continued to do during a period of three years; and the people raised an outcry against him, and fled with their daughters, and there remained not a virgin in the city of a sufficient age for marriage. Such was the case when the King ordered the Wezir to bring him a virgin according to his custom; and the Wezir went forth and searched, and found none; and he went back to his house enraged and vexed, fearing what the King might do to him.

Now the Wezir had two daughters; the elder of whom was named Shahrazad; and the younger, Dunyzad. The former had read various books of histories, and the lives of preceding kings, and stories of past generations: it is asserted that she had collected together a thousand books of histories, relating to preceding generations and kings, and works of the poets. . . . [The Wezir] related to her all that had happened to him with regard to the King: upon which she said, By Allah, O my father, give me in marriage to this King: either I shall die, and be a ransom for one of the daughters of the Muslims, or I shall live, and be the cause of their deliverance from him. I conjure thee by Allah, exclaimed he, that thou expose not thyself to such peril: — but she said, It must be so . . . .

Now she had given directions to her younger sister, saying to her, When I have gone to the King, I will send to request thee to come; and when thou comest to me, and seest a convenient time, do thou say to me, O my sister, relate to me some strange story to beguile our waking hour: — and I will relate to thee a story that shall, if it be the will of God, be the means of procuring deliverance.

Her father, the Wezir, then took her to the King, who, when he saw him, was rejoiced, and said, Hast thou brought me what I desired? He answered Yes. When the King, therefore, introduced himself to her, she wept; and he said to her, What aileth thee? She answered, O King, I Have a young sister, and I wish to take leave of her. So the King sent to her; and she came to her sister, and embraced her, and sat near the foot of the bed; and after she had waited for a proper opportunity, she said, By Allah! O my sister, relate to us a story to beguile the waking hour of our night. Most willingly, answered Shahrazad, if this virtuous King permit me. And the King, hearing these words, and being restless, was pleased with the idea of listening to the story; and thus, on the first night of the thousand and one, Shahrazad commenced her recitations.[2]

The many similarities between this opening to *The Thousand and One Nights* and the first chapter of Esther illustrate that Esther's story takes place on alien territory. Both works start with an incident that turns the king against women. Each narrative begins by giving the impression that the king is the main character. The language carries the air of a court chronicle and seems designed to astonish the reader with the vastness of his empire. Comparing the two:

It happened in the days of Ahasuerus—that Ahasuerus, who reigned over a hundred and twenty-seven provinces from India to Ethiopia. In those days, when King Ahasuerus occupied the royal throne in fortress Shushan, in the third year of his reign . . . (Esther 1:1–3)

There was, in ancient times, a King of the countries of India and China, possessing numerous troops, and guards, and servants, and domestic dependents. (Lane, *Stories from the Thousand and One Nights*)

In both accounts, the king appears supreme, with a kingdom more vast and powers mightier than all other monarchs. (Not surprisingly, therefore, the ancient Rabbis interpreted some mentions of Ahasuerus as coded references to God, the King of Kings.[3]) Perhaps because the Persian court would be unfamiliar to biblical readers, the Bible proceeds to describe the luxurious court scene in some detail: "[There were hangings of] white cotton and blue wool, caught up by cords of fine linen and purple wool to silver rods and alabaster columns; and there were couches of gold and silver on a pavement of marble, alabaster, mother-of-pearl, and mosaics. Royal wine was served in abundance, as befits a king, in golden beakers, beakers of varied design" (Esther 1:6–7). Within books from other cultures, this kind of opulence would signify the height of civilization: the king as the embodiment of earthly desires. For the Bible, however, such lavish display is normal only for God's palace,[4] not for human habitation, so this description seems decadent, rather than pleasurable and becoming. Note that the author of *The Thousand and One Nights* does not begin with an opulent description of the court; this may suggest that native readers or listeners of these tales already knew what to expect in a king's palace.

While in both the book of Esther and *The Thousand and One Nights* the initial impression is one that the king would wish to make, in both cases the story rapidly moves to show him in a less favorable light. After enjoying an indeterminate period of marital bliss, both monarchs discover their wives' infidelity and dispatch them in short order. Shahriyar's first, unnamed wife had lived in splendor. Her sexual betrayal is compounded in manifold ways: It takes place with a slave; it transpires in the open, in the king's gardens, in full view of the royal window; it is part of an orgy of twenty women and twenty black slaves, conveying the impression that such debauchery and adultery are pervasive.[5] The king is so overwhelmed with shock and anguish that he now believes all women possess the same deceit and treachery. Just as he was once overly trusting, so is he now misogynist and entirely mistrusting. He proceeds to have his wife executed and then devises an unsettling plot to decrease the female population one by one, killing each woman only after marriage and a night of sex. This king seems borrowed from the pages of the Marquis de Sade, who was said to "inspire" psychopaths such as Jack the Ripper and the Boston Strangler.

The outlines of this same story are visible in the book of Esther and its portrait of its debauched monarch. King Ahasuerus too feels deeply betrayed by his first wife, Vashti, who refuses to appear in public and show off her beauty as he has asked her to do. While there is no infidelity or other tawdry scandal, Vashti's unwillingness to obey the king nonetheless similarly inflames his anger. Ahasuerus consults the law (as if there should be a law for marital disputes!), turning to "the seven ministers of Persia and Media" to adjudicate the case (Esther 1:13–15). Indeed, the word "law" appears twenty times in Esther, starting with the wine at the royal banquet — "And the law for the drinking was, 'No restrictions!'" (1:8) — hinting from the beginning at the absurdity of such laws. Meanwhile, the incident causes Ahasuerus, like Shahriyar, to find all women suspect for the "sin" of one; just as Ahasuerus needed to assert his authority in the home, he enjoins all men to do the same: "For the queen's behavior will make all wives despise their husbands" (1:17). After all, if the king's authority over his wife is challenged, no husband is safe. Indeed, the seven ministers of Persia and Media issue a verdict: The king should pass a new law that Vashti be banished from the king's presence.

Notably, in both Esther and *The Thousand and One Nights*, the law and powers of state are instruments of insecure, paranoid rulers. In both, the king's vast and nearly omnipotent powers can nevertheless be challenged, ridiculed, and imperiled by the queen's defiance.

Esther Rabbah, a midrash on the book of Esther, brings out the resemblance between Ahasuerus and Shahriyar implicit in the biblical story. Ahasuerus did not merely beckon Vashti to show off her beauty; at the behest of his drunken colleagues, he asked Vashti to appear naked — except for a royal diadem! This sexually explicit detail adds more justification to Vashti's refusal. The midrash also aligns the two Persian kings in their wives' brutal end: It depicts Vashti not merely as deposed and exiled but beheaded and, like John the Baptist, her head brought back on a platter to confirm the deed. This supplementary story renders Ahasuerus monstrous like Shahriyar (although toward one woman, not many). The embellishment also serves to illuminate Esther's bravery in approaching the king later on, when she fears being killed for approaching him without an official invitation. Judging from his treatment of Vashti in the midrash, she had much cause to fear.

A further parallel lies in the striking contrast between the misogynistic kings and their loyal advisers, Mordecai and the vizier. Both advisers raise girls alone — no mothers or wives appear in either story — and they dote on their female charges. In both cases the children are exceptional, and the father or stepfather gives them every opportunity for education and advancement. Although the Bible says nothing of the way Esther was raised, one may imagine that she was given some of the attention received by Scheherazade: "[Scheherazade] had read various books of histories, and the lives of preceding kings, and stories of past generations: it is asserted that she had collected together a thousand books of histories, relating to preceding generations and kings, and works of the poets." Both women excel in cleverness, courage, and beauty, all qualities cultivated by their fathers and caretakers. The major difference between the two advisers is that Mordecai seems to encourage Esther's candidacy as queen. He serves as a kind of coach to guide her through the beauty contest (Esther 2:10–11), whereas Scheherazade's father is horrified by her decision to marry the king—naturally so, since he presumes it spells her death. Mordecai also plays a greater role than the vizier: He continues coaching Esther even after she becomes queen, encouraging and at times prodding her to become a hero. Scheherazade, by contrast, acts heroically, on her own, right from the beginning.

This brings us to the most important resemblance between Scheherazade and Esther: their roles as saviors. They make their entrance at the same point of the narrative, when the first wife has departed (from the world or the palace) and the king's monstrousness has been revealed to all. Scheherazade enters just at the point when a hero is needed to save more women from senselessly dying at Shahriyar's hands; Esther arrives well before the heroic plot unfolds. Both marry kings who exhibit highly offensive behavior. Both harness their considerable intelligence and beauty to outsmart their respective kings to serve their will and correct injustice. Both are driven by the mission to save their "people"—women in Scheherazade's case, the Jews in Esther's. In so doing, both face substantial personal risk. Scheherazade's danger derives entirely from the king, while Esther confronts a capricious monarch and his genocidal counselor, Haman.

Finally, both queens influence their husbands not only through charm and food but primarily through storytelling. Scheherazade is the teller of all the subsequent tales, including such perennial classics as "Ali

Baba and the Forty Thieves," "Sinbad the Sailor," and "Aladdin and the Lamp." By contrast, Esther's tale is true and simple—she is no heroine for modern-day literary fabulists[6]—but she exerts all her strategic ingenuity to tell it at the right time, in the right place, and in the right way, the way that will get Ahasuerus to listen and act.

Fairy-Tale Queen

The most significant difference between these two Persian queens is that Scheherazade acts like a hero from the beginning, whereas Esther must grow into one.

Like many a fairy-tale heroine, Esther is an orphan; both her parents have died, and a bachelor uncle has raised her. Her orphan status suggests a poor background. She belongs to the Jewish people, a group exiled from their homeland and now living in Persia. The fact that Esther hides her Jewish identity on Mordecai's command indicates that the Persians generally consider Jews to be unwanted outsiders.

In just one chapter, Esther vaults up the social ladder. Her rags-to-riches trajectory takes her in just a few short steps from poor Jewish outcast to Persian queen. If this were indeed a fairy tale, the story would end here, with the couple living happily ever after. But the differences from a fairy tale clue the reader that trouble lies ahead, and the story is far from over. First there's the disturbing matter of the drunken, capricious husband—not exactly the prized, handsome prince. Second, the path to becoming a queen was far too quick and easy, without the trials and obstacles lending the sense that the married couple has earned each other. Third, Esther remains largely unknown to the reader, who has only the vaguest sense that there is some special quality within her. All that the narrator has mentioned to date is her physical beauty, a quality that is never sufficient for a heroine. As we shall see, instead of a fairy tale, the story of Esther is closer to a fairy tale in reverse, starting with the happy ending and working backward through the heroine's confrontation with danger and triumph through bravery.

Unlike Scheherazade, Esther does nothing of her own free will at the beginning of her story. The first verb concerning her is in the passive—

Esther "was taken" to the king's palace (Esther 2:8). This passive verb is emblematic of her entire condition during the forthcoming period; things will be done to her, mostly by Mordecai and the king but also by Hegai (the eunuch in charge of the king's harem and the virgin hordes competing for the throne) and other unnamed actors. In this first instance, we are not told who does the "taking"; Esther is a person who "is taken," a young woman controlled by men, with no sense yet of her own power. The king will control her through the mechanisms of the beauty contest to select the next queen; she will obey Mordecai by hiding her national origins and, later on, conveying Mordecai's message to the king alerting him to a rebellious plot. She will succeed in the contest by winning Hegai's favor and then spending the next twelve months being transformed at Hegai's beauty salon; seven maids will prepare her with a cocktail of perfumes and cosmetics and, coached by Hegai, she will repeat his words to the king and win his love. Throughout this time, she appears highly capable of acting on the instructions of others, but we never see her speaking in her own words or taking her own initiative.

Even more, we get no sense of what Esther's will is, what she is thinking while she goes through the motions of the beauty contest. We see her only on the exterior. At first glance, all we learn is that she is "shapely and beautiful" (Esther 2:7), qualities she will need for the succeeding events. Besides her beauty, Esther's most salient characteristic early on is her silence. She says almost nothing, and when she does speak, her words are merely the repetition of someone else's: "When the turn came for Esther daughter of Abihail—the uncle of Mordecai, who had adopted her as his own daughter—to go to the king, she did not ask for anything but what Hegai, the king's eunuch, guardian of the women, advised" (2:15). The text conveys that Esther's very life derives from the men in her life, living and dead. Abihail, Mordecai, Hegai, the king— they write her script, apply her makeup, coach her lines, and direct her every gesture. Even within these cloistered parameters, the sentence emphasizes her quiet—she "did not ask." On the previous occasion when we do see her take action, it too is by not acting: Esther "did not reveal her people or her kindred" (2:10). Her silence during this period is at times passive, a pampered girl in the harem waiting her turn, and at times more active, representing a concealment of herself and crucial information.

In logic, it is a mistake to construct an *argumentum ex silencio*, an argument that deduces proof from silence or the absence of evidence; but in a story, silence can be pregnant with meaning. In Shakespeare's play *King Lear*, Lear's daughter Cordelia refuses to give verbal proof of her affection for her father when Lear unreasonably demands such proof from his three daughters in order to apportion their inheritance. Cordelia's sisters have proffered extravagant professions of their love; rather than falsify her genuine love for her father through the debased currency of language, Cordelia chooses silence:

> *Lear*: What can you say to draw
>   A third more opulent than your sisters? Speak.
> *Cordelia*: Nothing, my lord.
> *Lear*: Nothing!
> *Cordelia*: Nothing.

Similarly, the story's reticence to reveal Esther's thoughts is prone to provoke wonder at what lies beneath her powdered face. Is she excited at this opportunity to rise in status from obscurity to royalty, caught up in the competition and pageantry? Is she instead merely a dutiful adopted daughter, following Mordecai's instructions but unsure of their ultimate purpose? Or does she share some of the qualms and intelligence of the implied reader, possessing some detachment and perhaps even disgust at the king's behavior and his beauty contest? Might this underlying intelligence be precisely Esther's edge, enabling her ironically to win the pageant itself?

These thoughts lead to the question of Esther's motives as she takes part. Does Esther want to win the contest, and if so, why? Does she seek glory and riches for herself? Or does she seek the power to influence the king on her people's behalf? In other words, does she foresee what's in store or more generally recognize that the Jews in Persia occupy a precarious position and need the king's protection—which can only be secured by someone in his inner circle? Does she participate in the contest in order to defend her people by acquiring a voice in the chambers of power, as does Scheherazade? Is there a sense in which her actions throughout the book are part of her calculations from the beginning?

It is possible that Esther's silence hides one or more of these motives, but it might also be true that she harbors a mix of emotions, thoughts, and goals that are not clarified or of which she is not entirely aware. She might be flattered by the attention, honor, and adulation one moment and brought back to the reality of the king's character and the Jews' situation the next. Her silence may cover a plan; it may cover no plan; or it may conceal a bewildering stew of feelings waiting for meaning, direction, and lucidity.

Why a Beauty Contest?

While the marriage of Jacob and Rachel establishes a precedent of love based on attraction, deriving in some measure from physical beauty (Gen. 29:16–18), nowhere in the Bible apart from the book of Esther is there a beauty contest, especially not as a method for determining a queen.[7] In royal societies, marriage was generally a political arrangement between powerful families meant to solidify military and economic alliances. This kind of marriage was common among biblical rulers as well: Ahab was matched with Jezebel, "daughter of King Ethbaal of the Phoenicians" (1 Kings 16:31), while Solomon had "seven hundred royal wives and three hundred concubines" (1 Kings 11:3). Clearly Esther did not bring any such advantage to the marriage. What did Ahasuerus have in mind when he decided on this method for selecting the next queen?

In her book *Marriage, a History*, historian Stephanie Coontz educes a couple of exceptions to the rule of marriage as political alliance that shed light on the beauty contest in Esther:

Ancient Chinese emperors also tried to restrict the influence of their in-laws and prevent wives from putting the interests of their kin or sons before those of their husbands. During the Ming dynasty, rulers purposely chose women from weak or low-status kin groups as their wives.[8]

In the centralized theocratic state of the Byzantine Empire, the powerful emperor didn't need to choose a wife for her family connections. In fact, Byzantine rulers often selected their wives at a "bride show" that resembled a modern beauty pageant. Prospective brides from around the empire were paraded before the emperor, who could pick any woman, of any class, who caught his fancy.[9]

In both these cases, the ruler of a vast, powerful empire sought to limit the influence of the wife's family. Ming emperors married women of low status so they and their kin would pose no threat to their rule. The Byzantine emperor employed a beauty contest, demonstrating his freedom to marry anyone he chose in the entire kingdom. Whereas other rulers needed to arrange political alliances to cement their rule, these emperors were already so powerful that they had no need of such alliances. In their situations, a powerful wife constituted more of a threat than an advantage.

These instances from monarchies distant in time and place may help explain the institution of a beauty contest by the Persian monarch and the subsequent selection of Esther. The notion that beauty was the most fitting qualification for a queen would have seemed natural in the Byzantine Empire. Furthermore, aside from her beauty, Esther's Jewish background (here indicating being of a foreign minority and an outsider) as well as orphanhood may have provided her with a distinct advantage in this contest, as it would have in ancient China, rendering her relatively powerless to interfere in matters of state. From the king's perspective, an alliance with Esther could represent a pure marriage of love, a happy separation of matrimony and political business. Without royal lineage and titled relatives with influence and ambition, Esther could be the beautiful face on the throne, with no stake or interest in the chambers of government. Moreover, because she owed everything to her husband, she could presumably be relied on to show absolute loyalty and obedience.

The Byzantine Empire provides a historical analogy as well for the prevalence of eunuchs in Ahasuerus's court. As Coontz explains:

> Because the Byzantine rulers did not have to enter political marriages to consolidate their power, they didn't need to dispense patronage to noble in-laws or risk taking secondary wives who might produce rival heirs. Instead, they minimized battles over succession to the throne by appointing eunuchs, castrated former slaves, as court officials. The eunuchs, incapable of producing children of their own and bitterly resented by the aristocrats, were far more dependent on their sovereign and thus far more loyal to him than the average royal wife and her in-laws in the West.[10]

In Esther's Persia, eunuchs primarily served as attendants, especially to the queen: Vashti has seven eunuchs attending her; the eunuch Hegai is in charge of the beauty contest and takes Esther under his wing; and the king later appoints a number of eunuchs to serve Esther (Esther 4:4–5). Their favored role in the court appears to derive from their removal as a threat to royal succession; without any family, their loyalty rests entirely with the king. Castration has its privileges. However, despite the advantage of loyalty that Byzantine emperors attributed to their eunuchs, in the book of Esther their lack of virility does not entirely uproot their political ambitions, as two of their number who serve as "guardians of the king's threshold" are caught plotting a coup d'état (2:21).

Dual Names, Hidden Plots

Entering Ahasuerus's court, Esther encounters a web of protocols and intrigues: a world full of schemers, mixed loyalties, and double-dealing. Vashti's disobedience immediately establishes a climate of suspicion: All wives are potentially traitors to their husbands. The men of Persia prove no more honorable or dependable: They either connive to win the king's good graces or plot to overthrow him. Aside from his bacchanalia, the king appears far from a benevolent dictator. His tyrannical power breeds plots, counterplots, concealment, and widespread uncertainty of people's true motives. There is a pervasive atmosphere of danger, the feeling that no one can or will be trusted.

The atmosphere of mistrust, secrets, and misconstrual emerges in full force at the beginning of chapter 6, where it is played for comic effect. Earlier, the eunuchs Bigthan and Teresh had plotted to kill the king; Mordecai revealed the plot and saved the king's life, but the king has either forgotten or never learned of the affair. One night the king's sleep is fretful, and he has an inkling that something important may have happened. Did he forget the planned coup because of his drunkenness, or because he was too busy running the beauty contest to notice the palace intrigue? Or did he never learn of the incident, and fortuitously his midnight insomnia is helping him to catch up on current events? From the reader's point of view, the king's ignorance appears to be just one more sign of his weak leadership. The plot lies hidden in the official "book of records, the annals" that are now trotted out and recited in his presence. The king thus recognizes Mordecai's patriotic action and asks whether he was ever rewarded for it.

At this very moment Haman enters the palace courtyard—the fact that he is up pacing in the courtyard in the middle of the night itself speaks volumes—all aflame to report to the king that Mordecai is disloyal and deserves death, with a stake having conveniently been assembled in his own yard for the impaling. The king asks Haman, "What should be done for a man whom the king desires to honor?" and vain Haman, who says to himself, "Whom would the king desire to honor more than me?" describes an elaborate hero's parade, which is then performed for his archenemy Mordecai. In this episode, in short, everything is hidden. The treasonous plot, Mordecai's heroism, and Haman's scheme are unknown to the king, while the king's intentions are unknown and misjudged by Haman.

Aware that Ahasuerus's palace is rife with such intrigue and connivance, Mordecai advises his stepdaughter Hadassah to use the name Esther and hide her Jewish background: "He was foster father to Hadassah—

that is, Esther. . . . Esther did not reveal her people or her kindred, for Mordecai had told her not to reveal it" (Esther 2:7, 10). Ironically, in this story the highly popular Jewish name "Esther" signifies "Persian, not-Jewish." She enters a world where everyone has something to hide and looks to get ahead at the expense of others. Being marked as a Jew in the Persian court would make her vulnerable, a target for the ambitions and manipulations of Haman and his ilk. Her Persian name endows her with a kind of protective armor, rendering her a palace insider. Indeed, Haman is deceived to believe that Esther favors him—a crucial deception that could not have transpired had he known her true name and identity.

The name Esther, then, is part of her disguise, along with her perfumes, costumes, and scripted lines.[11] Her Jewish name, Hadassah, is mentioned only once in the story—a secret that the reader is privy to but that no one in the story aside from Mordecai and Hadassah knows. In effect, Esther's two names signify her two identities, Jewish and Persian. The story's tension lies in the question: Which is she really? In changing her name, dressing as a Persian, and becoming the queen, does Esther forget that she is Hadassah the Jew? Will her personal success come at the expense of her people? Like Moses, Esther must decide whether she will be a Jew or a gentile. Will she align herself with her persecuted kin, or escape their fate by assimilating among their persecutors?

Significantly, unlike Joseph, a character with whom Esther has much in common (see below), the narrator never again refers to Esther by her Jewish name. Even though Pharaoh gives Joseph the name Zaphenath-paneah when installing him as an Egyptian minister, throughout the story the narrator and other characters call him only Joseph. Moses carries *Joseph's* bones back to the family burial plot in Canaan. Not so with Esther, who retains her Persian name throughout the book. So long as she remains the king's wife, she can never go back to being Hadassah. Thus, to a much greater degree than Joseph, Esther must adopt a foreign identity. In a telling bit of creative etymology, Rabbinic interpreters associate the name Esther with the verb *lehastir*, to hide. Just as Esther hides her identity in order to achieve her goals, so too in the book of Esther does God—whose name goes unmentioned throughout—hide

God's presence, as it were, behind the narrative threads that are woven into the desired pattern.

Esther, Like Joseph, and Joseph, Like Mordecai

At the same time, Esther shares many similarities with Joseph:

- Both Joseph and Esther live in the Diaspora (unlike the vast majority of heroes in the TANAKH), experiencing the pressures of being a minority living in a foreign land, under foreign rule, and amid a foreign population. As such, they exist at the mercy of others, who may not choose to act mercifully.
- Both find favor with a foreign king, who enables the redemption of the Jews (the Pharaoh, from starvation; Ahasuerus, from slaughter). Yet in both stories the Jews confront the threat of genocide (with Joseph, shortly after his death).
- Both characters hide their Jewish selves, or at the least cloak them by adopting foreign names and garb.
- In both stories, a man is apprehended and falsely accused of sexual assault: Joseph with Potiphar's wife, Haman with Esther (7:8, discussed below).
- Both protagonists marry powerful foreign spouses. Esther marries the king; Joseph marries the daughter of a priest.
- Both ascend rapidly to great power—queen and chief vizier, respectively. Esther's rise occurs earlier in her story, but once Joseph meets the Pharaoh and interprets his dreams, his promotion is immediate.
- Both become intimate advisors to the throne, the trusted confidants of kings. They demonstrate the importance of intelligence and strategy in acquiring and maintaining power.
- In both instances, family relations are detached when they are in power. Joseph's ties to his family, of course, are cut off after the brothers sell him into slavery, whereas Esther maintains secret contact with Mordecai via messengers.

- Both reveal themselves at the climax of the story—Esther to the king, Joseph to his brothers. In both cases, the characters have hidden their Jewish origins up to this point.
- Both are Jewish saviors. Joseph saves his family; Esther saves her people.
- Uniquely in the Bible, these two stories feature the hidden workings of God "behind the scenes," not as an explicit actor in the story.[12]

Some striking resemblances are also apparent between Joseph and Mordecai rather than Esther—not so surprising, perhaps, since Joseph works alone, while Mordecai and Esther plot their moves together:

- The kings forget or are not told of Joseph's and Mordecai's help—Joseph's decipherment of the butler's dream, Mordecai's report of the coup plot.
- Both Joseph and Mordecai are paraded in fine clothing, riding on a horse or in a chariot, as a sign of honor (Gen. 41:42–43; Esther 6:8 and 6:11).
- Most significantly, at the end of the book of Esther, Mordecai, like Joseph, is raised to second in command of the kingdom, Ahasuerus's right hand (Esther 10:3).

Thus, by the conclusion of the story, Mordecai, as much as or perhaps even more than Esther, becomes a second Joseph.

In their relation to power and unintended roles as representatives of the Jews to the throne, Joseph and Esther are the same type of hero. As heroes, they are relatively limited in their potential scope of action: Their main decisions first pivot on the courage to choose to defend their people and then concentrate on strategizing to execute this defense successfully by garnering the king's favor. Both acquire considerable power for themselves, but of a second order; the king harbors all the real power, while their power depends entirely on his trust and whim.

The Bible, and the biblical God, I would argue, do not quite know what to make of these diaspora saviors. They are not as threatening as Israelite kings, who sit on the hot seat of judgment, constantly under God's (and the narrator's) watchful eye lest they overstep the line between royal and divine realms. Yet despite all of the kings' pomposity, the hand of God always appears clearly in their stories, whether to grant them victory or strike them down. The biblical God establishes a demonstrable relationship with a sovereign Israel. Outside of their land, under foreign power, that relationship becomes diluted. For this reason, God's role in these stories is muted, and at best must be inferred by the faithful. The biblical God is accustomed to making grand gestures on a national-historic stage, not operating by finesse and subterfuge. God's absence from these stories thus renders Esther and Joseph apart from other biblical heroes—and perhaps closer to our own age, when God's presence is rarely so clearly visible.

Sleeping Beauty Awakens

As discussed earlier, at the beginning of Esther's story the reader is given no purchase on Esther's mind. We glimpse her only from the outside, like an expensive oriental vase. She is described largely in the passive or as the object of verbs; she takes no independent action. We are not told how she feels about the beauty contest and being queen, nor what sort of cultural and familial ties or practices remain with her. The dramatic turning point of the book comes when Mordecai presents her with a stark choice: "Mordecai had this message delivered to Esther: 'Do not imagine that you, of all the Jews, will escape with your life by being in the king's palace. On the contrary, if you keep silent in this crisis, relief and deliverance will come to the Jews from another quarter, while you and your father's house will perish. And who knows, perhaps you have attained to royal position for just such a crisis'" (Esther 4:13–14).

Esther's note to Mordecai just prior to this provocation accentuates her state of continued submissiveness. Mordecai has copied and shared with her the text of a proclamation, authored by Haman with the king's imprimatur, exhorting Persians throughout the empire to massacre the Jews one year hence. When Mordecai then urges Esther to plead with the king to change the decree, Esther replies in the kind of formal, impersonal language of the court: "All the king's courtiers and the people of the king's provinces know that if any person, man or woman, enters the king's presence in the inner court without having been summoned, there is but one law for him — that he be put to death. . . . Now I have not been summoned to visit the king for the last thirty days" (Esther 4:11). At this earlier point in the narrative, Esther is still hiding behind her Persian mask. *Don't ask me to help the Jews,* she tells her uncle; *there's nothing I can do. What you want is against the law; how can you ask me to risk my life?* At this point, she could not be further from Scheherazade.

Esther's reply impels Mordecai to goad Esther into accepting her destiny and her mission. *Don't dream that you will be spared while the rest of the Jews are slaughtered,* he warns. *You too will be found out.* Mordecai is understandably disturbed by Esther's passivity in response to the impending crisis for the Jewish people, but it was Mordecai, after all, who initiated Esther on her path of achievement through passivity. Now, only through words — and in just a few sentences, since they have to be memorized and transferred by messenger — Mordecai must fully transform Esther's orientation from passive acquiescence to heroic action.

The strategy behind Mordecai's words is essentially twofold. First, he scares her, removing her sense of security. Esther's previous reply to Mordecai had communicated her sense of safety in her current status. She has just won the contest and become queen; how can she immediately put everything at risk by seeking an audience with the king when not summoned? Mordecai answers: *Don't fool yourself — everything is already at risk. Your life is in danger along with all the other Jews. Unless you take action, you will go down with the rest of us.*

Second, once Esther loses her complacency over her new status, Mordecai can provide her with a new perspective. As Esther revisits the situation from Mordecai's vantage point — moving from believing she has everything to lose by taking action to realizing that she has nothing to lose and everything to gain by speaking to the king — in between, she must experience a moment of vertigo when she's uncertain why she undertook to enter the beauty contest and what good came out of winning. At precisely this moment, Mordecai offers her a novel outlook: *Perhaps you have attained to royal position for just such a crisis.*

In effect, Mordecai radically reframes Esther's story for her, proposing a different way for her to make sense of everything that has happened in her life thus far. His feat is comparable to how new experiences and discoveries impel the narrator of Marcel Proust's *Remembrance of Things Past* to reinterpret characters and incidents in his life in novel ways. Until now, Esther has undertaken a lone journey, a personal quest for glory and recognition. Questions concerning her loyalty and identity have slumbered beneath the surface of her superficial happiness; Esther has not yet been forced to reconcile the two cultures that claim her. Mordecai makes Esther and the reader aware that the attainment of success comes with a high price tag.

Mordecai's call to action suggests that Esther harbors a mix of motives, both selfish and honorable, fearful and brave. For the first time in the story, Esther now has a choice; she must think through the situation by and for herself, deciding what she believes is right and hence what she wants to do. In this regard, Mordecai proceeds to give her a sense of her own authority and destiny. Esther has already demonstrated trustworthiness in her actions that essentially constitute following the dictates of others. Now she has the permission and duty to follow her own mind and will. From this point forward, no one can tell her what to do. She must devise her own goals, strategy, and tactics.

Mordecai's reframing of Esther's story again parallels Joseph's famous comment to his brothers at their reunification: "Now, do not be distressed or reproach yourselves because you sold me hither; it was to save life that God sent me ahead of you" (Gen. 45:5). *Put away all of the guilt you feel over selling me as a slave and telling father I was dead,* Joseph is saying. *Your actions that seemed so wicked were in fact the workings of God, enabling me to rise to power and our family to settle in Egypt during this time of famine. In fact, if you hadn't sold me into slavery, we would all be starving now in the land of Canaan.* Similarly, Mordecai suggests to Esther that all the questionable activities she has so far endured or desired—competing in the beauty contest, marrying a corrupt king—may be considered as serving the higher purpose of raising her to the position where she can now save her people.

In true biblical fashion, the crisis goads Esther to recognize her loyalty to her own people. The book of Esther transforms the basic message of fairy tales—be true to yourself—into the biblical terms of national identification: Be true to your people. Self-fulfillment, according to the Bible, can never come at the price of national commitment. When Esther accepts her destiny, she transmogrifies from fairy-tale hero to biblical hero.

A Flurry of Heroic Activity

From this point forward, Esther issues instructions. She sends her eunuch Hathach to deliver a message; she orders Mordecai to convene the Jews of Shushan; she has him arrange for them all to fast on her behalf before she approaches the king. For the first time, Mordecai is obeying *her* commands.

She is also prepared to risk her life by acting on behalf of her people: "If I am to perish, I shall perish!" Her fear of the king's reaction, seemingly belied by the king's favorable reception of Esther (5:2–3), again suggests a darker, capricious, and violent side to the king. In the world of his court, even a queen is not safe in seeking an audience with the king when he does not wish it. Perhaps he is not so different from Scheherazade's sultan after all.

After two days of fasting, Esther has a plan—her own plan, a plan no one else told her, and no one else even knows about. She will, in effect, entice and entrap the two people who plotted the Jews' destruction, Haman and the king, together. She invites the two men to a party alone with her—a "wine feast," the narrator calls it, perhaps not unlike the continual party Ahasuerus threw at the story's outset. Her wine party accomplishes several feats at once. It makes the king feel at home with his new queen, initiating her into the decadent culture he so prizes; unlike Vashti, Queen Esther is the consummate party girl! When she invites them to a second party, she confirms for the king the excellence of his selection of her in the beauty contest and suggests that her reign will ensure perpetual drunken bliss. Esther has lowered Ahasuerus's guard altogether. Now, he is receptive to her bidding.

At the same time, by inviting Haman to a private party exclusively with the royal couple, Esther stokes his vanity, thus blinding him to her intentions. Here is where her disguise as "Esther the Persian queen" serves her well: Haman has no idea that she is Jewish. Of course, he knows that Mordecai is Jewish—his hatred of the Jews arose when Mordecai would not bow down to him on principle—but he seems unaware of Mordecai's relation to Esther. Haman sees her only as an extension of the king, another ally in his lust for power. With the queen's favor secured, Haman thinks his rise in status is guaranteed and his plot to eradicate the Jews cannot fail.

Before the climax of the story at the second feast, the narrative is interrupted by the episode of the king's fitful sleep and the elevation of Mordecai to high office—a turning of fortune that anticipates Haman's rapid descent in the subsequent scene. Just as importantly, this scene plays out the beginning of a switch between Mordecai and Esther. Previously, Mordecai had been the one advocating for his people—the biblical hero—while Esther saw to her own personal success and rise in status—the fairy-tale hero. Starting in chapter 6, these roles are reversed: Esther saves her people, while Mordecai rises in power. The change (and Mordecai's parallel to Joseph) is signaled as Mordecai rapidly ascends in the king's favor and is paraded through town. For the rest of the book, Esther will complete her heroic part in the story, but afterward, the ending suggests, she will gladly withdraw from the cutthroat world of Persian court politics, to the extent possible for a queen.

First, however, comes the moment that requires all of Esther's newfound daring and bravery. For the third time, the king asks Esther, "What is your request? Even to half the kingdom, it shall be fulfilled." At last Esther plunges in and reveals her secret, perhaps sensing and certainly hoping that Ahasuerus has started to mean what he says: "If Your Majesty will do me the favor, and if it pleases Your Majesty, let my life be granted me as my wish, and my people as my request. For we have been sold, my people and I, to be destroyed, massacred, and exterminated. Had we only been sold as bondmen and bondwomen, I would have kept silent; for the adversary is not worthy of the king's trouble" (Esther 7:3–4). At last, Esther removes the mask; she identifies herself with her people. She openly calls the Jews "my people," and she uses the pronoun "we" for the first time. She mentions an "adversary," namely, the Jews' adversary. Wrapped in the elaborate, overwrought language of the court is a personal, desperate plea for the king's salvation.

Ahasuerus acts as if he is utterly unaware of the situation Esther describes: "Who is he and where is he who dared to do this?" The king's question here is bewildering. In chapter 3, Ahasuerus is fully aware of Haman's plot against the Jews. Furthermore, after hearing Haman's complaint against the Jews and his request that "an edict be drawn for their destruction" (Esther 3:9), the king lends Haman his imprimatur — his signet ring — and material support for his cause. Now, four chapters later, does the king fail to understand that Esther is Jewish, and thus does not realize that "my people" refers to the ones he allowed to be threatened with annihilation? Or does he know that Esther is Jewish, but has forgotten Haman's notorious decree? Another possibility: Perhaps Ahasuerus here, like Esther earlier, has a change of heart when he realizes that the edict affects not just the nameless Jews beyond the court, but his own wife. Regardless, Esther undertakes one last bold step. Staking her own reputation against that of Haman's in the king's eyes, she names the author of the decree — "The adversary and enemy is this evil Haman!" Her gambit pays off. The king walks out in fury, feeling betrayed by the actions of his trusted advisor.

Esther embarks on one more clever turn to entrap Haman and seal his doom. Reverting to a passive stance, she lies down on her couch, allowing Haman to plead with her, perhaps even throw himself at her in desperation. All the while, Esther is playing Potiphar's wife, and when the king storms back into the chamber, the scene is set for false assumptions to be made: "Does he mean to ravish the queen in my own palace?" In the haze of duplicity rife in the Persian court, Esther finds it easy to deceive the king about Haman's intentions. Immediately Haman is removed and impaled on the stake he himself had built for Mordecai.

Conclusion

By the end, Esther seems quite like Scheherazade as a heroine. Beyond the aforementioned parallels, both women succeed by capturing the narrative out of the hands of destructive, powerful men. Scheherazade disrupts the repeated story of virgin wives married and murdered by the king to avenge his first wife's betrayal; Esther negates Haman's story of the dangerous Jews, "whose laws are different from those of any other people and who do not obey the king's laws" (Esther 3:8), by presenting the king with a Jew up close who follows and obeys him, whom he has gotten to know and care for. Like Scheherazade, Esther risks her life by approaching the king and talking to him, finding his weak spots (stories, wine) and exploiting them, until the king cannot resist her will and agrees to annul the harsh decree. Ultimately, Esther exercises questionable tactics to advance herself in an ugly environment in order to secure a necessary and noble goal: the redemption of her people. Her heroism is inseparable from the messiness of her story and the murkiness of her motives.

4

ABRAHAM

Pilgrim

Within the Bible, Abraham represents a new beginning for humanity—the creation of a new family, eventually a new nation, that lives in relation to God and testifies to God's presence in the world. Within the history of world heroes, Abraham also represents a new beginning. His loyalty and concern for others, along with his relationship with God, isolate him from the surrounding people, and also empower him to endure that isolation, to have faith in the new society he creates. In his sense of isolation, Abraham establishes the pattern for subsequent founders of religions: Buddha, Jesus, Muhammad, and so on. These figures all experience a calling that separates them from other people. Their intimate relationship with God (or the Godhead) confers upon them tremendous spiritual strength, wisdom, and confidence that raise them above their fellow mortals as teachers and exemplars.

Unlike these later figures who resemble him, Abraham does not give the impression of being innately above his fellow man. Also, whereas the other founders of religions appear to be spiritually if not physically invulnerable—suffused with metaphysical certainty to the point of arrogance, rendering them frighteningly powerful—Abraham comes across as almost always vulnerable, wounded both physically and psychologically. The Bible emphasizes Abraham's loneliness, uncertainty, pain. Abraham shows doubt even at the seemingly most inappropriate times, such as when God seeks to reassure him by revealing the future. Time and again, Abraham finds God's promises troubling and questions them. Perhaps the fact that Abraham is seen more as a forerunner, a forefather, than as the true founder of Judaism or the Israelite religion (a role ascribed to Moses) points to something unsettling about Abraham's character and story.

Abraham's constant movement renders him an outsider. He lives independent of anything resembling a society. He generally flees or fights the communities he encounters, while his own family dramas appear to be staged in a vacuum, far from other human contact or habitation. At the same time, however, this outsider status embodies and confers certain benefits. Whereas for Cain, being forced to wander is a punishment, for Abraham, it is a sign of God's favor.[1] It leaves Abraham open to extraordinary experiences with people and supernatural beings. It also empowers him to see things others can't and to learn from all, both human beings and God. Still, for Abraham, as for Cain, wandering exacts a similar price—solitude, the dearth of lasting, meaningful human contact. Not until the creation of modern literature in the sixteenth through seventeenth centuries, with the introduction of figures such as Don Quixote, Hamlet, and the Princess of Cleves, do we encounter heroes who experience comparable isolation and confusion, albeit in vastly different ways.

A Hero in Tension

God's command to Abraham at the beginning of his story is both extremely concrete—"Go forth from your land, from your birthplace, from your father's house"—and maddeningly open-ended: "to the land that I will show you" (Gen. 12:1). This mix of the concrete and the abstract typifies Abraham's entire saga, for even after he gets to a place, he hasn't entirely arrived. He is not permitted to get established, to stay put. Right away something goes wrong, an unexpected crisis develops that forces him again to move on. Each step in the journey seems to offer him short-lived hope that his wanderings are over. His story is in fact purposeful and progressive—Abraham learns and matures, his adventures are not merely episodic but cumulative—but still, the reader experiences a powerful sense of dread uncertainty over where the next story will lead and how it will test Abraham's character. For Abraham, life is a pilgrimage whose triumphs can scarcely be enjoyed, whose destination is half mirage, whose mission is constantly imperiled.

Another tension arises from Abraham's status as the most solitary figure in the Bible (apart from the prophets). (Moses resembles him in this regard, though his is the loneliness of a leader who bears the burden of a nation on his shoulders, while Abraham is alone with only his wife and sometimes his servants as company.) From the time he leaves his father's house in Haran for "the land that [God] will show [him]," up to the moment when he almost sacrifices his son, Abraham's entire life as an adult is spent in thinking, deciding, and acting independently. Although he is usually surrounded by people close to him—Sarah, Hagar, Isaac, Ishmael, his servant, Lot, even God—the Bible continuously emphasizes the distance between Abraham and everyone else. Generally, there is a gap in knowledge or perspective between the characters, creating an emotional separation that weighs heavily on Abraham. Often, his closeness with God creates a wedge between him and others.

As the first fully developed character in the Bible, Abraham thus reveals the biblical hero as one whose life is replete with tension. At every turn, his story is drawn forward by the tension between promise and (lack of) fulfillment. All of his relationships likewise suffer the rack of persistent strain that at times slackens or pauses but never finds true release. His exchanges with God mingle intimacy, protection, and love together with anxiety and suffering until all the elements appear inseparable. These larger tensions overshadow his relationships with members of his family, rendering his scenes with them as stoic dramas full of silence, distance, and misunderstanding—forerunners of Ingmar Bergman as much as the saga of the Israelite tribes.

Adam: The Origins of Human Tension

This depiction of the hero as a figure encircled by tension can be traced backward to Adam. At first, Eden, his home, is a paradise largely because of its absence of tension. Adam's solitude is blissful. He feels at one with the earth because he *is* one with it, having been formed from the elements of earth and air. The land produces trees and a garden that he solely tends (rather than works in the manner of agricultural land). Rivers flow in the land, precious metals lie for the taking; birds flutter, cattle graze, and wild beasts roam with little regard for this late hominid interloper. Adam exists as one element within a natural world ruled by harmony.

It is God who first introduces a discordant note to threaten this harmony: "Of every tree of the garden you are free to eat; but as for the tree of knowledge of good and bad, you must not eat of it; for as soon as you eat of it, you shall die" (Gen. 2:16–17). For centuries, readers have wrestled with the implications of this verse for our understanding of God. Why did God create this temptation for Adam, and later Eve? Were Adam and Eve truly capable of comprehending this law, having previously lived in a world where everything was permitted to them? Could they fathom the consequences of breaking the law, the meaning of "death," which did not yet exist? If the answer to these questions is no, was God tyrannically cruel, setting God's creatures up for failure?

The implications for our reading of Adam's descendants, biblical heroes from Abraham on, lead in a different direction. The harmony that reigned after Adam's creation could only be short-lived, for humankind always contained the power to disrupt it. Through this first law, God calls Adam to be conscious of his own nature so he can try to master it. The law raises awareness of three tensions that at first remain latent: tension with nature, tension with God, and tension within the human being—in this case, between Adam's desire to taste the forbidden tree versus his instinct for obedience. These tensions and others break into the open as the story unfolds. The law creates a narrative tension as well, comparable to Ibsen's famous law of the theater: If a gun is introduced in the opening act, it will go off before the end of the play. God's law in scene one will be broken later on— the only question is how and why.

By forbidding the eating of the fruit of this special tree, God initiates Adam into a life lived in complex tension with the Divine, in which God's will and human will become bound together in a dance that frequently spirals at cross-purposes. Humankind requires the law's test in order to discover its own ambitions as well as its limits. Without the law, people have no sense of who they are, and the moral stage on which the entire Bible plays out loses all meaning. Rather than a cruel setup for inevitable punishment, God's command is a necessary step in the development of human consciousness.[2]

After Adam receives God's command, his desire for knowledge, control, and companionship are progressively awakened. Whereas previously he was content merely to live among the flora and fauna, he now desires to know animals, to name them. This act of control, of giving nature a man-made order and meaning, inserts a separation between Adam and the natural world that renders him suddenly lonely. Previously, he had no consciousness of being alone; now, being alone is a problem that requires a solution. The animals no longer feel like companions, so he needs a new kind of creature to be his partner: one just like him, endowed with his consciousness. Just as Adam came from the *adamah*, "the earth," signaling harmony with nature, so too does the *ishâh*, "the woman," come forth from the *ish*, "the man" (a new name). The two promise to create their own Eden together as creatures in harmony only with each other. Unsurprisingly, this promise—like the initial harmony between Adam and the earth—is fragile and will not survive. Throughout the Bible, with precious few exceptions (Ruth and Boaz perhaps unique in this regard), marriage is no Eden.

The arrival of woman furthers the development of human consciousness through an awareness of naked flesh and sexual longing. Although the narrator jumps to an etiological message—the power of sexual attraction originates in man and woman being "one flesh" (Gen. 2:24)—the implication is that Adam and Eve felt this attraction and perhaps acted on it. The next sentence continues the emphasis on flesh: "The two of them were naked, the man and his woman, yet they felt no shame." With heavy foreboding, they did not *yet* feel shame, but for the first time they were growing aware of their bodies as subjects and objects of desire. Both Adam and (now) Eve experience a growth of desire as an enlargement of their senses of self: desire to know, to control, to possess.

Their expanding desire now bumps against the one limit God has erected against it: the tree. The nature or "law of desire"—never to be satisfied, always to want more—leaves Adam and Eve vulnerable to the serpent's wiles. When their inner law confronts God's law, they are incapable of suppressing their desire, or sustaining the psychological tension between their desire and sense of right.

As a consequence of their disobedience, the humans are expelled from Eden. Women come to endure pain in childbirth and are ruled by their husbands; men struggle to obtain food from the ground, which grows only by their hard work, not the fruit of God's planting like the Garden of Eden. All of the initial harmonies enveloping Adam are gone. Human life is now largely a tale of hardship and enmity leading back to the dust whence people came.

The first thing Adam and Eve do after the expulsion from Eden is to have children, who serve as a consolation for newfound human loneliness and mortality. Yet their children, Cain and Abel, also embody the new condition of human pain (childbirth) and, furthermore, integrate the faults of the world their parents made: "The sins of the parents are visited on the children." The succeeding chain of generations will bring ever-new forms of contention and woe. By the time Abraham comes on the scene some twenty generations later, these tensions and lack of harmony are given features of the human condition.

Present Pain and Future Promise

Abraham experiences all of the realms of conflict first lived out by the primordial couple, and more. For him, too, the land is no longer a garden with food that grows of itself, but a source of famine that he must flee. Beyond the pain of childbirth is the pain of childlessness; his prayers for an heir will only be fulfilled in old age. On top of all this is a profound sense of loneliness in his encounters with others. Abraham does have moments of triumph and joy, but they seem fleeting compared to the numerous intimate scenes of torment. His life unfolds as a drama of inner suffering staged almost exclusively within the family.

Abraham's story begins with an instruction and elaborate blessing (Gen. 12:1–3). God cares about Abraham and will take care of him; God will protect him and make him famous, an example to other people. On the surface, this opening appears to presage a life story of security, growth, fame, and envelopment in God's love—in short, a story very different from the one about to transpire.

Abraham is seventy-five years old when his saga commences. The Bible says almost nothing about his prior life and never explains why God chose him from all those cited as Noah's descendants (Gen. 11:10–26). A midrash about young Abraham's behavior in his father's idol shop provides a backstory that sets Abraham well apart from his relatives:

> A woman came bearing a bowl of grain. She said to Abraham, Take it and sacrifice it to them. He took a stick and smashed the idols, placing the stick in the hands of the largest one. When his father came he said, Who did this? Abraham replied, Can I hide anything from father? A woman came with a bowl full of grain and said to me, Sacrifice this to them. This one said, I'll eat first, and that one said, I'll eat first. The big one arose and smashed them all. His father said, Do you take me for a fool? Are they capable of anything? He said, Are they not? Let your ears hear what your mouth is saying.[3]

The midrash neatly embellishes on the biblical story's lacunae. It explains why Abraham was uniquely worthy of God's special blessing and his prominence in the Bible—because he proved the falsity of idolatry. It also reveals why Abraham needed to leave his native land—because his family and people in the larger society felt mocked by him and sought to kill him.

There's only one problem with this midrash: The text gives no indication that Terah (Abraham's father) and Abraham differed in the slightest. In fact, the text states that it was *Terah* who left his native land, taking Abraham, Sarah, and Lot with him; under the father's direction, they left Ur of the Chaldeans, heading toward the land of Canaan (Gen. 11:31). They settled in Haran, short of their destination, and dwelled there together until Terah died—with no break in the generations. Of course, God's words in Genesis 12:1 convey a very different impression: "Go forth from your native land and from your father's house to the land that I will show you." But Abraham has already left his native land long before, and his father has died!

Perhaps the biblical text aims to suggest the opposite message from the midrash: God chose Abraham because of his remarkable *loyalty* to his father. Abraham's willingness to obey his father and part from Ur demonstrates his profound faith in his father that will subsequently be transferred to God. Abraham is willing to abandon all ties, confront an unknown future in an unfamiliar land, accept the perilous risks of a wanderer, all out of trust in paternal authority. By continuing on to Canaan, Abraham is finishing the last leg of the journey that his father originated and did not get to complete—comparable to Joshua entering the Promised Land after Moses has died across the Jordan.

The text continues:

I will make of you a great nation,
And I will bless you;
I will make your name great,
And you shall be a blessing.
I will bless those who bless you
And curse him that curses you;
And all the families of the earth
Shall bless themselves by you. (Gen 12:2–3)

Despite the grandeur of God's initial speech to Abraham, closer examination reveals a yawning disconnect between God's promise and Abraham's life at that moment, between future blessings and present circumstances. Where is the land? Why is it not named? How will a single man become a great nation? Among whom can Abraham's name become great when he has just left the two cities housing everyone he knows? Which nations will bless him and which will curse him? Why will they choose to do either? How will they know of him? What does it mean that "all the families of the earth will be blessed by you," especially when he has just been told that some of these families will curse him?

How is a family or nation blessed by a person—will Abraham actually say a blessing over every country, or if not, what will he do to spread this blessing?

God's entire speech to Abraham comes to seem impossible, inscrutable, fantastic. The most unsettling promise is surely "I will make of you a great nation." Yes, Abraham has possessions, servants, a wife; he is an important man. But he is old—seventy-five—and childless![4] The narrator never mentions a child, only Abraham's unmarried nephew Lot, whom Abraham is still watching over. When Abraham gets in the saddle and looks over at his nephew, does he say to himself, *There rides the great nation?*

God's opening speech sets a pattern of promises and blessings repeated throughout Abraham's life (Gen. 13:14–17; 15; 17; 18:10; 22:15–19). All the assurances—enormous territory, countless descendants—extend the tension between abundant bounties offered in the future and the meager circumstances of present life. The foretellings suggest that the entire history of the Jewish people has been solely determined by the meritorious actions of this one man—as if the history was over just when it began, "a chronicle foretold" in the words of biblically inspired novelist Gabriel García-Márquez. Of course, the story of Jewish history told in the Bible, with all its twists, cycles, and debacles, belies this promise. Nonetheless, there always remains the sense that God's special providence hovers over the Jewish people, thanks to the extraordinary relationship God has with this first Jew. No matter how many generations intervene, the Jewish God always remains the God of Abraham.[5]

In this way, there is a crucial difference between Abraham and the primordial family. Adam, Eve, and Cain all seek to evade God and, thereby, their challenges and responsibilities. Adam attempts to reattribute blame: "The woman You put at my side—she gave me of the tree, and I ate." Cain similarly tries to dodge accountability: "Am I my brother's keeper?" Abraham, though, never eludes God. He stays fully present. He possesses and harnesses enough inner strength to confront the circumstances of his life, no matter how excruciating they may be.

Singularity within Variety

One of the most striking features of Abraham's character is the consistency of his presence despite a remarkable diversity of experiences, from religious ceremony to warfare, from mystical visions to household drama, from bargaining over land purchases to arguing with God over human destiny. On the surface, he acts differently depending on the circumstances. Sometimes he is utterly silent, strong, and/or suffering; at other times he waxes eloquent or even verbose. He capably adapts his speech and manner to the person with whom he is speaking; he sounds distinct speaking to God, Pharaoh, Sarah, Hagar, Isaac, or the Hittites.

Yet, despite Abraham's dramatic skill, there is a powerful sense of consistency in his character. One invariable quality is his uprightness, an unwavering concern toward others, no matter whether they are family or stranger; a related characteristic is his forthrightness, his unstinting desire to express his sense of right in words and deeds. He moves speedily to do what he believes is right. He argues with God on behalf of Sodom; he rushes to protect Lot by mustering an army when Lot is captured in battle (Gen. 14); he remains ever-ready to carry out God's challenging commands, whether to circumcise himself and Ishmael or to sacrifice Isaac. True, at certain key times, when he feels his life is in danger or he needs to work a deal with dishonest or untrustworthy people, Abraham does not uphold the highest ethical standard. Nonetheless, from welcoming and feeding his guests the angels, to reproving Abimelech for stealing his well (21:25), Abraham insists that his words match his moral intention whenever possible.

Adding to the reader's impression of consistency in Abraham's character is that no matter where he is and what role he has to play, Abraham comes across as a man who is uncomfortable with words, who would prefer silence above all else. We sense this from repeated silences in the text: when he's listening to and wondering what to make of God's promises; when he's fighting to save Lot and no speech is narrated; when he silently buttresses his courage to confront God about God's sentence on the people of Sodom; when he is disturbed by Sarah's banishment of Hagar but cannot talk to either woman; and when he and Isaac walk silently up the mountain together. Moses may be the Bible's stutterer, "heavy of mouth and heavy of tongue," but Abraham precedes him as one who would prefer to dispense with language altogether. Speech itself, for Abraham, seems to be one of his trials.

The Pilgrim: The Goal and Its Costs

In embodying the image of the biblical hero as pilgrim, driven by God's command as well as war and the human hunger to wander, Abraham bears notable similarities with other famous pilgrims of literature. A comparison with the protagonists of John Bunyan's *Pilgrim's Progress* and Virgil's *Aeneid*, Abraham's literary descendants, sheds light on the type of hero Abraham establishes and some of the ways Abraham's story diverges from later examples. An underlying theme of all these pilgrim stories is the pursuit of an overriding goal alongside ample attention to the costs of the hero's pursuit.[6] Forced to flee Troy after its destruction by the Greeks, Aeneas, like Abraham, sets out on a voyage to an unknown destination but with a strong sense of destiny — in Virgil's words, Aeneas is "driven by fate" to go on a mission. Both Aeneas and Abraham receive a series of prophecies, omens, dreams, and often highly ambiguous divine signals about their futures. Divine messages repeatedly intrude in both stories, giving them an urgent forward thrust. Additionally, these journeys are not only personal but national. These heroes are the founders of new nations on new soil: Abraham as the first Israelite, and Aeneas as the progenitor of the Roman Empire.[7]

One surprising absence in *The Aeneid* is a prevailing sense of triumphalism for Rome's recently acquired regional military supremacy. One might expect a glory-in-domination motif from an established poet authoring an official myth of the country's founding, yet much of *The Aeneid* is devoted to emphasizing the high price of the enterprise of empire building. For sure, Virgil articulates the noble-sounding ideals of Pax Romana, a world subdued by Roman authority:

Roman, remember by your strength to rule
Earth's peoples—for your arts are to be these:
To pacify, to impose the rule of law,
To spare the conquered, battle down the proud.[8]

In Virgil's accounting, the entire purpose of empire is to establish justice—the rule of law—among peoples. Only a powerful nation can repress the bellicose urges inherent in human society and enforce the desired state of civilization: a universal peace.

In contrast to these noble goals that constitute the end result of Aeneas's destiny, Virgil does not hesitate to depict the severe toll imposed by the pursuit of that destiny. Despite moments of relaxation, Aeneas generally experiences his wanderings as relentless burdens punctuated by violence, cruelty, and despair. The Greeks sack and raze his native city of Troy; his wife, Creusa, dies as they make their escape; he carries his father, Anchises, on his back to flee Troy, only for him to die shortly thereafter; and the rest of his adventures are soaked in the blood of mortal combat. Even in the final scene, when Aeneas defeats his mortal enemy, Turnus, leader of the Italian army, Aeneas is not permitted to revel in victory: Virgil drenches the text with sympathy for the fallen general, including Turnus's gracious speech acknowledging his loss. At the end, Aeneas becomes embroiled in hatred, unable to see his enemy's humanity; he taunts Turnus before plunging in the blade. Like Abraham's pilgrimages, Aeneas's journeys have impeded his friendships. After the deaths of his wife and father, Aeneas cannot form a new family. Finally, suffused by loneliness, he becomes a raving madman.

Nowhere are these costs more evident than in the tragic love story between Aeneas and Dido, the queen of Carthage who hosts Aeneas and his men. After hearing Aeneas recount the story of Troy's downfall and his escape, Dido falls in love with him—mad with love, thanks to the efforts of Venus, Aeneas's mother and protector. Juno, the patron god of Carthage, arranges with Venus that Dido and Aeneas should seem to marry, with torches ablaze and nymphs singing, when the pair find themselves together in a cave, hiding out from a storm during a hunt. Juno hopes that Aeneas will stay with Dido, and thus prevent a prophecy that Rome, the city that Aeneas is destined to found, will destroy Carthage. Jupiter gets wind of the plot, however, and ensures that Aeneas flees Carthage to continue on his mission. Dido goes insane and commits suicide. Dido is essentially sacrificed to the greater cause of Aeneas's journey.

Biblical stories reveal a similar pattern. Compare Abraham's strained relationship with Sarah—who forces him to banish Hagar against his will and mocks his ability to bear children—and the seemingly more troubled relationship between Moses and Zipporah, who vanishes from the story after their son's belated circumcision. For these biblical heroes, as with Aeneas, a divine being compels the protagonist to shoulder a burden and travel on a mission, thereby straining or severing his relationship with a wife or near-wife.

As the Dido episode illustrates, Aeneas is portrayed as a victim of the gods, caught in the crossfire of competing favorites and jealousies among the feckless, vain figures of the Greco-Roman pantheon. Despite suffering from these divine antagonisms, Aeneas remains true to the moniker "pious Aeneas," obedient to the gods, no matter what befalls him. This posture toward the gods closely resembles Abraham's relationship with God. Abraham remains willing to fulfill God's command to him, however difficult or, in Kierkegaard's term, "absurd," it might be.

The main difference in the biblical narrative is that all commands and events come from one God; no opposing deities can be blamed. In monotheism, adverse adventures are seen as trials that serve to strengthen the tested person and his/her relationship with God. In biblical terms, the person who passes a test from God has earned the right to be considered a hero. Aeneas's suffering, by contrast, is the outcome of clashes between gods hostile and friendly to him; his predicament is not a meaningful challenge designed by a single intelligence, but rather the whim of deities striving among themselves, with people as unwitting pawns. When God calls and commands Abraham to act, Abraham has a choice of how to respond; Aeneas, "driven by fate," has no such option.

Closer in this sense to the biblical model, John Bunyan's *Pilgrim's Progress* depicts characters for whom choice is all. Human beings are confronted with one stark choice, freighted with dire consequences: the choice to become a pilgrim or not. Christian, the protagonist and the embodiment of all Christians, undertakes a journey of faith that leads to redemption in Jesus, and hence eternal life. The people who choose not to embark on this journey, or do so halfheartedly, are doomed to destruction. For Bunyan, the pilgrimage represents the true inner life of a Christian; the one meaningful choice in life is whether or not to undertake this pilgrimage.

Abraham's story does not hinge on choice, at least not explicitly. The emphasis falls on God. God commands, God promises; Abraham accepts, Abraham obeys: "Abram went forth as the Lord had spoken to him" (Gen. 12:4). (In Genesis, God changes Abram's name to Abraham in 17:5, and Sarai's name to Sarah in 17:15.) Biblical stories are famously reticent about the characters' motives. Here, it's not clear that Abraham regards himself to be in a position to choose whether or not to accept God's command. In principle, he has a choice—Abraham is not "driven by fate." However, that choice is never articulated, by God, Abraham, or the narrator. All we are told is that Abraham follows the command. Likewise, in the biblical account, Abraham does not choose to follow God of his own accord. God sets Abraham apart, God chooses him for a special relationship. Abraham's pilgrimage thus has a very different significance than Christian's. Abraham is not on a quest; he is not a seeker who later becomes a finder. His journey represents stages in his relationship with God—a voyage of love, testing, and fidelity.

As the archetypal lone biblical wanderer, Abraham surely served as a model for Bunyan's conception and depiction of his pilgrim.[9] But the influence—or, rather, the ability of one character to inform how we read the other—does not flow in just one direction. Bunyan helps us to see the pilgrim in Abraham; the later character sharpens the lineaments of this essential role Abraham plays. It's easy to find the similarities between them. Most saliently, both Abraham and Christian must leave their cities, homes, friends, and family (in Christian's case, his wife and children) for unknown destinations. God has promised to show their destinations to them both; as they set out on their journeys, their fears of the unknown are balanced by their faith in God's promised providential care.

Both leave a city marked by corruption: Ur, tainted by idol worship (at least according to Rabbinic folklore), and Bunyan's unnamed city, doomed to perish at God's hand. The threat of annihilation hovering over Bunyan's city derives from the model of Sodom and Gomorrah, fled by Abraham's nephew Lot. Both characters endure their trials largely or entirely alone. Occasionally Abraham has Sarah beside him; Christian abandons his family (see the text below). These similarities notwithstanding, Abraham suffers more than Christian. Abraham lives with the tension between fealty to God and to his family; Christian is purely and everlastingly devoted to God. Several degrees removed from the reality of human life, Christian's trials appear less lifelike and less terrifying to us.

For Bunyan, of course, a pilgrimage was a real occurrence undertaken for centuries in Christian Europe. In England, Chaucer's pilgrims wended their merry way to Canterbury Cathedral, as did many in real life. In mainland Europe, pilgrims have flocked for centuries to Rome and Santiago de Campostela, among various shrines; Crusaders and other adventure-seekers occasionally headed to Jerusalem. Meanwhile, Bunyan's contemporaries, passengers on the *Mayflower*, were British Puritans who called themselves Pilgrims, fulfilling physical and spiritual journeys that in their minds were akin to the Bible's and Bunyan's quests.

For Christian, there is a considerable cost to his pilgrimage: abandonment of friends and family. But the gains are so great, and the need to undertake the journey so severe, the costs pale in comparison. To him, they never present an obstacle or even cast a mild pall of regret. The burden of his sin, the urgency to flee the depravity of the city before it is engulfed by destruction — these are so overwhelming as to render the ties of kinship utterly superfluous.

Most importantly, the choice of whether to leave with his family is not his to make. It is up to his wife and children whether or not to follow the path of salvation (which they do in the second half of the book).

Moreover, his own family seems to play no factor in his calculus to set out on his pilgrimage:

Mr. Worldly Wiseman: "Hast thou a wife and children?"
Christian: "Yes; but I am so laden with this burden, that I cannot take
    that pleasure in them as formerly; methinks I am as if I had none."[10]

Christian's pilgrimage is an individual spiritual quest that he alone must take. It is also profoundly personal: the salvation of a single human being out of a damned society. This is a central tenet of Bunyan's theology: You can only save yourself. Even though the pilgrim is an everyman, standing for all other people who are urged to adopt this path, each subsequent pilgrim must make the journey alone. Furthermore, each pilgrim will not find comfort in a new society here on earth. Only in heaven will these escapees be able to join in the fellowship of the blessed.

Christian's wife, Christiana, and a friend, Mercy, express a kinder but similar sentiment when they embark on their own pilgrimage in the second part of the book:

Mercy: Alas, said she, who can but lament, that shall but rightly
    consider, what a state and condition my poor relations are in that
    yet remain in our sinful town? And that which makes my grief
    the more heavy is, because they have no instructor, nor any to tell
    them what is to come.
Christiana: Bowels [compassion] becometh pilgrims; and thou dost
    for thy friends as my good Christian did for me when he left
    me; he mourned for that I would not heed nor regard him; but
    his Lord and ours did gather up his tears and put them into his
    bottle.[11]

Christiana believes it is entirely her own fault that she did not join her husband. He showed her the right path that she would eventually follow. Even more, God ensured that the tears Christian shed over his wife's inaction were "gathered up" to influence her as well. Christian pilgrims influence others through their example and their compassion, not by remaining behind in sin city.

Abraham too flees a city, for a semipastoral life at the desert's edge. But he must make his journey in concert with his family. He also has different goals: to flee corruption and idolatry, settle a new land, build a new society, determine new principles for social life and morality that his descendants will observe and respect. He never travels entirely without his family; always one or another of them is present, and, for most of his life, a considerable retinue of household servants accompanies him as well. Christian travels to escape the world; Abraham travels to establish a better world.

Like Abraham, Christian does care deeply for other people. He cries for his family, enjoys the company of others, and shows some concern for the welfare of those who do not succeed in making or completing their pilgrimage. More often than not, however, he is content to point out their errors and trust in God's decree. He lacks Abraham's independence of judgment, a strong inner moral compass, and a willingness to argue even with God over the fate of the world. If there was a scale on which each figure's relationship with God appeared on one side and his relationship with humanity on the other, the balance would be precisely even for Abraham, whereas for Christian it would tip heavily in God's favor.

Christian would never show Abraham's daring to counter God's judgment for Sodom and Gomorrah, both because he himself is too pious and too selfish. His view is, *Sauve qui peut la vie* (roughly, "Every man for himself"): Nobody can redeem another person. This attitude could not be farther from Abraham's. He tries (but fails) to save Sodom and Gomorrah, two entire cities of people. And, on several occasions, he does save others: Lot, Sarah, the four kings.

The Spiritual Pilgrimage

In a traditional allegory, such as Dante's *Divine Comedy*, the literal level of the story is allowed its own integrity, no matter the other levels attributed to the work. The same cannot be said for Bunyan's allegory. In his pilgrim's journey, the spiritual landscape overtakes the physical one. Indeed, his journey is described as though he were walking through real places and meeting real people, but all the place names — Slough of Despond, Vanity Fair, Valley of Death — and the human names — Master Worldly Wiseman, Pliable, Mr. By-Ends — show that the spiritual meaning *is* the surface, not under the surface. One would be hard put to claim that there is a physical journey at all. The book is an allegory on steroids, a narrative at war with realism.[12]

Besides the obvious, if comedic, names, the spiritual, nonphysical, meaning is reinforced in other ways. The story is told as the dream of an anonymous narrator. Like Joseph's, the dream reverberates with allegorical significance meant to be interpreted. Even within the dream that makes up the story, the characters themselves have dreams relaying parts of the story, thus further distancing the narrative from earthly physicality. Additionally, Bunyan sprinkles notes throughout the book that spell out the spiritual significance of certain actions, presumably when he feels their real meaning might be obscure to the reader.

At one point in the book, Bunyan explicitly discusses the reason behind his use of a dream narrative. After Mercy recounts her dream, Christiana assures her that her dream can come true, and then generalizes about the meaning of dreams: "'God speaketh once, yea twice, *yet man* perceiveth it not. In a dream, in a vision of the night, when deep sleep falleth upon men, in slumberings upon the bed' (Job xxxiii. 14, 15). We need not, when a-bed, lie awake to talk with God. He can visit us while we sleep, and cause us then to hear his voice. Our heart ofttimes wakes when we sleep; and God can speak to that, either by words, by proverbs, by signs and similitudes, as well as if one was awake."[13] Thus, to Bunyan, dreams are God's allegories. At night, without the distraction of worldly matters, people are more receptive to hearing God's word. Alluding to the Song of Songs, "I am asleep and my heart is awake" (5:2), a poem interpreted as an allegory of the passionate relationship between God and humanity in Jewish and Christian traditions, Bunyan regards God as the lover who comes at night, conveying a special message to God's beloved.

Abraham's journey appears to have little in common with Bunyan's otherworldly allegory. The biblical characters have real names (even though their names do bear larger meaning, for example, Abraham, "father of a multitude of nations" [Gen. 17:5] and Sarah, "princess"). Abraham also travels among places that really exist, many still to this day. His actions take place largely in the noonday sun, not in a dream of night. The biblical author never explains hidden messages as Bunyan does. True, Abraham, like Christian, is not certain where he is headed—and yet, Abraham appears to arrive at his destination in just a few verses; he passes from Shechem to Beit El to the Negev, where he settles down (12:6–9). In what sense, then, can Abraham's story be considered a pilgrimage at all, if he arrives at the end point right away? Where is the spiritual dimension to his story?

The narrative of Abraham is not a journey story culminating in his arrival at a specific location. Abraham has already arrived. His story is about what happens *after* he gets there, the struggles and conflicts he needs to confront in the very place he is. Whereas Aeneas must continually escape to fulfill his mission, Abraham must ultimately stay put. Yes, he often needs to leave his home, but only for short periods, and always with the goal of returning as soon as possible. His spiritual journey revolves around his familial tent.

There are other ways to view the spiritual side of Abraham's story. For one, Abraham may be a pilgrim even after he has completed his pilgrimage. Such a pilgrimage is not just a one-shot or a multiple-site venture; it is a life-changing experience that lives with the pilgrim the rest of his or her life. After a pilgrimage, a pilgrim always remains a pilgrim. Abraham's life is marked by having traveled away from his home at God's command. Because of the formative experience of departing from his homeland, and also because he never returns to his original home, Abraham is forever a pilgrim.[14] Even as he settles down, somewhat, with his wife and family, he knows that this settling is only provisional, since his "offspring shall be strangers in a land not theirs" (Gen. 15:13).

The second spiritual perspective is embodied in the view of the ancient Rabbis, who considered the episodes in his story as tests from God.[15] God gives Abraham challenges to see to what degree he can rise to meet them. The prolonged intervals until the attainment of God's promises constitute yet another form of test. These delays also provide a sense of journey to the episodes: Abraham is moving toward a time and place when he will have a son, his offspring will produce a nation, and the nation will settle on the land. Even if Abraham himself will not witness all of these promises fulfilled, his story is propelled forward like a pilgrimage in the sense that he is traveling his whole life toward receiving God's beneficence.

Perhaps, then, Abraham is best viewed as a pilgrim in time even more than a pilgrim in space. He undergoes more than episodic adventures; his saga leads toward goals promised by God, and that larger vision imbues his story with spiritual depth. Abraham needs to keep the unseen promises in his mind so that God's tests and the familial imbroglios that beset him do not lead him to despair. To the Rabbis, Abraham the righteous test-taker is a spiritual archetype, a model for emulation. Our challenge as his heirs is to recognize the tests we face, confront them as best we can, and accept that they come from God.

Close to God, Far from People

When we look closer, Abraham does resemble Christian in a crucial way: The nearer he comes to God, the further he gets from other people. As Abraham heeds God's call to leave the comfort of his native land and surroundings, his relationship with God intensifies while his ties to people grow weaker and more contentious. In order to pursue God's command, he must essentially abandon the social web of friends and family that tie him to Haran (he departs only with Sarah, Lot, and perhaps his servants), just as Abraham's father did when he left Ur. This same dynamic appears when Abraham, alone with God, argues over the destiny of Sodom and Gomorrah (Gen. 18:16–33). God manifests closeness to Abraham by revealing to him God's plan for the cities: "Shall I hide from Abraham what I am about to do . . . ? For I have singled him out, that he may instruct his children and his posterity to keep the way of the Lord by doing what is just and right, in order that the Lord may bring about for Abraham what He has promised him." In other words, God is acknowledging having invested a great deal in Abraham. Abraham is the seed of God's plan for history that will extend to his descendants for generations. God must then go beyond a relationship based on command and obedience, sprinkled with promises; he must show trust in Abraham, and give him space to develop his own moral voice. God must allow Abraham to be a confidant, an advisor, even an opponent who has the freedom and courage to protest God's plans.

Indeed, Abraham finds fault in God's plan to destroy the two cities. In effect, Abraham's justice challenges God's justice. Abraham questions whether God would destroy the good with the wicked; he bargains with God over the number of righteous people required to save the whole. God will spare the city for fifty righteous, forty-five, forty . . . down to ten. The argumentation here is fostered by intimacy—only because Abraham and God are so close to one another are they free to passionately disagree. At the same time, Abraham's nearness with God pulls him from the world of people, the social reality where people congregate, where whole cities go astray. Even as Abraham contends with God, he is isolated from the people on whose behalf he is pleading. Abraham himself has no ties to the people of Sodom and Gomorrah; this time angels, not he, go there to save his nephew Lot (unlike the war among kings in which Abraham fights, in chapter 14). Meanwhile, his lack of personal investment elevates his moral status. He is someone who cares for people he does not know; in effect, he serves as a God-appointed defense attorney.

The sense of detachment from human society is brought out by the indeterminacy of the location of the dialogue. It is difficult to stage this scene: Where does it take place? Abraham has walked away from his abode in Mamre, accompanying the angels to see them off. He finds himself on an empty road, in no-man's-land. Now the earthly, human landscape seems to momentarily fade to the background as Abraham confers with God on a different plane of existence. Is Abraham temporarily swept up to heaven? Does God descend to earth as in Eden? Is God talking from the skies and Abraham from the ground, with the two in close proximity, as in a medieval drawing? Or should we envision the encounter as when the curtain descends on the stage and two characters speak to each other before the proscenium, with the realistic setting hidden behind? In the language of theater, is God here "breaking the frame," interrupting the drama to communicate directly with the audience?

This staging is suggested by God's interior monologue, to which the reader is privy in advance of Abraham's argument: "Shall I hide from Abraham what I am about to do . . . ?" God seems to anticipate Abraham's objections—and cherish them. This scene spells out something that remains largely hidden for the rest of the story: Abraham's spiritual life, his dialogue with God, his thoughts, passions, and struggles. The narrator pulls away from the physical locales so abundant elsewhere in order to dramatize Abraham's inner life in conversation with God. Moreover, given God's intimacy here with Abraham, we can surmise that their moral and intellectual conversation had to have been long in incubating. The exchange suggests a spiritual plane of Abraham's existence that lives in the shadows of the rest of his saga—a whole other life comparable to the one Bunyan describes for his protagonist.

Genesis 15 gives us another glimpse into Abraham's life in dialogue with God. Again, the location is not specified, most likely for similar reasons; the space where Abraham communicates with God is amorphous, beyond physical coordinates. Abraham receives a "vision," suggesting not a dream but a heightened form of consciousness known to the prophets. One unusual feature of this vision is that the first part comes while he's awake, and the second part when he's asleep. This vision brings to the fore the tension between God's grand promises and Abraham's concerns over their seeming impossibility. Twice Abraham questions how God will carry out God's promises, for a child and for the land. In the first instance, Abraham seems convinced that God's promise *cannot* come true, "seeing that I shall die childless, and the one in charge of my household is Dammesek Eliezer!" (15:2). Abraham seems either despondent or defiant and perhaps both, despondent of repeated promises that seem empty of hope, defiant in his unwillingness to accept such promises any more. God reassures him, by making his promise concrete—not Eliezer but Abraham himself will father a son who shall be his heir—and cosmic: Your offspring shall be as numerous as the stars you see in the night sky.

These answers satisfy Abraham: "And because he put his trust in the Lord, He reckoned it to his merit." Yet, immediately afterward, Abraham again questions God's promise, this time regarding possession of the land. When God says, "I am the Lord who brought you out from Ur of the Chaldeans to assign this land to you as a possession," Abraham replies, "O Lord God, how shall I know that I am to possess it?" Abraham is likely asking for a sign from God that this promise will come true, just as God gave Abraham a sign regarding his descendants when God asked him to look at the stars. This time the sign comes in the form of an elaborate and surreal ritual, known as the "covenant between the pieces," in which Abraham cuts a number of animals and birds in half, a vulture descends on the animal parts, and a smoky oven and fiery torch pass between them.[16] Then God puts Abraham into a deep sleep (the same Hebrew word, *tardeimah*, is used for Adam's sleep when God takes his rib) and reveals to him the history of his descendants: slavery and redemption from Egypt, return and conquest of the land. Significantly, for the biblical author as well as for Bunyan, sleep is a state of receptivity to messages from God. Visions and dreams offer a window into Abraham's spiritual life of communication with the Lord.

A comparison with the figure of the pilgrim raises a further irony in the promises God makes to Abraham. Abraham will become the father of a great nation, a nation modeled on the intimacy and responsibility of a family. Yet, those family feelings are precisely the most difficult ones for Abraham to maintain. Abraham's desire for intimacy and his sense of responsibility repeatedly clash rather than complement each other.

The tension between Abraham and Sarah becomes patent during crucial moments in their quest for a child. Since Sarah herself is childless, she urges Abraham to have a child through her servant Hagar. After Hagar becomes pregnant, Sarah grows jealous of Hagar and projects her feelings onto Abraham: "The wrong done me is your fault! I myself put my maid in your bosom; now that she sees that she is pregnant, I am lowered in her esteem. The Lord decide between you and me!" (Gen. 16:5). Sarah blames Abraham for obeying her wishes, and she invokes God to judge between them! Here, for the first time, God is serving as a wedge between the couple (at least in Sarah's mind). Abraham seeks to appease Sarah's anger: "Your maid is in your hands. Deal with her as you think right." However, when Hagar gives birth to her son, Ishmael, Abraham shows him paternal care and affection. Not only does Abraham refuse to abandon Ishmael per Sarah's wishes; he also bestows on Ishmael his name, meaning "God has heard." This, in turn, suggests that Ishmael's birth is at least in part an answer to Abraham and Sarah's prayers for a child—even if Sarah clearly would not agree. Likewise, Abraham remains concerned about Ishmael's fate. When God first announces to Abraham that Sarah will bear him a son, his second reaction, after initial astonishment and laughter, is to implore God not to discard Ishmael: "O that Ishmael might live by your favor!" (Gen. 17:18). Later, when Sarah finally gives birth to Isaac and tells Abraham to send Hagar and Ishmael away, a deeply conflicted Abraham heeds God's counsel to follow Sarah's wishes. God has assured him not to fear for Ishmael, for God will protect him and make a great nation of him as well.

During the second annunciation of Isaac's birth, this time in the presence of both Sarah and Abraham, God drives a deeper wedge between husband and wife (Gen. 18:9–15). God's messenger informs the couple that in one year they will have a son. Sarah's reaction is identical to her husband's in the previous episode: laughter, astonishment. Whereas God did not react to Abraham's laughter, God does react to Sarah's, telling Abraham, "Is anything too wondrous for the Lord?" implicitly accusing Sarah of a lack of faith. Overhearing God's words, Sarah is stung, and frightened, by God's rebuke. She denies her action: "I did not laugh." This time God contradicts her directly: "You did laugh." God embarrasses Sarah twice, first almost inadvertently through God's speech to Abraham, the second time directly to her. Abraham says nothing. The man who rises to plead for his wife's maidservant and a city of wicked inhabitants is apparently powerless to defend his wife. Here again, Abraham's intimacy with God distances him from Sarah.

How can a nation emerge from such a family of broken parts? Is the covenant between the pieces symbolic of Abraham's lack of wholeness in his family life? In this conflict between responsibility to God and destiny on one hand and his family on the other, Abraham foreshadows the same conflict we will find in Moses. But Moses breaks the tension by parting promptly from his family, which disappears near the beginning of his story. For Abraham, with no nation yet to shepherd, his family is his Children of Israel, whom he must lead, cajole, suffer, and love. God is his guide, but no refuge or comfort.

Akedah: Climax of Abraham's Pilgrimage, and God's

The episode in Genesis 22 in which Abraham nearly sacrifices his son (known in Hebrew as *akedat Yitzchak*, "the binding of Isaac," or simply the *Akedah*) encapsulates all of the main themes woven throughout Abraham's stories. God calls on Abraham to move, to leave his home for an unnamed location. He endures loneliness; his devotion to God places a wedge in his relationship with his family. He takes God's tests and undertakes their costs. His faithfulness to God is ultimately rewarded with God's reciprocation. Of course, there is one new aspect—the utter unreasonableness of God's command: "Take your son . . . and offer him there as a burnt offering"! This is the only time we are explicitly told in the Bible that God "tested" Abraham. Here, the tension implicit throughout Abraham's saga reaches its snapping point. Will Abraham continue to trust in God? Will he obey God? Will he continue to believe God's elaborate promises in the face of their imminent annihilation—at God's command?!

So many things trouble the reader of this scene. They trouble us precisely because the characters are all so real, so believable, because the Bible has gotten us invested not just in caring about the characters, as would most books, but in caring about the moral quality of their behavior. We have witnessed Abraham's fine moral sensitivity operate throughout his numerous challenges, in concert with his keen strategic awareness. He has shown compassion for the most vulnerable, for Hagar and Ishmael within his household, for the strangers traveling at noontide in the hot desert. He has rescued his nephew from mortal danger during warfare, and challenged God over the injustice of destroying an entire city despite its repute for iniquity. And yet he appears to display not the least qualm for God's justice when he himself is called to slay Isaac.

How could God, who chose Abraham for a special destiny and revealed a special bond with him over and over—how could God require Abraham to kill his son? What happened to all the promises of offspring, land, a nation? How could Abraham, who has waited his entire long life for God's promise of offspring, now follow God's command? How could he be capable of carrying out God's order to the end, looking in his son's eyes and raising the knife for slaughter? Not only does God test Abraham—the Bible itself is testing the reader, pushing *us* to the limit of what we will accept from these two characters who mean so much to us by now. How awful a test can God place on a person before the *reader* loses faith? How great a burden must Abraham silently bear before the reader expects him to cry out like Job? Is Abraham truly the hero of this story, and if so, in what way?[17]

Significantly, the framing of this climactic scene strongly echoes the opening scene of Abraham's story. God again commands Abraham to leave his home and *lekh lekha*, betake yourself, go forth. The place he is headed toward, again, is unnamed, only "the place that I will show you." God again presents Abraham with a string of synonyms loaded upon the object he must lose. In Genesis 12, the synonyms reinforce the home he is leaving; in Genesis 22, God gives three synonyms for Abraham's son before directly naming Isaac, the son whom he is about to lose. Both of these bookend experiences are cast as difficult journeys toward unknown destinations containing religious tests—Abraham's twin pilgrimages. This similarity reinforces the sense that Abraham's life consists of one long pilgrimage. Finally, at the conclusion of the *Akedah*, God returns to the promise God made in Genesis 12:2–3. Now we find all the "nations of the land," as compared with all the "families of the earth," being blessed through Abraham's "seed," rather than through Abraham himself. Abraham's own story is nearly done, but his impact on history will be profound.

The idea of the pilgrimage offers some help in understanding this most challenging of religious narratives. For Abraham, life is a journey whose path is determined by his unfolding relationship with God. Not God alone, not Abraham alone, not other people alone set the path;

the journey is shaped in the space between, through their interactions. Throughout Abraham's pilgrimage to date, God has been his trusted guide and companion. God and this man have revealed their inner plans and thoughts to one another; they can respectfully disagree. During the *Akedah*, God pushes their relationship to the limit, but because that relationship has been strong and founded on trust throughout his whole life, because he has walked with God all this long way so far, Abraham will not abandon God, even now. Without this history, Abraham's silent obedience would appear the act of a pious madman.

The notion of a pilgrimage may give us some insight into God's actions in the *Akedah* as well. In Abraham, God discovers the extent to which God can trust a person. Until Abraham, human history has presented God with a string of disappointments. Adam and Eve could not be trusted to carry out God's first command; in Noah's time, God determined that the "devisings of man's mind are evil from his youth" (Gen. 8:21). God chooses Abraham because in him God senses the opportunity for a new beginning to God's relationship with human beings: At last, here is someone worthy of God's trust. The story of Abraham thus also represents the story of *God's* pilgrimage, a journey in which God changes God's view of people and develops a sense of trust in them. Abraham restores God's faith in humanity—in fact, in the whole project that starts with Creation.[18] Abraham's saga can thus be seen as having two protagonists, Abraham and God. The *Akedah* is the final stage in the restoration of trust between God and people. Will Abraham remain faithful to that relationship even when his reason, his emotions, his closest personal ties tell him not to? By passing the test, Abraham creates a model for a relationship based on trust that has been nourished by God and people throughout the generations.

As the first monotheist and the first Jew, Abraham stamps his character on all who follow him in time, in descent, and in faith. Abraham imbues his descendants, the Children of Israel, with the qualities of a test-taking pilgrim. After all, the whole Torah is a story of a pilgrimage, with the entire nation embarking on a journey quite similar to their father Abraham's. They leave their country of residence for an entirely unknown Promised Land. Pitfalls, family strife, and tests shape the physical landscape of the wilderness in which they encamp and travel. Moses is their pilgrim-in-chief, and it is no coincidence that the first place where he strikes the rock (Exod. 17:7) is called Massah and Meribah, "Testing and Strife."

Abraham's role as the father and exemplar of the Jewish people plays out especially in the notion of the test. In the wilderness, God tests the Children of Israel through the manna (Exod. 16). They come to see the story of their own destiny in the plotlines of their founder's saga: as a succession of tests large and small, requiring all their reserves of faithfulness and preparedness. They devote their lives to fulfilling the minutiae of God's commandments, just as Abraham devotedly embarked on God's all-too-often incomprehensible commands (leaving home, circumcision, sacrificing his son). Abraham's willingness to carry his devotion to the farthest limits imaginable has inspired Jews throughout history to be faithful to their tradition in the face of untold persecution and suffering.[19] Like Abraham, they too have had faith in God's ultimate intervention and redemptive power, even when the knife of their tormentors was unrestrained.[20]

The Practical Abraham

Despite being wracked with anxiety, tension, doubt . . . despite living in flight, episodically tested, suffering from periodic family traumas—this same Abraham repeatedly reveals a remarkable acumen and shrewdness in his relationships outside his immediate family. In his deals and trades, his deft diplomacy and public relations, Abraham appears at his most content, unburdened by the existential concerns that often engender strife among people in his inner circle.

His uncanny ability to maneuver, form alliances, and defeat enemies emerges in the story of Abraham's military triumph in Genesis 14. Its emphasis, however, is not on his might, but on his capability. Suddenly, as soon as he learns that his nephew Lot has been taken captive, Abraham musters the tactical and organizational leadership of a secretary of defense. He recruits his allies, Mamre, Eshkol, and Aner, with whom he has already formed an agreement (*brit*) in case of warfare; enlists the sizable cadre of retainers in his household; and goes on the attack. Further, he deploys against the enemy cleverly, at night. Presumably his band is outnumbered and inferior in weaponry, but when the enemy is taken by surprise in the darkness, they will not know any of this. Indeed, the strategic ruse succeeds—the enemy retreats, Abraham rescues Lot and other captives, and plunders his adversaries' possessions. Throughout this episode of physical conflict, the psychological and moral conflicts that engulf Abraham elsewhere are absent. Strikingly, too, in this episode and elsewhere, when Abraham evinces his inner strategist, God is nowhere mentioned. Only after the battle is over do people invoke God again: King Melchizedek of Salem, "a priest of God Most High," gives thanks to God, and Abraham swears to God.

Aside from warfare, Abraham's calm proficiency is evident in his supreme talent for negotiation. Time and again, he finds himself needing to negotiate for his family's survival (and others' as well). There is an effective pattern in Abraham's negotiation strategy: By beginning with a stance of openness, flexibility, and generosity, without a trace of belligerence, he is ultimately able to receive what he truly needs or wants. We see this early on, in Abraham's conflict with Lot (Gen. 13:5-13). They both possess sizable herds, and "the land could not support them staying together," causing their herdsmen to quarrel. Abraham and Lot agree to separate, and Abraham leaves the choice of destinations to Lot: "If you go north, I will go south; and if you go south, I will go north." Lot picks the rich pasturage by the Jordan River, while Abraham stays put in the Negev. The last line of the section informs the reader that "the inhabitants of Sodom were very wicked sinners against the Lord," foreboding Lot's miserable experience there. Between the lines, there's a sense that Abraham and Lot know, or should have known, the wickedness of the "cities on the plain." Lot chooses to ignore their reputation for the promise of valuable land, and Abraham happily remains behind. Thus, here as elsewhere, Abraham's apparent generosity masks a keen tactical and strategic intelligence.[21]

Abraham's strategic judgment comes to the fore at times of even greater necessity, including his numerous encounters with people of foreign cultures. Starting with the foreknowledge that he cannot trust the people with whom he needs to deal, he anticipates that they likely regard him with an equal dose of suspicion, sizes up the danger, and tailors his actions accordingly. The two sister-wife scenes (Gen. 12:10–20, 20:1–18) elucidate how Abraham manages to survive in foreign territory. The logic is simple and brutal: Abraham has his wife Sarah claim to be his sister, so the ruler (first Pharaoh, then Abimelech) will not want to kill him in order to marry the beautiful woman with him. While the narrator never describes either Pharaoh or Abimelech as considering Abraham's murder, the fact that Sarah is quickly prized for her beauty and taken to the palace in both stories suggests that Abraham correctly assesses the risk. Both times God intervenes at the eleventh hour to rescue Sarah from having illicit relations, and inflicts an ailment on the ruler and his household as punishment (although neither ruler committed a crime, since neither knew the true nature of Sarah and Abraham's relationship and the relations did not take place). In the end of both episodes, Abraham and Sarah leave considerably richer in possessions, with gifts of animals and servants.

Abraham's strategy in these scenes might be described as Realpolitik, the willingness to employ unsavory means toward what he believes are necessary ends. To ensure his own survival, Abraham lies to his hosts, in effect tempting them to immoral behavior by introducing them to a beautiful woman who appears to be available when in fact she is married. The rulers are subsequently exposed to physical peril as well when God acts as a deus ex machina, swooping in at the last moment not only to extract the vulnerable Sarah from a close scrape but also to punish the rulers. Worse, Abraham shows no qualms about placing his own wife in danger. The reader is left to consider whether Abraham's actions were in fact morally justifiable — did his ends justify his means? Shouldn't he have put himself in peril before his wife? Couldn't he have found another winning plan of action? Wasn't he presumptuous in the extreme to rely — twice — on God's last-minute intervention — something he does nowhere else?

As is often the case, strategic success rests on moral dubiety.[22] Both episodes feature this tension between strategy and morality, with the ruler insisting on his innocence and questioning Abraham's behavior and God's justice. In the second tale, Abimelech turns the tables on Abraham, summoning and interrogating him over the incident, forcing Abraham to produce a fact hitherto unreported: Sarah is "technically" his half-sister, hence his ruse was not a lie. Pharaoh's and Abimelech's assertions of innocence, of course, may only be technically true; both rulers may have been thoroughly unworthy of Abraham's trust. Yet again, in the Bible, the narrator's reticence leaves the question of the characters' true natures open to the court of reader opinion.

Abraham's negotiation with the Hittites to purchase a burial plot for Sarah (Gen. 23) also calls forth all of his resourcefulness and subtlety. Initially the Hittites' position appears quite puzzling: Why do the Hittites first, and several times thereafter, offer to give him a burial place for free? Why does Abraham refuse them and ask for the plot owned by Ephron? Furthermore, why does he insist on paying, and what appears a hefty price at that, after Ephron again offers to give it to him for nothing? And why does Genesis devote an entire chapter to this horse-trading over Sarah's burial plot? The entire dialogue seems like ritual theater, prescripted and repetitious, with recurrent bowings and words that may express the opposite of the speakers' true intentions.[23]

Abraham aims to ensure that his ownership of Sarah's plot by fair purchase is publicly acknowledged and completely legitimate.[24] He wants a place where he can return and be buried alongside his wife, and where his descendants can also be buried—something that would not be at all certain if he buries her in one of the Hittites' fields, at their invitation. He has predetermined what he deems to be choice land for his wife's and family's interment.

The Hittites' true motivations are hidden throughout the encounter. Are they sincere in their respect of Abraham: "You are the elect of God among us"? Do they genuinely want to give him a plot for nothing? Or are they motivated instead by gain? Are their protestations of generosity a mere pose, perhaps a cultural norm, serving to preface the actual financial haggling?

Humbly but forcefully, Abraham persists in his request until he succeeds. By having started his negotiations with the Hittites, the leaders of Kiriath-arba, Abraham guarantees that the transaction will be sanctioned and accepted by all. He then negotiates with Ephron, still in the same public forum in view of the Hittites. The text repeats the phrase "in the hearing [literally, ears] of the Hittites" at the beginning and end of Abraham's exchange, the implication being that in an era long before official written records or receipts, such public pronouncements constituted legal recognition.

Ephron first repeats the Hittites' offer of free burial; Abraham again bows down and begs him to accept his money. Then Ephron presents his price, in the most oblique and coy terms: "My lord, do hear me! A piece of land worth four hundred shekels of silver—what is that between you and me? Go and bury your dead." Astonishingly, Ephron gestures as if Abraham and he are old friends, as if an enormous sum of money means nothing to him, as if he would gladly overlook such a sum and welcome Abraham to bury his wife on the plot regardless. His true intentions are, of course, precisely the opposite. He has moved from offering Abraham the plot for nothing to naming a princely sum for it.

By voicing such a steep offer, is Ephron seeking to deter Abraham from making a purchase, or setting the bar high for an anticipated sally of counteroffers? We do not know. What Ephron presumably does not expect is Abraham's reply: an immediate acceptance of his tender. Abraham sought a public and hence nonretractable offer; had Abraham attempted to bargain for a lower price, Ephron could have denied his bid and the cave would have been lost. There is a final touch: The silver with which Abraham makes the purchase is "at the going merchants' rate"—strictly weighed and counted. The deal is signed, sealed, and delivered.

Abraham behaves very differently when he is residing in the security of his own turf. At home, he displays to strangers the exemplary generosity and humility of a leader worthy of God's trust and promise. When three strange men pass by his tent (Gen. 18:1–8), Abraham treats the men not as accidental passersby but as his invited guests, welcoming them with honor, haste to serve, and ample generosity.[25] The scene is evocatively set with the expression "in the heat of the day," like the midday sun in an old Western, when people take a siesta and wait for the sun to move on. This is a time of day when people lie in their tents and brush off flies.[26] Yet as soon as Abraham espies his visitors, he gets up and runs to greet them. The sun provides no hindrance or excuse for indolence. He considers it his duty, as the lone master of a household in the area, to assist people wandering by—in those times, quite possibly a rare occurrence.[27]

Abraham adopts a posture of servitude, begging the men to rest and eat with him as if they were paying him a great favor. The men show no token of wealth or possessions, so Abraham could have hardly had an expectation that they would somehow reciprocate his kindness. He offers to bring them a "little water" to bathe their feet and a "morsel of bread" to sate their hunger, the modest quantities perhaps intended to assuage the men that he is not troubling himself much on their behalf. He then does the exact opposite, rushing to and fro, issuing commands, rousting his household, all to prepare a sumptuous feast in minimal time. He, Sarah, the serving boy all "rush." He "runs" from the tree to the tent to the sheepfold and back to the tree; he gives Sarah three quick commands: rush, kneed, make; he takes a young calf and gives it to the boy to prepare; he fetches milk, curds, and veal and gives them to the men. In three verses he metamorphoses from dozing street-watcher to chief chef and bottle washer. The episode reveals the face of Abraham when he has no need to dissimulate. His guests, more divine than human, reward his treatment with the promise of a son in one year.

Given Abraham's craftiness, diligence, and social intelligence, it is not surprising that he "was very rich in cattle, silver and gold" (Gen. 13:2). Abraham possesses many of the requisite qualities for material success. Under other circumstances, he might have been a prosperous yeoman and patriarch of a flourishing brood. Indeed, we glimpse just such a life in the last phase of Abraham's story (25:1–6), when he remarries and fathers six sons, some of whom are recognizable as eponyms of other biblical peoples (most notably Midian). These verses stand out for their complete lack of incident; they make Abraham sound like just another father in the chain of generations listed elsewhere (e.g., Gen. 11:10–25). The potential for conflict inherent in Abraham's bequest to Isaac and banishment of his concubines' sons eastward, which would have surely emerged had this story taken place earlier, fails to materialize here. Having borne and passed his tests and suffered the death of Sarah, Abraham is finally permitted to enjoy the fruits of his accomplishments, to taste an ordinary life without tension. The effect is not lost on his family: Isaac and Ishmael reunite harmoniously to bury their father.

Conclusion

As the first father of the Jewish people, and the first to fulfill a commandment specifically enjoined upon the People of Israel (circumcision), Abraham broadly establishes a model of heroism followed and developed by his descendants. He is often credited as the first monotheist, although his predecessors from Adam to Noah are not depicted as worshipping multiple deities. Nonetheless, he is singled out in Genesis—not so much for his belief in monotheism or the specifics of his faith, but as the first human being to develop a mutual faithfulness with God. God confers special rewards and trials on Abraham; Abraham is ever prepared to follow God's commands, no matter the difficulty of the challenge or the implausibility of the promised reward. Over time, God and Abraham develop the intimacy of close friends or family members more than that of king and servant, the Bible's common God-human metaphor. God trusts Abraham's judgment and reveals God's plans to him; God gives Abraham marital counseling when the patriarch is torn between Sarah and Hagar. At the same time, Abraham's relationship with God unfailingly complicates, even obstructs, his relationships with the people closest to him. He leaves his father's home, parts from his nephew, argues with his wife, banishes Hagar and Ishmael, attempts to sacrifice his son and, according to legend, causes Sarah's death in the process.

Still and all, Abraham reveals himself to be a remarkably capable leader, able to read other people and cultures, strategize, and improvise to accomplish a needed goal. In his mix of reliance on God and self-reliance, in his being a family man whose choices sometimes alienate him from his family, in his tormented though confident and resourceful leadership, Abraham embodies the complexity characteristic of biblical heroes.

5

JACOB

Trickster

Like Samson and Esther, the biblical Jacob also evokes a classic kind of hero story utterly alien to the Israelite ethos. Yes, this is true of Jacob, one of Israel's Patriarchs and early heroes from whom one might least expect this sort of foreign influence. After all, Abraham, Isaac, Jacob, Joseph, and Moses set the heroic mold for the entire Bible, and this mold emerges in pristine form with Abraham and Moses, unaccompanied by the polemic against popular foreign heroes we saw with Samson and Esther.

Unlike those of the other Patriarchs, Jacob's story is riddled with motifs found in a foreign kind of hero: the trickster, popular in folktales around the world.[1] In fact, Jacob's character as trickster is inscribed from the beginning in his very name, according to biblical etymology: "Then his [Esau's] brother emerged, holding on to the heel [ʿekev] of Esau; so they named him Jacob [Yaʿakov]" (Gen. 25:26).[2] In the Hebrew, the name for Jacob, *Yaʿakov*, contains the root letters of the word "heel," ʿayin-kof-vet. Jacob knows how to find his brother's heel, grab onto it, hold his brother back, and advance himself. The related Hebrew word ʿakov means "twisted, deceitful"—the connotation Esau attaches to his brother's heal-grabbing.[3] Esau's heel is also reminiscent of the strongman Achilles' heel, his point of vulnerability. Achilles' heel is pierced at the peak of his military prowess; Esau's heel is caught when he has yet to exit the womb. Esau is thus doomed from the start. His might will be no match for his brother's wiles.

The immediate revelation of Jacob's trickster identity differs considerably from early depictions of Abraham and Moses, which cast them unambiguously in a heroic light. It is harder for the reader to regard Jacob with that same esteem. He will develop into a different model of hero: one who relies on cleverness to triumph over enemies and escape from peril. And just as, after wrestling with the angel, Jacob will become Israel, the eponymous father of the nation, over the course of the Bible Jacob the trickster will imprint his character on the nation as a whole, as the Children of Israel are forced to negotiate a perplexing and ever-shifting array of encounters with foreign powers and exercise their wits to survive and prevail.

How are we to understand a patriarch of the holy nation that established a Covenant with God who is portrayed in far-from-flattering terms? Even in biblical times, people considered Jacob to be deeply flawed. As the prophet Hosea proclaims (Hosea 12:3): "The Lord once indicted Judah, / And punished Jacob for his conduct, / Requited him for his deeds." Yet the Bible never tells the reader that Jacob's actions are immoral, certainly not in any explicit way.

Nonetheless, despite the narrator's ambiguous reticence, Jacob's wiles do not remain altogether lauded and unpunished. The collection of stories known by scholars as the "Jacob saga" are tightly woven together for the very purpose of bringing the trickster in line with the biblical view that human actions take place within the parameters of a moral universe. According to this view, found throughout the Bible, a wrong action will eventually meet with its appropriate recompense. For instance, the Canaanite leader Adoni-bezek, who regularly cut off the toes and thumbs of his vanquished enemies, acknowledges the justice of his receiving the same punishment: "As I have done, so God has repaid me" (Judg. 1:7). The verb for "repaid," *shilam*, is related to the word *shalom*, "peace, wholeness," here betokening a sense of "cosmic balance" in the world's moral scales.[4] The design of Jacob's story indicates a similar, if much more protracted, act of cosmic balancing: by depicting a world in which no good trick goes unpunished. Meanwhile, Jacob expands the reader's notion of the qualities that inform the biblical hero. Just as the Bible's sense of cosmic balance shapes its presentation of Jacob as trickster, so too Jacob's heroism throws that balance slightly off-kilter, where it will remain for the duration of the Bible's long journey.

The Trickster

Trickster stories make heroes out of often poor, downtrodden, outmuscled characters who rely on no one and nothing but their own ingenuity to survive. In these stories, a person is never rewarded merely for being righteous. By definition tricksters are skeptical about morality, not because they're opposed to virtue, but because they are unwilling to suffer or lose for the sake of upholding it. The cultural historian Robert Darnton's observations about French folk tales hold true for trickster tales more broadly: "As no discernible morality governs the world in general, good behavior does not determine success in the village or on the road.... True, the hero often wins a magic helper by a good deed, but he gets the princess by using his wits.... The tales do not advocate immorality, but they undercut the notion that virtue will be rewarded or that life can be conducted according to any principle other than basic mistrust."[5] Tricksters are arch-"realists," shrewdly assessing people's true characters and always advancing one step ahead of their more dim-witted but ever-present antagonists. Their art of deception can rise to the level of tradecraft; a survey of medieval Arab tricksters notes that "whatever morality and law might decree, at a certain level of expertise, theft was both acceptable and admirable."[6] Tricksters' actions are not animated by lofty goals or grand faith; they aim merely to slip through the grasp of their enemies and move on. Nonetheless, in triumph they may jab at their enemies, rub salt in the wounds of the vanquished. In the trickster's universe, life is brutal even if humorous; gloating appears to be one of the few pleasures he or she can afford.

Tricksters operate with the assumption that ordinary rules of morality don't apply to them. They don't operate out of a sense that they are necessarily above such rules; that is, they don't usually present an inflated sense of themselves as worthy of being allowed to "get away with murder" while the rest of humanity keeps sheeplike to the fold. Instead, like precocious children (as they are often depicted), they quickly home in on what is illogical or unjust in those rules and flaunt them. Tricksters are improvisatory anarchists, blazing their own ways around barriers erected by friends or foes. In a world where there is black and white, right and wrong, the powerful and the weak, the trickster invents a third way that makes such oppositions seem foolish.[7] A story about the young Krishna, the Hindu god, for example, relates how he stole butter out of a pot after his mother explicitly forbade him. Krishna's reply: "I didn't steal the butter, Ma. How could I steal it? Doesn't everything in the house belong to us?"[8] His reply both disarms the situation—his mother laughs—and reframes it by upending a conventional notion of property. Krishna as trickster thus challenges not only his mother's individual authority but implicitly the authority of all parents over their children—and he gets away with it. He accomplishes all this by wits alone.

An easy way to demonstrate the trickster aspect of the Jacob stories is to compare his numerous similarities to one of the most famous tricksters in Western literature, Odysseus. The fact that the two characters emerge from the same Mediterranean culture and during roughly the same time period (late Bronze to early Iron Age, ca. thirteenth to twelfth century BCE) suggests the existence of a common fount of narratives (if not a direct influence) that both storytellers draw on.[9] Both characters are travelers, wanderers; both are away from home for twenty years (Odysseus to fight in the Trojan War, Jacob to get married and escape his brother Esau's wrath). Both are trapped for a long time in a place against their wills (Odysseus, Circe's island; Jacob, Laban's farm). Both are renowned for living by their wits and outsmarting their opponents.[10]

Odysseus, like Jacob, is a trickster from before his birth. Odysseus possesses the finest in a trickster pedigree: His grandfather Autolycus was "one who excelled the world at thievery, that and subtle, shifty oaths,"[11] and his great-grandfather, Autolycus's father, was the god Hermes, the original Greek trickster-hero. Autolycus gets the honor of naming the boy. In an act of etymology as punningly creative as for the biblical Jacob, Autolycus names the boy Odysseus, "the Son of Pain, a name he'll earn in full."[12] True to the prophecy, Odysseus, like Jacob, will both cause pain and suffer in like measure, a pattern that holds true for all trickster heroes.

Both protagonists escape more powerful foes who threaten to kill them. Odysseus is pursued by the Cyclops after outsmarting him, and later fights off a host of suitors who have lived off his castle and courted his wife while he was away. Jacob is pursued by Laban after sneaking away with considerable wealth, and later goes to enormous lengths to appease his brother Esau, whom he clearly fears. Both are trapped by erotic choices—Circe holds Odysseus on her island for a year, while Jacob must remain on Laban's farm another seven years in order to marry his beloved Rachel, after having being deceived into marrying her sister. Both are threatened by erotic danger to women in their family—Odysseus's wife, Penelope, manages to evade the suitors' clutches through her own tricks, but Jacob's daughter Dinah is raped. Both Jacob and Odysseus suffer a devastating loss on their respective journeys (Rachel, Odysseus's crew) that haunts them, resulting in grief and loneliness. Nevertheless, each enjoys the watchful eye of a personal guardian deity.

Similar tales of cunning deceit cement the close cousinage between these characters. Odysseus and his men escape notice of the blinded Cyclops and succeed in fleeing from his cave by strapping themselves under sheep that pass in and out: When the Cyclops feels the woolly beasts, he does not detect the men beneath. Jacob tricks his blind father, Isaac, into trusting he is his brother, Esau, by wearing hairy gloves his father feels and believes to be Esau's skin. Odysseus makes the Cyclops slumber through a gift of food and wine; Jacob too plies his father with wine and prepares a gift of Isaac's favorite meat, deceiving Isaac into believing that Esau, a hunter, has brought it. Just as Isaac misrecognizes and mislabels Jacob as Esau, so too the Cyclops thinks that Odysseus's name is Nobody, the name that Odysseus has told him. Just as Jacob's mother, Rebecca, disguises him in order to deceive Isaac and win the birthright, so too Odysseus's guardian, the goddess Athena (daughter of Zeus), alters his appearance when he lands back at Ithaca, so that no one, especially the suitors out to kill him, can recognize him: "She shriveled the supple skin on his lithe limbs, / stripped the russet curls from his head, covered his body / top to toe with the wrinkled hide of an old man / and dimmed the fire in his eyes, so shining once."[13] Finally, both protagonists have encounters with the supernatural: Jacob has a vision of a ladder (or ramp) with angels ascending and descending and God perched above; Odysseus's voyage is interrupted midway for a long excursion into the Underworld.[14]

Other episodes in Jacob's saga are typical of trickster narratives more generally. Jacob's wrestling with the angel is reminiscent of the common motif of tricksters defying and struggling against established, more powerful deities. Often the trickster is a "culture hero" who creates, or steals from the gods, something such as language or healing, to benefit humankind. Similarly, Jacob becomes the Israelites' culture hero by receiving the name of Israel and fathering twelve sons whose names are given to the nation's tribes. He, not Abraham and Isaac, thus becomes the father of the Jewish people, who are henceforth known as *B'nei Yisrael*, the Children of Israel, the name the angel endows upon Jacob.

And yet, despite the many elements in Jacob's saga that chime with trickster conventions, the Bible (as we might expect by now) renders Jacob more frail and human than the panoply of tricksters outside the biblical realm. Whereas early on Jacob succeeds as a trickster, his trajectory falters shortly thereafter when he encounters other tricksters more devious and deceitful than he. He matures and seems to lose his taste for this side of his character. His relationships with God, his wives, and children sober his outlook, bending his personality toward a stronger sense of righteousness and justice. Yet, ultimately, for all of his changing, Jacob never entirely sheds his trickster psyche.

A final element, most salient for the Jacob saga: Trickster characters generally live in a world of tricksters. While they frequently deceive innocent people or deities, oftentimes they are matched against antagonists determined to outtrick them. In opposing the rules established in all societies they encounter—whether human, animal, or divine— tricksters in effect set up their own antinomian rules, the rule of "every creature for itself," that other characters in turn are forced to adhere to or oppose. In other words, tricksters create a narrative universe where the characters around them also become tricksters through their influence. Tricksters bring out the trickster in others. Tricksters beget tricksters.

One Trickster and Two Half-Tricksters

The struggles between Jacob and Esau reprise the sibling rivalry between their father, Isaac, and his brother, Ishmael. The clash also continues the pattern of brotherly rivalry found throughout Genesis: the contest between the social order and God's order. The prevailing social convention (which continued well into the Middle Ages) heralded primogeniture: Firstborn sons, such as Esau and Ishmael, were to inherit their father's property. The Genesis stories do not question the justice of this convention; rather, they affirm God's might through God's ability to overturn the convention. God's power can be discerned both in nature—in the heavens, the mountains, the stars—and also in human society. God "raises the poor from the dust, lifts up the needy from the refuse heap" (Ps. 113:7); similarly, God overturns the social hierarchy enacted by human beings to ensure stability of power and resources. By subverting human laws, God is the ultimate trickster, the disrespecter of established norms—an astonishing role for the universal Lawgiver, the One who has set all the rules of Creation!

Despite the resemblance between Jacob and Isaac in this narrative pattern of the younger displacing the elder, Jacob differs fundamentally from Isaac, who plays no role himself in obtaining his father Abraham's legacy. Isaac is the beneficiary of God's command ("For it is through Isaac that your offspring shall be called," Gen. 21:12) and Sarah's jealousy toward Hagar and Ishmael ("Cast out that slave-woman and her son," Gen. 21:10). By contrast, Jacob himself is largely the agent of his own destiny. Since he cannot rely on God's help alone to reverse ancient custom, he must muster the resources—namely, the powers of deception—he requires within himself.

Jacob's triumphs over Esau constitute a classic case of brains over brawn, the weak outsmarting the strong. In emphasizing the reversal between them, the narrator first portrays Esau as the worldly one: He is "a skillful hunter, a man of the outdoors." Jacob, instead, is "a simple man who stayed in camp" (Gen. 25:27), implying that he is inexperienced in matters beyond the familial hearth. Yet for Jacob to succeed at his father's and brother's expenses he only needs what he already possesses by having stayed in camp: an intimate knowledge of his own relatives' weaknesses.[15]

Jacob's expertise in relationships resembles traditional depictions of "feminine intuition," perhaps explaining both his closeness to his mother as well as her work in shaping his endowed gifts toward her desired end of Jacob's predominance. Jacob's smooth skin likewise marks him as effeminate compared to his brother. The storyteller implies that Jacob honed his wily craft at the foot of his maternal master and teacher, developing the subtle insight into human psychology that has often been the domain of women. Rebecca will similarly outsmart her husband by employing the same set of tools.

At first glance, the contrast between the brothers seems simple: Jacob is the spindly trickster, Esau the outtricked rugged outdoorsman. Rabbinic tradition, however, considers the true situation in reverse: Esau is the real deceiver, winning his father's favor through feigned piety,[16] while Jacob's tricks are merely the steps needed to entrap the trapper in his own snare. Although the Rabbis' desire to salvage Jacob as the clear and unadulterated hero is transparent, nonetheless there is license to regard Esau as a trickster like his brother. Tricksters are famous for their enormous appetites, for both food and sex. They are hunters who can never be satisfied no matter how much they eat. In many stories, the trickster's voracious appetite is his downfall, enabling his opponents to vanquish him, at least until the next story. In other tales, the trickster succeeds in suppressing his appetite, allowing him to outsmart his opponent.[17]

Esau fits perfectly into this archetype of the trickster hunter undone by his appetite. As the literary scholar Lewis Hyde observes, "[A] trickster is at once culture hero and fool, clever predator and stupid prey. Hungry, [a] trickster sometimes devises stratagems to catch his meal; hungry, he sometimes loses his wits altogether."[18] The biblical narrator calls Esau "a skillful hunter, a man of the field," and yet, the moment he returns from the field, Esau feels tired, consumed by hunger: "I am at the point of death, so of what use is my birthright to me?" (Gen. 25:32).

Note that the text does not say whether or not Esau succeeds in his hunt. If he is such a great hunter, why does he return so ravenous? Why the dramatic exaggeration, "I am at the point of death"? One possibility is to align Esau with this pattern of tricksters who are depleted by their own appetite. The more he eats—the more there is "game in his mouth"—the more he needs to eat. He will give up anything to supply his craving.[19]

Jacob is the opposite: the trickster who suppresses his appetite. By relinquishing his food, Jacob gains the upper hand over his brother. Jacob's self-mastery over his appetite enables his triumph as a trickster: to deceive and not be deceived. In fact, Jacob is never seen eating, unlike Abraham (Gen. 21:8) and Isaac (26:30); even on the road he seems unencumbered by appetite. In this reading, the twin brothers are two sides of the same character, acting out different plots in the widespread narrative of the trickster and his gargantuan appetite.

Similarly, Jacob's mother Rebecca is part trickster herself. Indeed, although in world literature tricksters are overwhelmingly male, in the Bible we find many female tricksters, even in Jacob's family alone. Rebecca, not Jacob, orchestrates the entire deception of Isaac (Gen. 27). Overhearing Isaac's instructions to Esau to bring him food and then receive his father's blessing, she immediately conceives a plot and directs Jacob's next steps: He is to bring her two goats, which she will slaughter and prepare just as her husband likes. Jacob is concerned: It's easy to fake the source of the meat, but how can he hide the contrast between Esau's hirsute body and Jacob's smooth skin? "If my father touches me, I shall appear to him as a trickster and bring upon myself a curse, not a blessing" (27:12). Rebecca dismisses his question, because she has already thought through the whole scenario: "Your curse, my son, be upon me! Just do as I say and go fetch them for me." Like most tricksters, she is convinced that her success is inevitable, so sure is she of her mastery in manipulating others.[20] And when Jacob finally wrests the birthright from Esau (here, too, savory cooking blinds the judgment of the devourer), he is now a mere actor reading the lines of his mother, the playwright. Rebecca, it seems, has not only helped Jacob to perform the illusion that will get him what he wants; using Jacob as her tool, she has effectively carried out her own deception of her husband to secure her own goal: the guarantee of Jacob as the true heir of the family's physical and spiritual legacy.[21]

However we might understand Jacob's motives—perhaps he truly believed he was the right son to inherit his family's mission—it is hard for most contemporary readers to justify his actions: taking advantage of Esau's hunger to steal the birthright and tricking his blind father to reap the blessing Isaac mistakenly believes he is giving to Esau. Is lying, deceiving, taking advantage of others justified by these stories? Are these the Bible's values?

Taking stock of Jacob as a trickster character offers one solution to this quandary. It has been said of the film director Quentin Tarantino, "Violence is a color in Quentin's palette."[22] Similarly, in the repertoire of trickster legends, cruelty is a color in their palette. Think of the familiar cartoons of Road Runner and Wile E. Coyote: an anvil drops on one, who recovers, chasing the other off a cliff, ad infinitum. Jacob's deceptions are far milder than the often brutal exchanges found in most trickster tales. Furthermore, as we shall see, the larger story does not glorify Jacob's deceptions; rather, through the Jacob saga, the Bible bends the arc of the trickster plot toward its familiar moral universe.

After her favorite son, Jacob, has obtained the prized blessing, along with the bounties usually apportioned to the firstborn, Rebecca continues to write Jacob's script by having Isaac send him away to her brother Laban. Rebecca comes across as the model for Jane Austen's Emma, smoothly manipulating the other characters toward her intended outcomes yet again. She has already demonstrated her savviness in intuiting Isaac's and Esau's desires and forecasting their actions. Thus, not surprisingly, she is in place to discover the hateful words Esau has said "to himself"—his intention to kill Jacob: "The words of her older son Esau were reported to Rebecca" (Gen. 27:42). Who told her? How were Esau's internal thoughts discovered by his mother or, perhaps, his mother's spy? Rebecca's powers of observation, of surveillance, render her a proxy for the narrator, singularly capable of moving the plot forward along its desired course.[23]

On the Road I: Boundary Crossing

Jacob is the first character in the Bible whose experiences on the road are described for the reader. While Abraham is similarly forced to travel, we read uniquely about Jacob's adventures on the road, alone, in a strange place. "Jacob left Beer-sheba, and set out for Haran" (Gen. 28:10)—these are fateful words. In the Bible, to be on the road, journeying from one location to another, is not a condition for romance or envy. Consider what happens when Joseph gets lost on the road: He meets a stranger, who points him toward his brothers, who ambush him, throw him in a pit, and nearly kill him; then he is sold to a passing caravan of traders, who in turn carry Joseph to Egypt and sell him into slavery; the brothers dip his cloak in goat blood and tell their father Joseph was devoured by a wild animal—an outcome entirely plausible to Jacob. The road is a lawless expanse between the comfort, familiarity, and safety of inhabited spaces, a place where people can disappear or die without anyone finding out. The most fearsome instance of this danger can be found in the episode of the broken-neck heifer in Deuteronomy 21, which conveys a ritual to be performed when a person is found slain in the no-man's-land between cities.

It is not surprising, then, that the road is where we find Jacob, for tricksters are, to cite one famous example, roadrunners by nature. Their fierce native independence renders them eager to cast off societal bonds, or to antagonize and threaten society to the point where they are forced to flee. The Yoruba trickster Eshu, for example, goes on the road to seek "escape from the prescription of social laws."[24] For his part, Jacob seeks safety after provoking his brother's rage (his mother is further concerned for his marital prospects). Still, flight often comes with a cost. The Winnebago trickster Wakdjunkaga is "desocialized, to be represented as breaking all his ties with man and society."[25] Jacob is shorn of family ties and exposed to unseen dangers.

These experiences illustrate another aspect of the trickster tradition he shares: Jacob as boundary crosser. Tricksters are characterized by their fluidity: They cross boundaries sometimes out of defiance and provocation, but just as frequently change form as an adaptation to new circumstances. Their very bodies are amorphous and changeable, able to alternate between human, animal, and divine forms. These forms can shift so subtly and rapidly that the reader may not know what form a particular trickster inhabits until the middle of the tale.

While Jacob does not display this full range of crossings typical of a mythological trickster—he doesn't actually become an animal, a deity, or a woman—he does freely cross boundaries. His earlier triumph over his brother is partly rooted in his ability to cross back and forth over the gender divide. By donning goatskins, he deceives his father about his masculinity while inhabiting an animal body. Even more so, on his travels, when he first lies down to sleep, Jacob experiences being on the crossroads of human and divine encounter in a way that blurs the distinction between these two realms.[26]

Jacob's dream of a stairway introduces his entry into this alternative, sacred dimension: The narrator emphasizes something particular about the place that Jacob encounters on his voyage, using the definite article with the word "place" three times in the same sentence: "He came upon a certain place. . . . Taking one of the stones of that place . . . and lay down in that place" (Gen. 28:11). Clearly this is not just any place to rest his head! Rather, it is a portal, a wormhole to a higher level of reality.

"He had a dream; a stairway [sullam] was set on the ground and its top reached to the sky, and angels of God were going up and down on it" (Gen. 28:12). In the view of biblical scholarship, a sullam is most probably a ramp instead of a stairway (or, as often translated, "ladder"), evoking the kind of incline with terraced landings found at a Mesopotamian ziggurat.[27] The ramp or stairway is a human vehicle; it extends to the earth, to where Jacob is lying, enabling him to ascend it and join the heavenly ranks. Whereas Abraham's angels pass by his tent, indistinguishable from human passersby, Jacob's are clearly walking another kind of path, crossing the divide between celestial and sublunary beings—and inviting Jacob to join them. In the next sentence, it is ambiguous whether God is standing above the ramp or directly above Jacob—"And behold, the Lord was standing above it [or him]"—though it may be most sensible to conjecture that Jacob has ascended the ramp with the angels and arrived at the heavens, where God speaks to him. Even if only in a dream, Jacob is the first human to "shoot the moon" and achieve a spiritual ascent to God's dwelling place.[28]

God offers Jacob a long and elaborate promise of protection throughout his sojourn and eventual return home. Jacob's blessing here is nearly identical to God's initial blessing of Abraham—blessings that both patriarchs receive at the beginning of their journeys: "All the families of the earth shall bless themselves by you and your descendants." Jacob awakens with a sense of awe and awareness of God that he has not hitherto shown. He names the place Bethel, the House of God, a name that is also mentioned in relation to Abraham (Gen. 12:8). In both cases, the patriarchs dedicate the place as a shrine to God.

Along with Jacob's feeling of awe in God's presence comes a newfound experience of surprise: "Surely the Lord is present in this place, and I did not know it!" The dream is a turning point for him. Previously, he always seemed to know how to handle situations to his advantage, and this knowledge gave him power over others. Now, Jacob's not knowing—and, furthermore, his recognition of not knowing—signifies a change in his character, a departure from the trickster who exercises control through knowledge. His admission of ignorance amounts to a cognizance of vulnerability. From here on he will not always be able to prevail by his wits. Moreover, his destiny will not always work out as he would like.

However, immediately after this brief glimpse of self-awareness, Jacob returns to his trickster ways: "If God remains with me, if He protects me on this journey that I am making, and gives me bread to eat and clothing to wear, and if I return safe to my father's house—the Lord shall be my God. And this stone, which I have set up as a pillar, shall be God's abode; and of all that You give me, I will set aside a tithe for You" (Gen. 28:20–22). Jacob is attempting to manipulate God, and scarcely differently from how he has tricked his brother and father. He is trying to entrap God in language by enfolding his pledge of loyalty within multiple conditions: *If God protects me, feeds and clothes me, and brings me back home safely, then and only then will I recognize the Lord as my God.* Jacob then ends his prayer with what appears to be an attempt to bribe

God: *God, if You give me all of these things, then I will build You a house and tithe my crops to You.* For the moment, even after ascending to heaven and experiencing a theophany, Jacob has not manifestly changed. He is still the heel grabber.

God as Trickster

Jacob does succeed; the gods—at least the gods of literature—love tricksters. God accepts Jacob's conditions and stays with Jacob throughout his story. Jacob even brings out God's trickster side, for indeed often in the Bible, God acts as a trickster.[29] As noted, all through Genesis, God is the upender of rigid social conventions such as primogeniture, as the younger rather than the elder son receives the inheritance.

In the Torah, the classic story in which God acts as trickster is the episode of Balaam the prophet (Num. 22–24). Fearing that the Israelites who are encamped nearby will destroy him, Balak, the king of Moab, seeks God's aid to drive them off. He sends for Balaam to curse the Israelites. Balak believes that prophecy can be bought: If he pays Balaam generously, Balaam will agree to curse Israel, and that curse will be effective. Thus, Balak holds that God's agency is up for sale. Balaam (whose fame is attested in an ancient writing outside the Bible) acts only on God's command, which comes to him in his dreams. At first God tells him not to go, because he cannot curse Israel; the second time, God allows Balaam to go, provided he follows God's word. Along the way, Balaam strikes his donkey three times when the donkey refuses to move; the donkey speaks and complains, and Balaam discovers that the donkey has received a heavenly vision that he himself could not see: an angel of the Lord bearing a drawn sword, blocking its path. Balaam travels to Moab, where three times he prepares altars and sacrifices; when he opens his mouth to utter a curse, three times God puts words of blessing in his mouth.

In this story, God plays the trickster who mocks the powerful. Balak thinks his money can empower him to win God's favor over the Israelites; God lets him go through all the effort and expense, only to have Balaam praise Israel. Balaam, the revered prophet, finds that a donkey has a clearer vision of God than he does. Just as God raises the lowly from the dung heap to sit with princes, sometimes God lowers the mighty beneath the donkey.

Perhaps the greatest demonstration of God's love for tricksters in the TANAKH is seen in the episode of Elijah's confrontation with the 450 priests of Baal (1 Kings 18:20–40). This scene doesn't even seem to belong in the Jewish Bible because the satire is so thick, the language so dripping with contempt, the Baal priests' actions so absurd, and Elijah's actions so brutal. The showdown between Elijah and the priests is framed by the ongoing rivalry between Elijah and Ahab. Prophet and king; loyal God-follower versus wanton idolater; lone, humble outsider against the mighty leader encompassed by sycophants — these are the terms that define Elijah's prophetic mission, terms so stark and memorable that they indelibly etch the image of the biblical prophet. A king's wealth, prestige, and arms, the Bible emphasizes time and again, have no substance without God's favor. When Ahab becomes an Israelite king, he marries Jezebel, daughter of a Phoenician king, and follows her god Baal: "[Ahab] erected an altar to Baal in the temple of Baal which he built in Samaria. . . . Ahab did more to vex the Lord, the God of Israel, than all the kings of Israel who preceded him" (1 Kings 16:32–33). Later, we are told explicitly that Ahab's idolatry and abhorrent behavior are committed "at the instigation of his wife Jezebel" (21:25), who personally arranges to "[kill] off the prophets of the Lord" (18:4).

Ahab and Elijah meet in private. They spar verbally, Ahab dismissing Elijah as a "troubler of Israel" (1 Kings 18:17), Elijah accusing Ahab of courting disaster by abandoning the Lord and following the Baals, Canaanite deities. Elijah then commands Ahab to summon "all Israel" along with the priests of Baal and 450 prophets of Asherah to Mount Carmel. Ahab agrees, for unmentioned reasons. Elijah's destruction of the priests, then, is explicitly an attack on Ahab and Jezebel, who brought idolatrous practices to the nation, all too many of whose members joined them willingly.

The confrontation is reminiscent of Moses' contest against Pharaoh's magicians, only here the stakes are higher and more savage. Elijah the trickster has prepared the script in advance: He will mock his opponents' practices and beliefs, exploit their ambition, and shred their power and authority, then hasten their end. Before all the assembled at Mount Carmel he announces the rules of the contest: Each side is to kill a bull, prepare it for sacrifice, but light no fire. Whichever bull is burned, that side's God is the true God. Elijah gives the Baal priests enough rope to hang themselves, and sure enough they appear like idiots. They shout Baal's name all morning. When there is no response, they perform a hopping dance; when that fails, they shout louder, gash themselves into a bloody mess, and still keep going. Elijah taunts them, as tricksters do: "Shout louder! After all, he is a god. But he may be in conversation, he may be detained, or he may be on a journey, or perhaps he is asleep and will wake up" (1 Kings 18:27). According to biblical scholars, the provocation here may be even more pointed: The Hebrew words, which are obscure, may mean, *Baal is hiding behind closed doors because he may be defecating or making love*.[30] There is no greater reductio ad absurdum of idolatry in the whole TANAKH. This scene is an enactment of the judgment in Psalms 115:4–8:

> Their idols are silver and gold, the work of men's hands.
> They have mouths but cannot speak, eyes but cannot see . . .
> Those who fashion them, all who trust in them, shall become like them.

Tricksters often dabble in magic, serving as conduits of supernatural powers, as we will see with Jacob and Laban's sheep. Here, Elijah renders his feat all the more remarkable and an indisputable sign from God by stacking the deck against himself, the way a magician would to demonstrate his powers. He has the audience douse his bull offering and the wood beneath it with jars filled with water, three times, to prove that, by natural means, this offering would never burn. When fire descends and consumes Elijah's offering, then, there can be only one conclusion, one the people immediately grasp: "The Lord alone is God!" The soggy altar of the single prophet of God is consumed, while the sacrifices of the 450 Baal priests lie cold. Elijah's mockery of his opponents' religious beliefs and practices, and his stacking the odds against himself to demonstrate his ability to channel God's supernatural powers, are moves from the trickster playbook. So is the outsized cruelty of the story's end: Elijah then has the people seize and massacre the prophets of Baal—an explicit attack on Ahab and Jezebel for having brought idolatrous practices to the nation. Much more explicitly than Jacob, Elijah the trickster acts as an agent of God the trickster.

Contrasted with the subtle, emotionally resonant portraits of Genesis, this scene with Elijah seems plucked from a different culture. Nonetheless, Elijah, like Jacob, is a recognizable trickster. The prophet, to a far greater degree than the patriarch, is able to draw on his close relationship with God to triumph over enemies much more powerful and numerous than his allies. Elijah's intimate identification with God renders him here an agent of God's tricksterism. Just as Jacob's deceit of his father and brother are scripted by his trickster mother, Elijah's bravura performance mocking and then obliterating his battalion of opponents reveals the will and attitude of a trickster God.

Jacob against Two Tricksters: Deceiver Deceived

Shortly after Jacob receives God's blessing, he arrives at his destination, his uncle Laban's home in Haran (Gen. 29). When his father had instructed him to take a wife from Laban's daughters, little did Jacob suspect what this mission would entail. Initially, everything works as planned. Although the text does not reveal Jacob's thoughts, we might imagine him saying to himself, "I can't believe my good fortune." As soon as he arrives in town, he sees a well with shepherds and a flock of sheep; he asks where they are from, and when they answer Haran, he asks if they know Laban; they alert him to the arrival of Laban's daughter Rachel. Overjoyed and overwhelmed with emotion, Jacob cannot even speak to Rachel before kissing her and crying. Only then is he able to reveal his identity to her (and remove the stone off the well for Rachel's sheep). Perhaps Jacob is recalling the similar story of his grandfather Abraham's servant meeting Rebecca at the well—a sign that she was the destined one for his father, Isaac. Jacob appears to be feeling the same sense of destiny in his encounter with Rachel.

She runs back and tells Laban, Laban runs to the well to greet Jacob, and they all head back to his house. Laban seals this newfound relation with words recalling Adam's rejoicing over Eve, "You are truly my bone and flesh" (Gen. 29:14), which, at least in retrospect, introduces the first jarring note into the story. Laban seems to be trying too hard to cement Jacob's role in the family, talking to him like a wife—in the absence of his own wife, never mentioned in the story—rather than a future son-in-law. Jacob, excited by his love for Rachel, flush with success, can hardly detect the discordance.

At this point, Jacob likely thinks his tribulations are over. He can put aside the deceptions of his youth; he can marry his love, reside with her father, and enjoy the warmth of his household, without further need of trickery. Jacob is ready for the curtain call, not realizing that he's only in Act 2. Having set the trickster epic in motion, Jacob will experience many more confrontations and plot twists before the story closes. Even when they triumph, tricksters never get to relax.[31]

Jacob and Laban's relationship will subsequently be defined by a long series of tricks and deceptions reminiscent of the rivalry between Coyote and Rabbit in Native American tales. Here's one example:

> One day Coyote was out walking. He was walking in the forest. He saw Rabbit. He started to chase Rabbit. Rabbit ran in a hole. Coyote said: "I'll get you out of that hole. Let me think." Coyote sat down to think. "Now I know. I'll get you out. I'll get weeds. I'll put them in the hole. I'll set fire to them. Then you will come out," said Coyote.
>
> Rabbit laughed. "No, I will not come out, my cousin. I like weeds. I'll eat the weeds."
>
> "Do you eat milkweeds?" asked Coyote. "I'll get milkweeds."
>
> "Yes, I like milkweeds. I'll eat milkweeds," said Rabbit. . . .
>
> "I know," said Coyote. "Piñon pitch."
>
> Rabbit looked sad. "You will kill me. I do not eat piñon pitch," said Rabbit.

Coyote was happy. He ran from piñon tree to piñon tree. He gathered piñon pitch. He put the piñon pitch in the hole. He set the piñon pitch on fire. He bent low. He blew on the fire.

"Come closer," said Rabbit, "blow harder." Coyote came closer. He blew harder. "I'm nearly dead," said Rabbit, "come closer. Blow a little harder."

Rabbit turned. He kicked hard. The fire flew in Coyote's face. Rabbit ran away. He was laughing very hard.[32]

If Jacob is Coyote, the trickster hero and often antihero, Laban plays Rabbit, nemesis and sometime friend. Laban, like Rabbit, is a second trickster providing the first with his comeuppance for his deceptive and arrogant ways. The fact that Laban "ran to greet him; he embraced him and kissed him, and took him into his house" (Gen. 29:13) leaves Jacob feeling welcomed and unaware that he is being manipulated. Jacob speaks to Laban with newfound honesty, telling his uncle "all that had happened" to him, concealing nothing. He thinks he no longer needs to deceive. He wants to establish a new, married life on a different basis than the relations he had back home. He does everything he can to demonstrate his trustworthiness—so, for the first time, he is vulnerable to the deception of others.[33]

After serving as host for a month, Laban is ready to entrap Jacob, through negotiation. Laban reveals himself to be a seasoned, wily negotiator, whereas Jacob is out of his depth. This brief exchange is reminiscent of Abraham's negotiation with the Hittites over the burial cave for his wife, but Jacob is no Abraham, lacking the maturity and life experience to perceive the intent of the other side, to know how to drive a good bargain. It needs hardly be said that Laban is not negotiating in good faith, nor does he show the slightest concern that his son-in-law-to-be is treated fairly or generously. Laban will squeeze Jacob as dry as he can; Jacob's eyes are too misty to see his pocket being picked. Laban begins by feigning concern, desiring not to cheat Jacob of his wages: "Just because you are a kinsman, should you serve me for nothing? Tell me, what shall your wages be?" (Gen. 29:15). Laban asks Jacob to name his price; and Jacob, like most first-time employees, is so overjoyed to be asked to "have a job," he does not know what to offer. He gives away the bank, offering to serve Laban for seven years in order to marry Laban's daughter Rachel. Through his egregious bargaining skills, Jacob in effect commits himself to voluntary slavery, like the biblical law regarding a servant who serves for six years and must be released on the seventh (Exod. 21:2; Deut. 15:12).

After Jacob's promised seven years of labor for no wages other than a bride, Laban exchanges Leah for Rachel, Jacob's beloved. While Laban's professed motive, "It is not the practice in our place to marry off the younger before the older" (Gen. 29:26), may be sincere, and indeed he may be concerned about Leah's marital prospects, these considerations do not justify Laban's breaking his agreement with Jacob. For her part, just as Jacob was a willing pawn of his mother Rebecca's trickery, Leah is her father Laban's agent and beneficiary, a parallel that a midrash brings to light (Bereishit Rabbah 70:19): "All that night he [Jacob] called her [Leah] 'Rachel' and she answered him. In the morning, 'Behold, it was Leah.' He said to her: Deceiver, daughter of a deceiver! Didn't I call you 'Rachel' at night and you answered? She said to him: Is there such a thing as a teacher without students? Did your father not call you 'Esau'—and you answered him?"

Genesis does not record a verbal exchange between Jacob and Leah in the nuptial tent, so this midrash casts light on this episode. Leah is not merely a pawn of Laban's deception; she is a trickster in her own right. She wears a veil to hide her identity from Jacob and gladly deceives him,[34] impersonating her sister like the expert imitator she is. Unlike in classical trickster stories, however, where the trickster is outtricked in response to his present actions, Leah's deceits are meant to punish Jacob for his past misdeeds. Moreover, Leah exacts justice for acts Jacob committed in another place and against other people. In effect, she and her father Laban become tools of God's vengeance.[35]

The biblical scholar Yair Zakovitch spells out the similarities between the stories of Rebecca and Jacob's deception of Isaac and Laban and Leah's deception of Jacob:

> The perceptive reader understands that Laban administers a measure-for-measure penalty on Jacob, and the perfectly mirrored symmetry between the two episodes seals the case: in the story of the stealing of the blessing, the mother, Rebecca, took advantage of the father's blindness to replace her firstborn son with the younger one. In the parallel episode, the father, Laban (who is Rebecca's brother), takes advantage of darkness (which prevents Jacob from seeing the bride's identity) to substitute his younger daughter with the firstborn.[36]

We will see that this scene repeats a third time at the end of Jacob's saga.

Counting Sheep

After twenty years of working for his father-in-law, fulfilling his agreement with him, and marrying his two daughters, Jacob is now ready to leave Laban and return to his native land. However, leave-taking is not that simple. Another contest between Jacob and Laban ensues. This episode begins like the first, with negotiations over wages. Once again Laban presents himself as an honest broker: "Name the wages due from me, and I will pay you" (Gen. 30:28). This time, however, Jacob does not name a price outright; instead he emphasizes his own significant role in Laban's accumulation of wealth. When Laban asks a second time, "What shall I pay you?" Jacob then names his price: "every speckled and spotted animal—every dark-colored sheep and every spotted and speckled goat." As before, Jacob seems to be selling himself far short: These unusual livestock are likely a very small percentage of the flock. Yet Jacob is actually summoning his trickster nature to outsmart his opponent, whom he now recognizes as a trickster like himself. He offers wages that seem so scant Laban can scarcely refuse them, and soon thereafter Jacob maneuvers these terms into a substantial gain.[37] First, though, Laban again tries to sneak out of the bargain: "He removed the streaked and spotted he-goats and all the speckled and spotted she-goats . . . and all the dark-colored sheep, and left them in the charge of his sons. And he put a distance of three days' journey between himself and Jacob." Begrudging Jacob even of the meager income he has agreed to pay him, Laban leaves Jacob without his promised mottled goats and dark sheep. Fortunately, Jacob is a worthy opponent, able to summon tools of the trickster trade. Using "fresh shoots of poplar, and of almond and plane," Jacob resorts to a special method to induce the flock to mate and produce baby goats and sheep of the desired coloration.

Jacob's feat with the sheep, while technically honest—a point he repeatedly emphasizes—is nonetheless redolent of the trickster's capacity to reinvent the status quo and to exploit possibilities hidden to others. In Hyde's words, "Trickster is the great shape-shifter . . . given the materials of this world, he demonstrates the degree to which the way we have shaped them may be altered."[38] Exhibiting a combination of magic and science, akin to Moses' legerdemain with the Egyptian wonderworkers, Jacob outsmarts his father-in-law.

For his part, Laban intended to keep Jacob dependent and exploited, as he had for the past twenty years—but in the struggle between Laban's Rabbit and Jacob's Coyote, the entrapped trickster has trapped and enraged the trapper. Balance is restored. In their game of wits and thefts, however, more reversals still await.

Rachel: Tragic Trickster

If the aforementioned midrash presents Leah as trickster, her sister Rachel even more patently fulfills that role in the biblical stories. Perhaps, aside from her beauty, that is why Jacob loved her so strongly: He recognized her as a kindred spirit.

Rachel's trickery first appears in the biblical text in the sisters' contest over the affections of their husband. This sense of competition and envy emerges in the meaning Leah assigns to her sons' names: for Reuven, "The Lord has seen my affliction . . . Now my husband will love me"; for Levi, "This time my husband will become attached to me, for I have borne him three sons." Bearing children thus becomes a means for Leah to compete for Jacob's love. Furthermore, God, fulfilling God's role as Master Trickster, overturns Jacob's favoritism for Rachel, giving Leah child after child: "The Lord saw that Leah was unloved and He opened her womb; but Rachel was barren" (Gen. 29:31). Only after Leah has had seven children does God then show compassion for Rachel by granting her children.

Rachel is not content to wait for God's favor. Supremely jealous, frustrated, and enraged at her fate, she rants to Jacob like a female Patrick Henry: "Give me children, or I shall die" (Gen. 30:1). Jacob, perhaps hearing in her cry an echo of his brother's exaggerated plea years earlier ("I am at the point of death, so of what use is my birthright to me?"), now expresses anger toward her for the first time: "Can I take the place of God, who has denied you fruit of the womb?" Rachel then gives Jacob her servant Bilhah and has two children through her. Rachel's explanations of their names reveal her participation in the sibling rivalry: for Dan — "God has vindicated me"; for Naphtali — "A fateful contest I waged with my sister; yes, and I have prevailed." (Naturally, Leah responds by having more children through *her* servant.) As with Sarah, who first had a child through her servant Hagar, however, this solution to Rachel's barrenness provides only temporary satisfaction. Ultimately, it does not dull the intensity of her yearning for children of her own.

Rachel seizes her opportunity when she spots Reuven bringing mandrakes from the field to his mother Leah. From the context it's clear that mandrakes were considered a fertility aid and perhaps also an aphrodisiac (properties attributed to it because of the alleged resemblance between its root and a person, and the similarity between its Hebrew name, *duda'im*, and the word for lovemaking, *dodim*). So convinced are both sisters of the root's magical properties, they wrangle over the prized mandrakes almost as much as over Jacob. In the bargain, Rachel wins the mandrakes, but Leah gets to lie with Jacob for just one night. God subsequently opens her womb three more times, making explicit that God and not a mandrake produces children. When Rachel then finally has children of her own, the text again assigns Divine responsibility:

"God remembered Rachel" (Gen. 30:22). Whether or not Rachel has inserted the mandrakes under the bed sheets, the narrator, unlike the sisters, does not consider them to be a factor in fecundity.

Note Jacob and Rachel's similarities here. Both resort to magical devices in service of fertility: Rachel obtains mandrakes; Jacob peels the rods for his motley flock. (The irony is that Jacob is able, and willing, to exert himself on behalf of his flock's fertility but not his wife's — he is "instead of God" for his sheep!) Both cases involve an act of bargaining with a close relative: Rachel exchanges the mandrakes for Leah's night with Jacob; Jacob receives the cast-off sheep for all the years of his service to Laban. And in both cases the magic works, albeit the role played by magic versus God's agency remains ambiguous. However, while the episode of the sheep shows that Jacob still has some of his trickster gumption, the episode of the mandrakes reveals him as the passive object of his trickster relatives — the predominant role he plays in his middle years.

A second incident demonstrates Rachel's resort to the trickster's tool chest. In a dream, Jacob receives a message from God that it is time for them to leave Laban and return home. He and Rachel flee from Laban without telling him, worried that he will force them to stay or not allow them to take their possessions. Before they leave, though, Rachel steals the *terafim*, Laban's figurines representing protective household deities. The text offers no explanation for this odd behavior. Does she steal them to get back at Laban for the thefts he has committed, taking all the money for the bride price and paying Jacob meager wages? Is she absconding with deities she still believes in, as the biblical scholar Robert Alter proposes? Perhaps the intent is the opposite: to remove Laban's statues as a sign of disrespect for idol worship, akin to Abraham's destruction of his father's idols in the famous midrashic legend?

Another explanation is that the idols were used for divination, and Rachel therefore takes them in an effort to prevent Laban from discovering their escape route. Alas, if this is her aim, the tactic is not successful. The pair have a two-day lead, but even so Laban overtakes them in just seven days. Laban himself admits that he would have harmed Jacob, had not God warned him in a dream. Now begins a series of tragic events that in the saga of Jacob's life appear as punishments for his deceptions. Laban accuses Jacob of stealing his gods; Jacob, not knowing that Rachel had taken them, is so certain of his family's innocence that he is willing to wager everything: "Anyone with whom you find your gods shall not remain alive" (Gen. 31:32).[39] As he did when he first met Laban, Jacob tries to "go straight," insisting on his integrity; as a born trickster, however, he is doomed to trick others or be trapped in their deceptions. Relationships for tricksters are always contests of power, ingenuity, and mastery. Jacob's attempt to be honest, to suppress his trickster nature, time and again ends badly.

The trickster Rachel, too, ensnares herself in her own web. At first she succeeds in tricking her father: When Laban comes to check her tent, she sits on top of the idols and says she can't move because she has her period. Just as Laban tricked Jacob about "women's customs" that may have been fabricated to suit the purpose, so too Rachel turns the tables here on Laban by manipulating or inventing a "women's custom." Although the ruse works, it ultimately boomerangs against her. She dies giving birth to her second son, Benjamin, thus fulfilling Jacob's curse. Even as she expires, the couple who love each other so powerfully wrangle over the child's name: She names the boy Ben-oni, "son of my vigor," or "son of my sorrow"; he corrects to Ben-Yamin (Benjamin), "son of my right hand" — "my right-hand man" (Gen. 35:18). Her death might also be seen as a punishment for transgressing the Fifth Commandment: "Honor your father and your mother, *so that your days may be long.*" Since she so blatantly disrespected her father, her days are cut short.

To an extent, Rachel and Leah reprise the sibling rivalry between Jacob and Esau, but the correspondence between the sisters and the brothers is not parallel. Rachel, like Jacob, is the younger one, favored above the elder. Yet she is also the one with superior natural endowments — her beauty, like Esau's talent for the hunt — and it is Leah who wins through deception, engineered by a parent.

Still, Rachel and Leah are both, ineluctably, tricksters inhabiting the narrative universe fashioned by their trickster husband and deceitful father. Living in Rome, they act like Romans. The capacity for wit and deception in the Bible knows no gender.

On the Road II: Double Ambiguity, Double Appeasement

Heading home, a boundary crosser for a second time in his life, Jacob intentionally renders himself alone. The first time he had no choice: He was fleeing his brother's wrath and making his way to his ancestral homeland to find a wife. This time, again fearful of his brother, who is coming to meet him, he consciously sends his family away over "the ford of the Jabbok" specifically so he can confront the dangers—of the road, of Esau—by himself.[40]

Jacob's messengers have returned with concerning news: Esau is coming to meet him accompanied by 400 men (Gen. 32:7). (Note that Abraham mustered only 318 men when he defeated the four kings in Gen. 14). Jacob only has "his two wives, his two maidservants, and his eleven children" (32:23), along with a handful of servants. Does Esau intend to attack? Or is he bringing a diplomatic retinue to greet his prominent, successful brother and his clan? The biblical narrator, normally so laconic, uses two verbs to describe Jacob's reaction: "Jacob was greatly frightened, and he was distressed" (32:8).

Jacob clearly fears Esau's intentions, but the double verb here suggests that it is the uncertainty that exerts particular angst. If Jacob knew that Esau was going to attack, he could prepare one way—flight, arms, reliance on God; if he knew that Esau would greet him warmly, burying the hatchet, he could prepare to encounter him in confidence and grace. It is the suspense, the not knowing, that animates Jacob, who prepares in excess for either possibility: praying to God that Esau means no harm; setting aside hundreds of choice animals as gifts. For indeed there is even a third possibility: Esau himself does not know how he intends to treat his brother, and thus brings his henchmen to allow for either possible course of action.

Jacob's prayer, uttered when he and his family are nearing Esau's territory in the region of Edom, introduces a new note in Jacob's relationship with God: humility, dependency, pleading. Just as Jacob's prayer after his dream of the ladder/ramp asked for God's support on the journey ahead, here too Jacob implores God for help in anticipation of his encounter with Esau:

> O God of my father Abraham and God of my father Isaac, O Lord, who said to me, "Return to your native land and I will deal bountifully with you"! I am unworthy of all the kindness that you have so steadfastly shown your servant. . . . Deliver me, I pray, from the hand of my brother, from the hand of Esau; else, I fear, he may come and strike me down, mothers and children alike. Yet You have said, "I will deal bountifully with you and make your offspring as the sands of the sea, which are too numerous to count." (Gen. 32:10–13)

Jacob tries everything to appease God and win God's support in facing his brother (just as Jacob does everything possible to win Esau's favor). With God, Jacob does not offer animals (as he does with Esau) but blandishments attempting to coax God's protection. He reminds God of God's relationship with Jacob's father and grandfather; he recounts God's promise to him, the same promise given to his ancestors; and he casts himself on God's mercy, for surely without God's help Jacob doesn't stand a chance. We see here the contours of the new Jacob: He does not stop being a trickster, here through his verbal artistry, but the trickster in him mingles with nobler sentiments and mature behavior.

Ironically, it is precisely this new Jacob who brings forth the confrontation with God. God recognizes Jacob's change and accepts Jacob's invitation to change their relationship. For that is what Jacob essentially does by sending forth his family and remaining alone across the river: In contrast to their first encounter, where God spoke to Jacob in a dream, Jacob now invites God to encounter *him*. Before Jacob can change his relationship with his brother, he first needs to adjust his relationship with God.

The angel who wrestles with Jacob, in the climactic moment of Jacob's life, is often identified with one of the human characters (Gen. 32:28–33). In a midrash (Bereishit Rabbah 77:3), Rabbi Hama bar Hanina identifies the unnamed "man" as the "prince [protective angel] of Esau." In other words, Jacob struggles with Esau here on a metaphysical plain, so that the actual encounter can go peaceably. Another popular interpretation today holds that Jacob is wrestling with himself, his "inner demons," as a path toward psychological and moral growth.[41] But the text suggests that this "man" is indeed a messenger of God, so that God, as it were, is the one wrestling with Jacob: "Your name shall no longer be Jacob, but Israel, for you have striven with God and men and prevailed." This literal interpretation of the story both makes the most sense and is most compelling. For Jacob, this scene is the equivalent of Abraham's argument with God over Sodom and Gomorrah: a moment of struggle, of deepening the bond, of enabling mutual assertion and conflict. Perhaps God does want to wound Jacob for his hubris, his presumption that he needs to and can outsmart God; perhaps in his wrestling Jacob expresses his neediness and will to hold onto God and bend God to his desire. For the first time in their long relationship, both God and Jacob can give expression to these yearnings, through a physical struggle that is also an embrace.

The name change is emblematic of the new, higher relationship between God and Jacob. Jacob no longer needs to hide himself behind his trickster persona—neither for God nor with people. He can bring both his vulnerability and strengths to his encounters. He cannot stop being a trickster—that is who he is—but his tricks, tactics, and strategies can now be channeled into genuine, mutual relationships, based on trust and wariness, self-preservation and reliance. This mature Jacob is the one worthy of being the father of the nation of Israel.

This new Jacob emerges in his encounter with Esau that follows. Yes, Jacob employs every trick he can muster: dividing his family in two, sending them and servants in waves, bequeathing an exorbitant present (Alter translates as "tribute"), bowing down seven times to his brother, treating him with more honor than the angel with whom he has just wrestled: "For to see your face is like seeing the face of God, and you have received me favorably." But the narrator suggests that much more than deceptions to appease his brother, Jacob is expressing his earnest regret and desire to find peace with Esau. Esau's reaction to Jacob attests to his perception of Jacob's sincerity: "Esau ran to greet him. He

embraced him and, falling on his neck, he kissed him; and they wept."
Neither Jacob nor Esau is faking it.

The peaceful denouement of the brother's reunion suggests a fourth
possible motive for Esau, beyond a desire to kill his brother, to reconcile, or to do something (to be determined) in between. Perhaps Esau,
just like Jacob, did not know which brother he would meet. Would he
be Jacob the deceiver, or a different, changed Jacob, a genuine brother
eager to restore their broken kinship? Their reunion enables both men
to recover their humanity and repair their ruptured ties.

Father of Tricksters

It is a rule of literary genetics that trickster DNA gets passed down
through the generations. As recounted in the popular medieval story
of the trickster Reynard the Fox, "There are many Reynards these days,
including most of those who creep and use holes as he does. . . . He's left
many heirs of his craftiness in this world."[42] With Jacob, this rule plays
out in the most painful fashion, as his trickster children repeatedly
inflict harm, embarrassment, shame, and aggravation on their father
and each other. Early on, their deceptive and often cruel actions are
like massive car pileups caused by the reckless abandon of unhinged
drivers, requiring great quantities of time and manpower to untangle.
His children's tricks often appear as a form of cosmic retribution for
Jacob's initial deceptions.

A couple of especially provocative and problematic stories bring out
this sense of tricksterism run amok. The most notorious episode is the
rape of Dinah and her brothers' revenge massacre (Gen. 34). Here, the
biblical narrator's reticence to cast judgment reaches its pinnacle in a
horrifying, brutal scene in which all characters except Dinah appear
blameworthy. Most striking in the narration is the rapid alternation
of sympathy and revulsion as the perspective switches back and forth
between characters. Dinah is out for a walk alone in her new territory
when Shechem, a Hivite (one of the Canaanite tribes) rapes her. Shechem
decides he loves her. He and his father Hamor propose marriage to Jacob
and his sons, offering to pay a high bride price and to allow Jacob's fam-

ily to intermarry and remain part of the city. Dinah's enraged brothers pretend to agree to this arrangement and tell Shechem that, according to their custom, for the marriage to commence, the men of the city must get circumcised. Shechem discusses this with the other men, who accept, and all of them are circumcised. While they are recovering, Dinah's brothers Simon and Levi gird themselves with swords and slaughter all the men, including Shechem and Hamor; they also take the women, children, and livestock as booty. Jacob appears to react fearfully: *When the other inhabitants of the land find out, they'll kill us.* His sons respond indignantly: *Can we let them treat our sister like a whore?*

This disturbing story leaves the reader with a bucketful of unanswered questions. Are the brothers right to seek vengeance? Is their deception of Shechem, promising to unify their families if Shechem's family undergoes circumcision, justified or barbaric?[43] They rail against Shechem's unethical treatment of Dinah, but what about the ethics of their murder and plunder? Can the biblical narrator possibly be condoning such behavior? Regarding Shechem, is his desire to marry Dinah a sincere act of repentance, or of love for that matter? Why does he tell his neighbors that they will get Jacob's "cattle and substance and all their beasts" if they consent to merge with Jacob's family? Is Shechem appealing to their avarice, and/or is avarice his own motive? And, if the latter, can Shechem's avarice somehow justify Simon and Levi's avarice in taking the Hivites' wives, children, and possessions?

As for Jacob, why is he silent until the end? Does Jacob's ultimate outcry to his sons, faulting them for the danger his family now faces, indicate that he does not judge what they did, only the lack of forethought for the consequences? To put it more starkly: If Jacob actually agrees with them that Shechem's act was so repugnant that it deserved such vengeance, how can he nonetheless assert that they still should have made peace with Hamor's family and merged with them for the sake of survival? On the other hand, if Jacob does in fact judge Simon and Levi for their violence (as he attests later on in his last testament), why doesn't he express moral outrage here? Why does he remain unseemingly silent?

Furthermore: According to biblical standards, to what extent should Shechem be considered guilty? Shechem's offer of marriage and a high bride price appears to fulfill the biblical law in such cases: "If a man comes upon a virgin who is not engaged and he seizes her and lies with her, and they are discovered, the man who lay with her shall pay the girl's father fifty [shekels of] silver, and she shall be his wife. Because he has violated her, he can never have the right to divorce her" (Deut. 22:28). However abhorrent we might find such an arrangement today, within ancient social norms, this law was intended to protect the victim.[44] In a society where a woman was expected to be either a virgin or a widow, the act of rape not only defiled the woman, but cast her as unmarriageable. Thus, as a result of this law, a woman who had been violated, and thereby rendered ineligible for marriage to someone else, was now guaranteed the protections of home and property (as repugnant as it was with her rapist). Her father, who would not get a bride price for an unmarried daughter, was awarded fifty shekels of silver—a high price (as borne out by other references to shekels in the Bible)—and the rapist was punished by being forced to pay such a price and to live with the fruits of his actions. In the instance of Dinah, although Shechem is not an Israelite, the fact that he is willing to own up to his actions and take upon himself the punishments and responsibilities that biblical law later established as normative seems to render his acts as somewhat less blameworthy and Jacob's sons' revenge as even more problematic. When we weigh this practice mandated by biblical law against the brothers' murderous rage, might the law have been intended to prevent just this kind of vigilante justice? Is the law an implicit condemnation of Dinah's brothers' behavior?[45]

Parallels with earlier scenes in Jacob's life help trace the contours of the trickster narrative, though they do nothing to untie this Gordian knot of judgment. The brothers employ a strategy and even language similar to Laban's when he tricks Jacob into marrying Leah. Both Laban and Dinah's brothers ground their contentions in local custom—Laban: "It is not the practice in our place to marry off the younger before the older"; the brothers: "We cannot do this thing, to give our sister to a man who is uncircumcised, for that is a disgrace among us." Bespeaking their identity as tricksters, the narrator informs us that the brothers utter this sentence *bemirmah*, "deceptively." Note that Isaac uses the same language to describe Jacob's theft of the blessing to Esau: "Your brother has come *bemirmah*, deceptively, and taken your blessing." The parallel clearly points to Dinah's brothers' lineage as tricksters. As Jacob was with Laban, Shechem is thoroughly convinced of the brothers' sincerity ("These men are wholehearted with us"). Instead of a surmountable hurdle leading to full admittance—Jacob to marry Rachel and become an equal partner in the family, Shechem to marry Dinah and become one family—the supposed customs become tools of surprise and domination, suckers' shills ending in betrayal.

In all its ambiguous and troublesome morality, or immorality, the episode reads as the kind of trick Coyote and Rabbit would have pulled on each other, but of course the differences are glaring. Coyote and Rabbit are immortal, and so their pain, loss, and death can only be temporary. Their stories are funny precisely because we know the inflicted damages are unreal—the characters can bounce back in a moment and execute ever-new methods of trickery and revenge. Biblical stories, by contrast, take place in the world as we know it, with mortal characters suffering the pains "that flesh is heir to." Dinah's story reveals what happens when tricksters with unbounded ambitions and outsized imaginations get shrunk to the dimensions of our world, with real, lasting, irreversible consequences.

Seeing this episode as part of the narrative arc of the Jacob saga— "the trickster outtricked"—helps to make some sense of its distressing content. Jacob's initial transgressions, his deceptions, lies, and thefts, set in motion a concatenation of other subterfuges that culminate in this episode's moral catastrophe. Here, the whole chain of chicanery catches up with Jacob. Now that he has arrived back in his homeland, where he will settle, he has nowhere left to flee. Jacob can hardly respond because he recognizes his own guilt in his sons' actions. His children have grown up to be tricksters like him; no matter that he tried to change his character, to correct his behavior, his past and his nature have returned to haunt him. His grown children have turned out to be a mirror image of himself. Powerless to change them, all Jacob can do is leave them to their devices, hoping that they eventually find a way out of the trickster's curse he inherited along with his blessings.

Joseph and His Brother Tricksters

The same pattern of trickery and strife continues throughout the stories of Jacob's favorite son, Joseph, and his brothers. Continuing in their father's footsteps, Joseph's brothers outtrick him, and then he outtricks them.

Joseph displays similar characteristics to his father. Using their brains alone, both father and son emerge from nothing, from a position of servitude (Jacob—servitude to Laban; Joseph, servitude to Potiphar and imprisonment) to achieve great wealth and, in Joseph's case, power. Both excel as managers (of Laban's sheep farm, of Pharaoh's kingdom), and both are endowed with supernatural powers (manipulating sheep fertility, interpreting dreams). At other times, however, Joseph's brothers are the ones who act like their father. As Jacob deceived his father, Isaac, with clothing, so too do the brothers deceive their father, Jacob, presenting Joseph's blood-soaked tunic as manufactured evidence that a wild beast has killed him. In this, the brothers exceed their father in cruelty, for they use the very symbol of Jacob's preference for Joseph — the multicolored tunic he bequeathed his favorite son—as the evidence of Joseph's demise.

Years pass. Driven by the great regional famine and rumor that Egypt has accumulated vast stores of food, the brothers descend to Egypt. Unwittingly, they face their brother Joseph, who over the years has transformed himself from the slave they made him into Pharaoh's vizier (trusted advisor). They cannot recognize him, as he bears the appearance of Egyptian royalty. A decade or two earlier, Joseph's life was in their hands. Now, the brothers' lives are in his.

This dramatic encounter raises a host of questions that hold the reader in sharp suspense. How will Joseph react? Does he bear a grudge, and will he seek vengeance? Even if he does not, how can the brothers possibly expunge the hard feelings and guilt from their youth, when they sought to kill him and sold him into slavery? How can the brothers regain their brotherhood? Through the genius of biblical storytelling, the narrator does not answer these questions for several chapters (Gen. 42–44). Instead, the suspense keeps rising, thanks to the Bible's reticence to reveal the characters' motives.

Like Jacob, the brothers are tricksters who will be tricked when they themselves try to "go straight." They conduct themselves with integrity in the Egyptian court—and suffer for that honesty, as Joseph manipulates his brothers several times. Driven by famine, the brothers come to Egypt and bow down to Joseph as Pharaoh's representative. Joseph pretends not to recognize them, accusing them of being spies from the land of Canaan sent to scout out the land. Jacob had withheld Benjamin from descending to Egypt along with his brothers, refusing to risk the life of Rachel's remaining son (since Jacob believes Joseph to be dead). Joseph insists his brothers return to Egypt with the missing brother, and he keeps Simon as hostage (even as he cries in private, and sends the brothers home supplied with ample food and money). Joseph knows that Jacob will not agree to part with Rachel's remaining son unless he's desperate from the famine; he also knows that Benjamin will not come to Egypt unless the brothers certify to Jacob for his safety. And so the contours of Joseph's plot slowly emerge: In order to reconcile, Joseph's brothers need to show they care for Benjamin to atone for the disregard they showed to Joseph.

The deceptions do not end there. The brothers convince Jacob that the urgency of the famine necessitates that Benjamin accompany them to Egypt. Joseph treats the brothers more sumptuously than the first time, giving them ample food and drink before sending them back with supplies. As he had the first time, Joseph packs the brothers' bags full of supplies as well as money. However, this time Joseph plants his special chalice in Benjamin's sack. When the brothers head back, Joseph sends his steward after them to accuse them of theft. Ignorant of the ruse, the brothers naturally protest; when the steward discovers the object, he insists that Benjamin stay as a servant while the others proceed. All the while, Joseph's tears reveal to the reader his brotherly intentions, that he is not seeking revenge but amends; yet he must maintain his stern composure in order to give his brothers the opportunity to demonstrate that they have changed and will remain behind to seek Benjamin's freedom.

Joseph's chest of tricks enables him to craft a plot that will not entrap but liberate his brothers and unite the family. Accusing them of spying, planting them with money, stashing Joseph's valuable chalice in Benjamin's sack—through these devices, Joseph harnesses the trickster's stock-in-trade one last time for good: to heal the family's rift. He deploys deception to end all deceptions. The brothers, led by Judah, rise to the occasion. Whereas previously the brothers sold Joseph into slavery and brought grief to Jacob by falsifying Joseph's death, now Judah explains to Joseph why Benjamin is particularly precious to their father, as the remaining son of Jacob's favorite wife, and insists they will not inflict sorrow on him this time. Judah asks Joseph to take him as a servant and release Benjamin; Joseph recognizes that the brothers have passed the test he devised for them, and reveals himself. Thanks to this final act of trickery, Joseph and his brothers heal the damage done years earlier. Perhaps they all see that they have more in common than they realized. Aspects of Jacob's character have been spread among the brothers, accounting in part for both their initial enmity and their eventual reconciliation as one family. They recognize themselves in each other; they are all *b'nei Ya'akov*, the "sons of Jacob," bearing reserves of guile and magnanimity in abundance. They acknowledge the damage they have inflicted on each other and, by acting together, strive to repair it.

In all its beautiful complexity, the story represents the untangling of the tragic knots of the trickster narrative. The tale of reunification closes the narrative disharmony that began with the rupture between Jacob and Esau. The destructive force of tricksterism is countered, and can only be countered, by tricksterism in the service of repair.

Nevertheless, the effects of the damage continue to live on in the book of Exodus: The family that becomes a nation does so on foreign soil, where their collective enslavement may justify the brothers' anxiety over the punishment they deserve for Joseph's suffering. Furthermore, to what extent is the forthcoming rift that will break the nation of Israel into two competing kingdoms—the nations of Israel and Judah—an indication that the harmony achieved in Genesis will always remain incomplete?

Indeed, the end of Genesis leaves the reader with uncertainties. After Jacob dies, the brothers panic, fearful that Joseph's kindness to them may have been a charade enacted for their father's benefit. They attempt one last deception: inventing a deathbed instruction from Jacob asking Joseph to forgive his brothers. What is more, so uncertain are they still of his intentions—seventeen years after they moved to Egypt!—they then offer to become Joseph's slaves. Joseph reassures them: He harbors no grudge; everything that happened to him was part of God's plan. And yet . . . the placement of this episode, well after the brothers have supposedly made their peace, leaves the reader with a queasy stomach. Have the brothers indeed put their tricks behind them?

Comic Coda: The Trickster's Last Return

The narrator has one last surprise in store.

At the end of Jacob's life, we think we have the message figured out. Jacob the trickster gets punished repeatedly; later, chastened, he changes his ways. He is no longer called *Ya'akov*, "heal grabber." He is a demoralized, bitter old man who's had to swallow many regrets, but has also learned his lesson. He's retired his mojo.

But no. At the very end, on his deathbed, Jacob upsets this pat narrative. Jacob still has one trick left in him—a coda to the long biblical saga that takes up half the book of Genesis.

By the conclusion of the story, all the narrative threads seem neatly bound up. The brothers have reunited, Jacob has descended to Egypt, and the family has a new temporary homeland—Goshen—where they can dwell in peace with their flocks and growing clan. But something doesn't seem right about Jacob. After an initial pulse of happiness on discovering that Joseph lives and thrives, he appears miserable, eager for death. Joseph introduces Pharaoh to his father, and in their exchange, Jacob is exaggeratedly bleak. Pharaoh tries to make small talk with him, asking his age; Jacob forecloses conversation with his depressing reply: "Few and hard have been the years of my life, nor do they come up to the life spans of my fathers during their sojourns" (Gen. 47:9). Jacob is already discussing his death, even though he is not even close to his deathbed; he will have another seventeen years to live! And, now, of all times, he has reason to be optimistic, to see his life as a triumph. Instead, he focuses on his hardships.

Indeed, throughout the story of Joseph and his brothers, Jacob seems a pathetic figure, a much-weakened father. He is unable to stem the brothers' developing enmity after Joseph reveals his dreams of dominating the family. Then, seemingly unaware of the depths of that enmity and/or the perils it poses, Jacob sends Joseph alone into their hands. He is easily deceived by the ruse of the bloody tunic—more so than his blind father Isaac was, who at least recognized Jacob's voice behind Esau's hairy hands. Jacob repeatedly wails that his sons will drag his "white head to Sheol [the underworld] in sorrow" (Gen. 44:29). Although Jewish mothers are infamous for supposedly instilling guilt in their children, in Genesis, it is Jacob who sets the mold. Once his sons travel to Egypt and experience Joseph's trickery, the fear for Jacob's emotional state continues to grow. When Joseph insists that Benjamin be brought before the Egyptian court, the brothers' hardest task is to convince their father to let Rachel's remaining son go. Reuben's unreasonable offer to Jacob, meant to assure him that Benjamin will not come to harm, "You may kill my two sons if I do not bring him back to you" (42:37), brings to a fevered pitch the helplessness and excessive emotionality surrounding Jacob during his long decline.

Additionally, Jacob becomes blind at the end (Gen. 48:10), and thus, like his father Isaac, prey to deception himself with seemingly scant power to defend himself or act upon others. The reader wonders: Is this broken-down, self-pitying shell of a man the same person who, entirely confident and self-possessed, repeatedly outwitted others as well as wrestled with and received messages from God? Or, when factoring in his earlier self, is Jacob's overarching weakness now yet one more disguise, like Odysseus's transformation into an old beggar when he lands back at Ithaca?

A final scene lends credence to the impression that Jacob's decrepitude may be one last subterfuge. As Jacob lies on his deathbed, eviscerated of strength and substance, with scarcely the power to move, Joseph tries to wring one more act out of his father: to bless his two sons. He places his sons in the "correct" order: Manasseh, the older, at Jacob's right hand; Ephraim, the younger, at his left. Joseph assumes his father doesn't have the strength or the power of vision to know who's who, or certainly to care about the birth order. But here the trickster comes back to life, just as in many stories where Coyote or his antagonist seem left for dead:

> [Joseph] bowed low with his face to the ground. . . . But Israel [Jacob] stretched out his right hand and laid it on Ephraim's head, though he was the younger, and his left hand on Manasseh's head—thus crossing his hands—although Manasseh was the first-born. . . . "Not so, Father," Joseph said to his father, "for the other is the first-born; place your right hand on his head." But his father objected, saying, "I know, my son, I know. He too shall become a people, and he too shall be great. Yet his younger brother shall be greater than he, and his offspring shall be plentiful enough for nations." (Gen. 48:12–19)

Jacob has one trick left to perform; one might even surmise that the temptation to perform one last trick revives him. Primogeniture is one custom the irrepressible trickster in him cannot leave intact.

This episode also reverses the earlier pattern of the sightless person being tricked. Jacob and Rebecca deceive Isaac into giving Jacob the birthright; Laban and Leah deceive Jacob in the darkness of the marriage tent. However, here the blind Jacob asserts his will—and Joseph, who in dreams and reality rules over his family, is now the one to bow down to his father. Jacob's crossed hands symbolize the final set of reversals being enacted in this scene, simultaneous with the reversal of inheritance: the old outtricks the young, the blind sees more than the sighted. Here, the patriarch is called Israel but acts like Ya'akov. Fittingly, in his final act, Jacob's two identities, the youthful trickster and mature patriarch, finally come together like two lenses in focus. In a last foreshadowing among many,[46] Jacob here reminds us of Moses when his weak arms rout the enemy army: His strength emerges precisely in a moment of apparent helplessness.

Jacob continues to assert his dominance over his children through his "blessings" for his sons, a series of prophecies from Israel to the future tribes (Gen. 49). Delivered in obscure language dense with punning wordplay and allusion, Jacob's last will and testament casts judgment on the tribes based on the brothers' individual characters. All of the rivalries, the competition among the brothers, the arts of deception, reemerge with a vengeance. Jacob had let Simon and Levi get the last word after they slaughtered Shechem, Hamor, and their city; now Jacob asserts their harsh decree: "Cursed be their anger so fierce, and their wrath so relentless. I will divide them in Jacob, scatter them in Israel." Neither brother's tribe gets its own territory. Jacob endows two of the brothers with a blessing from his own name, "heel": Dan is "a viper by the path, that bites the horse's heels so that his rider is thrown backward," and Gad "shall be raided by raiders but he shall raid at their heels."

The greatest and longest blessings by far are reserved for Judah and Joseph (Ephraim), in whose tribes the future capitals of the Southern and Northern Kingdoms will sit. Judah, Jacob proclaims, shall predominate both among his brothers and above external nations. Notably, Joseph's dream of the brothers' subservience is thus transferred to Judah:

> You, O Judah, your brothers shall praise;
> Your hand shall be on the nape of your foes;
> Your father's sons shall bow low to you. . . .
> The scepter shall not depart from Judah,
> Nor the ruler's staff from between his feet;
> So that tribute shall come to him
> And the homage of peoples be his. (Gen. 49:8,10)

Joseph's legacy now sounds simultaneously more glorious and more nebulous. Jacob summarizes Joseph as the son who was attacked but prevailed: though "archers bitterly assailed him," his "bow stayed taut . . . by the hands of the Mighty One of Jacob." Jacob invokes unnamed blessings on Joseph as "the elect of his brothers." The root word for blessing, *barech*, appears here five times—a striking reiteration, since this is the only time this word appears in the entire speech to all of Jacob's sons. In other words, Jacob sets the brother-tribes up for trouble by granting primacy to *both* Judah and Joseph. The future rivalry between the Northern and Southern tribes for claims of legitimacy and supremacy has its origin in Jacob's ambiguous testament. Jacob/Israel leaves the nation with the divided legacy embedded in his own divided character.

A Hero?

After all the twists in Jacob's story, we are left with . . . more questions. What kind of a hero is Jacob? Why is he placed among the Patriarchs? The answers may lie in the reader's understanding of Jacob as a trickster.

The narrative shows misgiving toward Jacob's tricksterism. As with other trickster heroes, Jacob succeeds in obtaining the prizes he seeks—his father's blessing, the birthright, wealth—through deception, ingenuity, and magic. But these qualities don't sit so well with the biblical storyteller; after his initial triumphs, Jacob repeatedly suffers, scene after scene, in a pattern that appears to be a measure-for-measure rebuke for his transgressions against Esau and Isaac. With the bestowal of his new name, Israel, Jacob seems to have put his Jacob-ness behind him: trickster no more, now patriarch of a nation. And yet, the full-throttle resurgence of Jacob's trickster side on his deathbed twists the plot, reshaping, and confusing, the reader's sense of the story's message.

Perhaps there are two ways of reading this story, depending largely on how we read Jacob's trickster character, as bad or good.

1. Overall, the saga seems to present Jacob's trickster character as it did Samson's superhuman strength: as a troubling quality out of place in the moral assumptions of the biblical universe. In some trickster stories from world literature, the trickster always wins out against one or more opponents; in others, a trickster alternately wins and loses against an antagonist equally endowed with cunning and guile (e.g., Coyote and Rabbit). The biblical trickster receives starkly different treatment. Jacob accomplishes one deception against his brother; for his next deception, against Isaac,

he is a puppet of his mother; after that he experiences a long train of deceptive comeuppances that far outweigh his initial damage. Jacob is made to perform penance and then some.

As he is popularly understood, Jacob is the biblical character who wrestles not only with the angel, and not only with God, but with the most difficult of opponents: himself. His setbacks and disappointments, along with his encounters with God, are significant because they lead him to reevaluate his own character, and to change it. He treats Laban and his daughters with respect. He will risk Esau's wrath to face him directly and reconcile. The name the angel confers on him, a reward from God, testifies to the new character he has acquired, through his own efforts. Jacob has become the hero of self-transformation, of second chances.

2. The surprise ending to the Jacob saga, however, opens up a vastly different interpretation. There is no mistaking that Jacob dies as an unrepentant trickster. He intentionally reverses the order of blessings to Joseph's elder and younger son, in explicit contravention of a father's wishes, and pours forth a mélange of grudge and praise in issuing his blessings for his sons' posterity. Now, with nothing left to lose, Jacob appears to return to his innate inclinations. Meanwhile, the narrator, who is rarely given to intrusive judgment, provides not even the subtlest indication that Jacob's final turn is blameworthy.

Perhaps, then, Jacob's story is not meant to bury the trickster, but to praise him. Yes, Jacob cheated his brother and father at the beginning of the story, but the fault lay in those deeds and not in Jacob's very nature. With Jacob, the Bible seems to recognize that human society does not always reward the upright and trusting. The idealistic qualities of "righteousness and justice" embodied by Abraham need to be augmented by Jacob's realism—the resources of skepticism, patience, and wit; the will to success and self-preservation; and, at times, even the urge to repay a bad turn. In the Bible's multifaceted portrayal, Abraham and Jacob are not so much opposites as complements: Abraham displays

Jacob's cunning in his negotiations with characters of uncertain trustworthiness, such as Abimelech and the children of Heth, while Jacob embodies Abraham's expectations of fairness and honesty, even as he is deceived by Laban and others. Indeed, one might argue that over the long haul, Abraham is the wilier and more successful trickster than his more notorious grandson. But without Jacob, we might never have seen this side of Abraham.

As a trickster, Jacob provides one model of a hero that proves useful to the people Israel at critical times. The trickster appears in David, who as "but a boy, ruddy and handsome" slays the fearsome monster Goliath with a mere slingshot when he lacks sword and armor (1 Sam. 17). The trickster appears in Yael, who graciously welcomes the enemy general Sisera into her tent, covers his body with a blanket, and gives him milk when he asks for water—in order to lull him to sleep so she can drive a tent peg into his head (Judg. 4). At still other times, prophets such as Elijah and Amos resort to trickster arts in order to satirize and then demolish their enemies who possess far greater numbers, social prestige, and military prowess.[47]

But there may be no greater argument in favor of the trickster than the fact that the God of the Bible shows favoritism to biblical tricksters and even employs some classic trickster strategies. After all, very often the world as people have constructed it is far removed from the world as God would have it—governed by honest dealings with God and fellow human beings, and driven to realize justice for the poor, the stranger, the widow, and the orphan. In such a topsy-turvy world of immorality and injustice, the trickster may be required to overturn conventions and right wrongs, just as in the world of Shakespeare, the fool is the character who proves the wisest.

6

DAVID

King

In the figure of the king, all of the Bible's mistrust of human heroism bursts forth.

The Bible has no problem with kings per se; if it did, the biblical narrator wouldn't use the term repeatedly to refer to God. Nor is the main tack of the Bible's criticism aimed at their power, even though some of the prophets utter aspects of such a critique. Instead, the Bible's objection to kings is theological. Power resides in God's hands. Human leaders can succeed only to the extent that they acknowledge God's supremacy. Kings, of all people, have the greatest difficulty in recognizing their subservience to an authority above them, whether human or divine. In his political tract in favor of American independence from England, *Common Sense*, the fierce defender of democracy Thomas Paine colorfully expresses the biblical view of monarchy: "Government by kings was first introduced by the Heathens, from whom the children of Israel copied the custom. It was the most prosperous invention the Devil ever set on foot for the promotion of idolatry."

In other societies, the king is the person everyone else wants to be, the one with all the money, prestige, power. In ancient Israel, this situation is turned upside down: The Bible portrays kingship as the least desirable role in society, the king doomed to failure before he is even anointed. After all, as society's most powerful figure, the king represents the greatest threat to God, the most likely candidate to usurp God's role and prestige. Kings, as we know, exercise control and/or ownership over people, territory, resources. They may marry exorbitant numbers of women, fulfilling their limitless appetites. Hence, in their very existence, by sitting on the royal throne, kings symbolically set themselves up as deities.

In God's eyes, the king is humanity's challenge to God: a one-man tower of Babel who arrogates the honor due to God. As such, the very institution of kingship is an affront to the biblical worldview. Unsurprisingly, biblical kings are nearly universally, and relentlessly, condemned. Of all the Bible's character types, the king is most vulnerable to God's wrath, as well as the most susceptible to the biblical narrator's harsh judgment and God's prophets' penetrating criticisms. The king is the Bible's Prometheus, a figure constantly trying to poach on God's domain, and constantly punished for it.

Biblical kings in particular are figures trapped in the bind of biblical leaders. The people look to them as substitutes for God, to serve as saviors by administering the political, military, judicial, and economic needs of society. The priests, however, expect them to serve as spiritual leaders, to obey God's law above their own edicts and pronouncements. The bind proves impossible for the kings; even the best fail in their obligations to God in the most extraordinary fashion. If they are fortunate to have a long reign, they may fail several times. Often, they are flanked by a retinue of hired prophets who serve them poorly out of a desire to flatter them. The true prophets largely conceive of them as false surrogates for the One Source of Power, quasi-idols who act with colossal hubris to usurp God's kingship, and thus are doomed to catastrophe. Furthermore, in the Bible the prophets get the last word. The long books of Samuel and Kings detail a revolving spectacle of failed, miscreant monarchs.

Into this minefield steps David, the most potent biblical symbol of national sovereignty. Among the dozens of kings named in the Bible, David almost single-handedly emerges from the narrator's gauntlet as—albeit not unscathed—still a hero who can be recalled as such for centuries later. Archaeological remains testify to his long-heroic status: The earliest external evidence of Israelite kings is the reference to Beit David, the House of David, in the Tel Dan inscription from the ninth-century BCE, about one hundred years after David's reign. His descendants include kings of both the Northern and Southern Kingdoms.

Many biblical stories about David lend evidence to his reputation as a hero. They tell of his unlikely rise and unparalleled bravery, his military exploits and fearsomeness as a warrior, his charisma and honesty to friend and foe alike, and his loyalty and reverence for God. Even so, the Bible's distrust of kings inevitability shapes the portrait of the Bible's greatest king. And the tension between David's heroic and antiheroic strains gives rise to an enigmatic character who is at turns upright and corrupt, powerful and impotent, riven by internal oppositions and yearning in vain for wholeheartedness.

Extreme Ambivalence

The biblical portrayal of kingship may be fraught, but it is hardly uniformly negative. More typical is an alternation of affirmation and negation, the literary equivalent of a rollercoaster ride tossing the reader from one extreme to the other, often in short, rapid strokes.[1] The last line from the book of Judges, which comes right before the rise of the monarchy in 1 Samuel, provides the final verdict on this form of governance and ultimate justification for the Israelite kingship: "In those days there was no king in Israel; everyone did as he pleased" (Judg. 21:25). During the reign of the judges (a name given to tribal chieftains), a degree of chaos took hold of Israelite society, leading to military weakness, exposure to enemy control, and increasingly widespread moral decay. The narrator offers an inescapable conclusion borne of historical experience: Without a king exerting centralized power, society falls apart; therefore, Israel needs to appoint a king. From a purely practical political, social, and military perspective — from a human vantage point — there is no alternative. It is remarkable that the narrator offers this line at all, let alone so matter-of-factly, with such authority. It's not often that the Bible presents the human perspective alone, or affords it the last word. The theological perspective that would routinely undermine this assertion is entirely absent.

A mere eight chapters later, before the first king, Saul, is even installed, the Bible offers the opposing judgment on kingship: "And the Lord replied to Samuel, 'Heed the demand of the people in everything they say to you [by asking for a king]. For it is not you that they have rejected; it is Me they have rejected as their king'" (1 Sam. 8:7). This quotation presents *only* the theological perspective. As far as God is concerned, it would seem, there can be no justification for a human king. The people's acclamation of a king is of a piece with the repeated rejection of God's authority in the Torah. There is a tone of weariness in God's statement. God offers comfort to Samuel, who is both a priest and prophet, and Samuel must convey to the people God's disapproval of their choice, incurring their displeasure. God is in effect saying to Samuel: *Don't take it personally; you can give in to the people's misguided inclinations; they are rebelling against Me, not you, and I, God, am thoroughly used to it.* God makes it clear that kingship itself is the heart of the issue. God alone is king; there can be no other. When the people insist on having a human monarch, they are forgetting their King in Heaven.

Clearly, these two assertions clash in the boldest fashion. On a practical level, kingship is necessary; on a religious level, kingship is apostasy. Both assertions are valid and true, as both exist on entirely different planes of reality. The narrative of biblical history as played out in the books of Samuel and Kings is riven by these conflicting truths. Israel's kings are shown to be uniters, protectors, legislators, builders, symbols of strength and national pride. They are also idolaters, oppressors, dividers, fomenters of destruction in themselves and the nation—accounting for the narratives' disjointed qualities, stark contradictions, and enduring fascination.

While God's attitude toward the institution of monarchy in Israel is harsh at base, often it is tempered in practice. God's stark alternation of denunciation and acceptance can be seen in 1 Samuel 10:17–27, one of two scenes in which Saul is chosen to be king. This scene begins with another condemnation of Israel's cry for a monarch. Samuel says to the Children of Israel, "Thus said the Lord, the God of Israel: 'I brought Israel out of Egypt, and I delivered you from the hands of the Egyptians and of all the kingdoms that oppressed you.' But today you have rejected your God who delivered you from all your troubles and calamities. For you said, 'No, set up a king over us!'" The language here recalls the Ten Commandments (Exod. 20:2), in which God's assertion of redeeming Israel out of Egypt is the premise for Israel's worship of God alone. By this parallel, Israel's establishment of a human king is equivalent to worshipping a second god.

Astonishing, in light of this condemnation, is the way God acts toward the people now. Idolatry is, after all, the gravest sin in the Bible, evidencing disloyalty to God and abandonment of the covenantal relationship between God and the People of Israel. Consider: Following the sin of the Golden Calf, Moses leads the Levites to purge the nation of idolaters; three thousand people die, after which God sends a plague to further punish the offenders (Exod. 32:25–35). Yet here, God does not punish the people for a sin expressed in starkly similar terms. Instead, they get off with a warning about the perilous nature of monarchy.

Why this discrepancy in punishment? Several possibilities come to mind. Perhaps God (through Samuel) is being hyperbolic, recognizing a difference between erecting a king and true idolatry. Kingship is *like* idolatry—it's close enough that the people need to be warned of its similarity—and it can lead to idolatry, the deification of the ruler, but in itself it is not identical and hence should not receive the same punishment. Samuel's words are not meant literally as much as rhetorically, to serve as a hortatory injunction against the dangers of erecting a king. Second, God may in fact acknowledge Israel's need for a king, thus upholding the legitimacy of the narrator's observation in Judges. Political necessity may not make it right, but does render it understandable, even somewhat forgivable. Third, a darker possibility: God may allow this historical development to progress because God knows where it will eventually lead—to disaster. The people have the right to choose, even to choose badly, and to suffer the consequences.

The permission of kingship is in itself a form of punishment, one not imposed from above or without but generated from within, reaping what is sown. In this and other ways, God's role has changed over time. In the wilderness, when the people are not yet ready to control their own destiny, God leads them at every turn. Once they have entered their land, however, their national maturity invokes a different relationship with God—less of a father to a toddler, more of a sage to be consulted and heeded, or ignored at their peril.

As such, God's punishment of the people changes correspondingly as well. Compare God's withholding of punishment for the people's choice of king in Samuel with God's reaction to the Israelites' complaint about their desert menu in Numbers: "[The Lord said to Moses,] say to the people: . . . The Lord will give you meat and you shall eat. You shall eat not one day, not two, not even five days or ten or twenty, but a whole month, until it comes out of your nostrils and becomes loathsome to you. For you have rejected the Lord who is among you, by whining before Him and saying, 'Oh, why did we ever leave Egypt!'" (Num. 11:18–20). God regards Israel's complaints as a rejection of God, because God has provided for their sustenance.

Both texts, in Numbers 11:20 and 1 Samuel 8:7, employ the same word, *ma'as*, "reject," "despise," to describe the underlying effect of the Israelites' behavior against God. In both situations, the Israelites yearn to be like other people—to eat luxurious foods like the Egyptians, to copy the form of government of Israel's Mesopotamian neighbors. In the wilderness, God's initial reaction is to give in, to let the people suffer through a surfeit rather than withdrawing the desired effect. God furnishes massive quantities of quail—but also punishes the people for gluttony, sending forth a plague the first day against those who cannot limit themselves. In Samuel, God holds back his present wrath for long-term disappointment and suffering. *The people want a king—let them have one! See what they'll be getting, the ingrates!* God displays a kind of schadenfreude toward a people who refuse to follow the wise path God advises and insist on learning through hard experience.

After expressing such stark disapproval, God proceeds to select Israel's first king (1 Sam. 10:20–24). The process is triply designed to indicate God's intervention. Samuel arrays all of the people, bringing each tribe forward one by one to determine which clan, then family, and then member is to be selected as king, by lot. At the end of the proceeding, Samuel selects Saul, through divination. When Saul is nowhere to be found, the people inquire of his whereabouts directly to God, and God answers, "He is hiding among the baggage." God's reply both subtly affirms that Samuel's selection of Saul is correct (or else, why bother mentioning the fact that Saul is hiding?), and indicates, humorously, Saul's extreme reluctance to serve as king (the resemblance to Moses reinforcing Saul's aptness). When Saul finally emerges, he stands a head taller than everyone else, prompting Samuel to exclaim, "Do you see the one whom the Lord has chosen? There is none like him among all the people." God's choice is confirmed through Samuel's reaffirmation and Saul's evident physical endowments.

As the scene concludes, Samuel "expounded to the people the rules of the monarchy." This action seals the astonishingly rapid transition from utter disapproval to utmost establishment. The law code, which is not enumerated in the text, institutes the norms that enable the monarchy to take hold as a permanent institution. God, and God's earthly representative Samuel the prophet, now accept the kingship, under strictly limited conditions. God's disapproval, however, will nonetheless endure, casting a dark shadow over the reign of all Israelite kings to follow.

Another telling feature of the Bible's view of kings emerges from Judges 21 and 1 Samuel 8. Both texts portray the king as a figure erected by the people. In Judges, the king represents a solution to the people's inability to form a viable government by other means; in Samuel, the king is the unwitting symbol of the people's rebellion against God. In neither view is the king the heroic figure depicted in other cultures. He is not the brave, lone warrior who defeats the monster, slays the tyrant, and earns the throne in glory. Israelite kingship is not about the king—it is about the people he leads. The king fulfills a role—an impossible role—and as such, his power can easily be taken away and given to others. In this respect, Israel's kings more closely resemble modern elected leaders than their ancient monarchical colleagues, although they were "elected" and removed from office not by the people, but by Divine fiat.

David's Strategy

The Bible's ambivalence toward its greatest political leader creates emptiness within the heart of David. He faces a quandary: to achieve political greatness, he needs to appear bereft of political ambition. Only God can appoint true leaders; humans who strive to rule, who attain power through their own efforts, are double usurpers, against both their political enemies and God. Thus, the narrator cannot portray David in mostly admiring hues. He has no choice but to depict David as a cipher.

The word "cipher" refers first to the number zero; metaphorically, it connotes a "person or thing without influence or value; a nonentity." David becomes a cipher in that his motives, inner life, true self all empty out. Most of the actions in the story, especially ones that propel his rise to power, are related as occurring without his agency, even despite his will. While glimpses of David's desire and activity pierce through this narrative, at the heart of his portrayal is a void chiseled out by the theological assumptions of biblical storytelling. David, who occupies the cultural space of an Israelite hero, is shown spending the majority of his life eschewing glory, denying his triumphs, rejecting and atoning for violent actions taken on his behalf, ignoring or misreading other characters and pivotal situations, and failing to take proper action when circumstances require.

David's ascent to the throne is quite similar to the paths of both historical and fictional kings throughout history. He begins as an outsider, a humble shepherd. Soon, his talents are recognized, and he is brought into the orbit of royal power. Once there, however, his bloody path to the throne is littered with corpses. Some of the victims are explicitly Israel's "enemies" (especially the Philistines), but a great many are members of Saul's family and supporters. Conveniently, nearly all the males in Saul's sizable family are killed off—leading scholars such as Baruch Halpern to speculate that, behind the apologetic text, David personally arranged for the dispatch of Saul's line.[2] How can a narrative tradition that prizes humble, generous, and faithful leaders justify and even extol a ruler who appropriates power under such brutal circumstances?

The narrator's solution is to employ the Bible's own theological assumptions and biases against heroes, against kings, against human power, ironically *in service* of the depiction of David's claim to heroic status. David is justified in becoming king, fully worthy of the reader's respect as a hero, precisely because he is cognizant of the theological trap that lies before him. For the duration of his rise, he avoids that trap by continually and forcefully denying his ambitions. He does not seek out advanced stature; he is sought out to be king. Far from pursuing Saul's demise, he repeatedly demonstrates service, magnanimity, and affection. Furthermore, any feats of strength or arrangements of good fortune come to him solely through God's bidding. In short, David achieves greatness on the Bible's terms in the only possible way: through the most strenuous assertion of his lack of agency.

David's strategy in these biblical stories affords him a double justification. In the eyes of his contemporaries, the narrator explains David's rise as legitimate owing to his military success; Saul's madness, mistakes, and erratic behavior; and David's ostensible innocence from the downfall of Saul and his house. In God's eyes, from which the narrative focus rarely strays, David's merit lies in his exemplary restraint from seeking power. He is able to "have his cake and eat it too," receiving glory by so assiduously renouncing it.

Even so, the habits of leadership David strategically acquires patently fail him after he gains office. There, he faces an entirely new set of challenges for which his previous behavior is unsuited and his prior dilemmas leave him unprepared. The same impulse to restraint that secured the throne—yielding to others when decisive action is called for—now appears as hesitation and weakness while upon it. David's inaction and poor judgment emerge particularly with his children. His self-restraint morphs into insufficient vigilance, and this abets a bloody contest for succession that nearly sinks the "House of David" at the beginning of the dynasty.

Julius Caesar: The Crux of Ambition

> BRUTUS: As Caesar loved me, I wept for him; as he was fortunate, I rejoice at it; as he was valiant, I honor him. But as he was ambitious, I slew him.
> —Shakespeare, *Julius Caesar* 3.2

The conflicting perspectives that the Bible harbors toward its kingly hero-villains finds a counterpoint in depictions of Julius Caesar, Rome's greatest leader, among the most successful warriors and conquerors of the ancient world. Caesar was a master strategist both in waging war and in political advancement. With his brilliant grasp of human psychology he secured crucial allies within Rome and on the battlefield, earned his soldiers' loyalty, and reveled in the love of the populace. Yet his success, popularity, and independence also won him the distrust and ultimately the hatred of the entrenched Roman aristocracy. The Roman Senate, led by Cato, comprised nobility ("optimates") who mostly despised him, though Caesar's two powerful allies there, Pompey and Crassus, joined with him to rule in the original triumvirate. The written record of Caesar's ascent and rule speaks to the bitter divide his personality and actions provoked among Romans. Like David, he left behind a mixed legacy.

Caesar's early biography positioned him to bridge the class and economic cleavages in Roman society. He was born to a royal family—descended from Venus, according to lore—but raised in a poor part of town (one even thought to have a sizable Jewish population). His modest upbringing attuned him to understand the Roman populace and win their respect and affection, while his family's noble heritage gave him credentials among the ruling class and inspired him to recapture his family's prestige.

Caesar went on to expand the Roman Empire from Britain to Egypt. He capably maneuvered the complicated terrain of Gaulish tribes, forging key alliances with enough chieftains to acquire both manpower and intelligence gatherers. Strikingly, he was known to alternate between remarkable generosity and vicious brutality. For the sake of peace or gratitude for loyalty, Caesar often surprised his opponents with extravagant mercy. As Cicero noted (with dire concern) after one such incident during the Roman civil war, "I truly believe that if he continues to spare all the lives and property, he will convert his most bitter enemies into ardent supporters."[3] On other occasions, however—especially if he was double-crossed—Caesar would wipe out entire tribes as punishment.

David's behavior, on and off the battlefield, is similarly portrayed. After his victory over the Moabites, for example, David "made them lie down on the ground and measured them off with a cord" (2 Sam. 8:2), killing two for every one spared. However, in a separate episode David shares war booty with men who remained behind and did not fight, against the wishes of those who took part in the battle. Both of these ancient rulers appear to have favored generosity *and* harshness — in each case whichever they believed was necessary to achieve military victory.

Events at the end of Caesar's life raised the pitch of opinions toward him, pro and con. First came the Roman civil war, thrust on Caesar by the Senate, under the consulship of Caesar's former ally Pompey. After Caesar's triumphant conquest of Gaul, the Senate attempted to limit his power by passing a law requiring him to return to Rome without his troops. Even as he feared arrest and punishment, Caesar nonetheless "crossed the Rubicon" into Roman territory, surrounded by one of his legions of soldiers, and continued on to the capital. Pompey, the chosen Senate commander, fled to Greece, where Caesar eventually pursued and defeated him. Afterward, Caesar had himself declared first consul and then perpetual dictator — a usurpation of Roman political authority that signaled the end of the Roman Republic and led to the establishment of the Roman Empire. (Shortly thereafter, he was assassinated on the Senate floor by a large bevy of conspirators, including, famously, Brutus, the central character of Shakespeare's play.)

The ancient historian Plutarch recognized both Caesar's heroic and ignoble qualities. Caesar's greatness in war far exceeded the claims of all other Romans, Plutarch wrote: "He excelled them all in the number of battles he had fought and in the multitudes of his enemies he had slain in battle."

Plutarch reported what happened next:

[T]he Romans, inclining to Caesar's prosperity and taking the bit in the mouth, supposing that to be ruled by one man alone, it would be a good mean for them to take breath a little, after so many troubles and miseries as they had abidden in these civil wars, they chose him perpetual Dictator. This was a plain tyranny: for to this absolute power of Dictator, they added this, never to be afraid to be deposed.[4]

Although Plutarch attributed Caesar's new position entirely to the Roman people's will after Caesar's triumph over Pompey, he still regarded the new powers bestowed on Caesar as reflecting badly on him and leading to his downfall. Plutarch explained: "The chiefest cause that made him mortally hated was the covetous desire he had to be called King: which first gave the people just cause, and next his secret enemies honest color, to bear him ill will."

A pivotal scene near the end of Caesar's life, just a month before his assassination, captures the same kind of deep ambivalence toward kingship found in the Bible. Drawing on Cicero and other ancient sources, the contemporary classicist Philip Freeman sets the scene this way:

> When [Mark Antony] came to the Forum, he found Caesar sitting on his golden throne and wearing a purple robe. Suddenly he pulled a diadem wreathed in laurel from somewhere under his goatskin and held it out to Caesar proclaiming: "The people ask me to give you this crown."
>
> There was a notable silence from the crowd at this supposedly popular gesture as Caesar sat staring at the gift in Antony's hands. Antony offered it to him again, but Caesar pushed it away and declared: "Jupiter alone is king of the Romans!" At which point the crowd erupted in wild applause.[5]

Was Caesar truly rejecting the kingship? Some ancient commentators say that Caesar staged this spectacle to quash any rumors that he desired the kingship. By refusing the crown in the most public of settings, he was making it abundantly clear that he had no desire to be king. But most sources take the opposite view: that Caesar had arranged for Antony to offer him the kingship so he might gauge the reaction of the Roman populace and accept the monarchy if the people approved. Since it turned out they did not, he made a great show of rejecting Antony's offer.

At the time, Caesar served under the title of dictator, a role that was supposed to be of limited duration under emergency circumstances. Instead, he arranged to receive the dictator's special powers for ten years.

Still, he did not have the title of king, presumably a higher function that was entirely foreign to Roman politics. Notably, the Plutarchian perspective was even more stacked against kingship than the biblical account, since the Roman Republic, for all its flaws, was considered a Golden Age. In the Bible, the historically preceding form of political structure did not hold redeeming virtues that kingship overturned.

On the question of Caesar's motives, the historical record remains ambiguous. Was the real Caesar the generous servant of Rome or the power-grabbing usurper? Or, was Caesar divided as far as his motives, and did they shift over time? After he returned to Rome victorious in the civil war he was compelled to fight, as the people gorged his vanity and encouraged him to seize greater power—did the calls go to his head? He seems to show a moment of uncertainty when he tests the popular reaction to Marc Antony's offer of the crown: Is this confident, resolute leader of military strategy suddenly unsure of his next move? Is he too blinded by power to see his way forward?

Or, perhaps, the issue is that, for a fleeting moment, Caesar tipped his hand and revealed his ambition—an ambition not grounded in stability of governance, not rooted in service of city, people, and country, but a raw ambition: the possibility of a power grab. Perhaps he was tempted to divest Rome of the inefficiency of a democracy for the unfettered authority of an absolute monarchy. If he became king, he could dispense with his enemies and the institutions that had established Rome's superiority and its rulers' political legitimacy for generations. Perhaps Caesar dared to aspire to become a god. Indeed, he would become the first Roman ruler to be named a deity, after his death.

From the reader's perch, David shares with Caesar an inscrutability about his ambition. Both men may have masked their aims in service of their ambitions—thus preserving their good graces with God and the people. Both may not have been entirely certain of their own ambitions. Both may have possessed conflicted feelings. As we will see, David, just as with Caesar, starts to lose his grip and moral compass once he reaches political and military heights.

God in Charge

He is the Lord; He will do what He deems right.

—1 Samuel 3:18

The books of 1 and 2 Samuel might more accurately be called 1 and 2 David, since David's story occupies the majority of the narrative space.[6] Yet the first half of 1 Samuel consists entirely of a prologue that seems disconnected from David. In particular, the opening section, chapters 1–6, presents an odd introduction to kingship, the main theme of the rest of Samuel and all of Kings. On the surface, these stories have nothing to do with Saul, David, and their descendants. Nor do they appear related to the larger narrative of Israel's political and national history as recounted from Genesis to 2 Kings.

They tell of a barren woman, Hannah, whose prayer for a son is granted. Hannah names him Samuel and sends him to live in the House of the Lord in Shiloh. There resides the reigning priest of Shiloh, Eli, on account of whose wicked sons God promises to destroy his dynasty. In time, Samuel is called as a prophet. The opening section of 1 Samuel also contains the "Ark Narrative," a strange story in which the Philistines capture the Ark of the Covenant and it inflicts havoc among them. The inevitable question is, what are these stories doing here? What is their relationship to the rise of the Israelite monarchy?

These stories set the stage for the presentation of kings in two ways. The first is through the literary device of foreshadowing: The tales briefly adumbrate both specific events and larger themes to follow. According to the biblical scholar Robert Polzin, Samuel's birth is parallel to the birth of monarchy, while Hannah's cry to God for a son anticipates the people's cry for a king.[7] Samuel's election by God as prophet resembles Saul's, and later David's, as king. God's lengthy rebuke of Eli and his sons (1 Sam. 2:27–36), delivered by a "man of God" (prophet), and God's promise to remove them from power, have both sons die on the same day, but not to "cut off all [their] offspring from [God's] altar," foreshadows the terms of the prophet Nathan's curse against David (2 Sam. 12:7–12). The Ark of the Lord, which wanders from the Israelites to the Philistines and back again in 1 Samuel 4–6, takes a similar journey in 2 Samuel 6. Overall, this section anticipates the rise and fall of the institution, individuals, and dynasties of the Israelite monarchy.

Second, these stories thematically prepare the reader for the royal history to follow. Designed to demonstrate the biblical thesis "God is in command of the world," the tales portray God as controlling the world and human affairs, sometimes in line with and often in opposition to human desires.

The story of Hannah, for example, explicitly recalls God's role in the conception stories of the Matriarchs in Genesis. Hannah, who is married to Elkanah, is a second Rachel, the beloved wife who is barren. Elkanah's other wife, Peninah, has children. Unlike Rachel's sister, Leah, however, Peninah openly taunts her childless co-wife that "the Lord had closed her womb" (1 Sam. 1:6). Like Jacob when Rachel weeps for a child, Elkanah too does not understand his wife's despair: "Am I not more devoted to you than ten sons?" (Just so, later on Samuel will not understand Israel's clamor for a king—isn't God's protective care more than ten human kings?) Eli the priest also does not understand, taking Hannah's silent prayer (1:12–13) for drunkenness. Yet later we learn that Hannah has had five children, "for the Lord took note of Hannah." God's intimate role in Hannah's pregnancies renders her a second matriarch for this new phase of Israelite history.

Hannah proceeds to offer a prayer of thanksgiving after Samuel's birth. Hardly a humble woman's expression of motherly joy, the poem instead resembles a war chant of a triumphal army: "I gloat over my enemies . . . / The foes of the Lord shall be shattered; / He will thunder against them in the heavens. / The Lord will judge the ends of the earth" (1 Sam. 2:1,10). To Hannah, the birth of her son represents a devastating victory over her taunters and doubters. God has led Hannah's troops into battle: "My heart exults in the Lord, I have triumphed through the Lord." Drawing on her most personal experience, Hannah now describes the God who will hover over dozens of kings:

The Lord deals death and gives life,
Casts down into Sheol and raises up.
The Lord makes poor and makes rich,
He casts down, He also lifts high.
He raises the poor from the dust,
Lifts up the needy from the dunghill,
Setting them with nobles,
Granting them seats of honor. (2:6–8)

Hannah's God is a trickster, a miracle worker who delights in overturning the orders of nature and society. God not only establishes the world and its rules; by violating rules that only God is capable of breaking, God demonstrates God's power and control of human destiny. By caring for the lowly and showing no obeisance to the mighty, God reveals "the wiles of a kind of guerilla divinity."[8] Hannah's God is the One whom Israel's kings bump up against at every turn, the God who troubles their sleep, hammers their sins, and treats them as the enemy army.

The Ark Narrative (1 Sam. 4–6) is another example of a story promulgating the biblical thesis that God commands the world. Essentially the account is a satire against false beliefs aimed at both the Israelites and the Philistines. This sequence hinges on the prevalent belief in the Ark's potency during battle. The Ark brings God to the front lines to wage war against Israel's enemies. When the Ark is present among Israel's army, God is literally on their side.

The narrator portrays both sides as credulous fools for harboring this belief. When Israel and the Philistines do battle, Israel is routed. The people return to the front with their secret weapon—the Ark. The Philistines hear the Israelites rejoicing over their now-certain victory and are terrified. Nonetheless, however convinced they are done for, the Philistines gird again for battle, and . . . rout Israel even more decisively. The Ark accomplishes nothing. Now, the Ark is in the Philistines' possession; thus they think God is in their possession and *they* are invincible. Rather, God shows the "wiles of a guerrilla deity" by chopping up the statue of their god Dagon in their temple and spreading painful hemorrhoids throughout the Philistine cities. When confronting their illness, all the Philistines can think of doing is to send the Ark off to the next city, hoping that there God's wrath will cease. After seven months, the Philistines have had enough; they send the Ark back on its way to Israel with a unique offering to assuage this divinity: five golden hemorrhoids and five golden mice, representing the five main Philistine cities. The Ark then returns to the rightful care of Israelite priests, but for good measure, God again strikes down vast numbers of Israelites, lest they take home the wrong message. God "will do what He deems right," not what the people try to dictate.

The Ark Narrative accomplishes several things at once. It demonstrates to both the Israelites and Philistines that God is in charge: God cannot be contained, manipulated, or expected to act in predictable, manageable ways. It mocks the pagans by depicting pagan beliefs as riddled with error, delusion, and fantasy. Meanwhile, it also ridicules the Israelites for holding the same erroneous belief in the Ark's talismanic power. Such a belief is a kind of idolatry no less than the statue of Dagon, for it assumes that God's will can be known, directed, and confined by human efforts. Aptly, in the next scene Samuel implores the people to "remove the alien gods and the Ashtaroth from your midst and direct your heart to the Lord and serve Him alone" (1 Sam. 7:3). Most importantly, the Ark Narrative illustrates the consequences of there being "no king in Israel." Lacking firm guidance and leadership, the people act in ignorance, and suffer greatly for it. The currents that have led them to God have all run dry. They long for a leader who can restore God's graces and return glory to Israel. They get their wish, in part. But the God who accedes is still Hannah's "guerilla divinity" who will not dwell in an Ark or be appeased by golden hemorrhoids.

Thus, these introductory stories foreshadow the rise and fall of multiple Israelite dynasties, hinting even before the kings step on stage that their reigns will come to an end. And the accounts forcefully assert that God, not people, controls the fate of individuals and nations. The kings have been put on notice: They will be kept on a tight leash.

Saul: Trial Run

As the first king, Saul as whipping boy becomes an emblem for the entire enterprise of Israelite monarchy.

Like David, Saul is plucked from obscurity by God. Two distinct traditions discussing his election (in 1 Sam. 9–10) emphasize this point. In the first story, Saul's father, Kish, sends him on a mission to recover his lost donkeys. Saul fails to find them and is ready to return home when his servant offers him direction, alerting him to the presence of a "man of God" nearby who might be able to help.[9] Ironically, Saul, the son of a "man of substance" (9:1, as Kish is known), must repeatedly rely on others to access Divine favor: first the unnamed servant, later girls drawing water, and finally Hannah's son Samuel, a prophet who will come to serve as Saul's necessary intercessor with God.

After God informs Samuel that God will appoint someone to "deliver My people from the hands of the Philistines" (1 Sam. 9:16), Samuel meets the wandering Saul. Now instructed by God that Saul is the chosen leader, Samuel treats Saul to a feast and later anoints him with oil, thus making him king. (Pouring oil over someone was how kings and high priests were invested with power in the Bible and beyond.) Saul regards himself as singularly unworthy of the role: "I am only a Benjaminite, from the smallest of the tribes of Israel, and my clan is the least of all [of Benjamin's] clans" (9:21). Yet Saul's personal humility here, and his humble stature in Israel's hierarchy, is of course precisely what makes him the most worthy candidate in God's estimation. (And, it is to be noted, Saul never finds his father's lost donkeys.)

In the second version of the story, discussed above (1 Sam. 10:20–27), the election of the Israelites' king takes place by lot, in public, in the presence of all the tribes. The lot falls first on Benjamin, then on Saul's tribe, finally on Saul himself; but as we saw earlier, the chosen king is nowhere to be found, "hiding among the baggage." This comic moment is the third depiction of Saul's reluctance; when he returns home from his failed quest for the donkeys, he does not tell his family about being anointed by Samuel, presumably out of disbelief and a sense of unworthiness. The narrator goes out of his way to note Saul's impressive physical attributes ("an excellent young man; no one among the Israelites was handsomer than he"), implying that Saul is someone whom the people can rally around, a quasi-matinee idol of his time. Yet as far as the selection process is concerned, the stray donkeys and the pick of lots emphasize the seemingly arbitrary nature of Saul's rise. Saul may have been the best candidate, but if so, no one but God would have recognized the shepherd from the smallest clan of the smallest tribe.

Significantly, after God lifts up Saul from nothing to become king, God will cast him down from the throne. The most serious misstep adduced against Saul seems like an overblown pretext drawn for a foregone conclusion (1 Sam. 15). In graphic terms, Samuel conveys God's decree that Saul exterminate the people of Amalek for attacking Israel when they left Egypt (Exod. 17:8–16): "Now go, attack Amalek, and proscribe all that belongs to him. Spare no one, but kill alike men and women, infants and sucklings, oxen and sheep, camels and asses!" (1 Sam. 15:3). Saul carries out Samuel's words meticulously, with just a couple of small exceptions: sparing the best of the flock to offer as sacrifices, and leaving the Amalekite king Agag alive. The narrative records God's immediate disapproval, as relayed by Samuel to Saul. According to Samuel, Saul's choice to spare Agag constitutes a rejection of God that justifies God's rejection of him as king. Samuel then summons Agag and slays him personally with his sword.

This is among the most troubling and morally challenging stories in the Bible. Has Saul done anything wrong, really, and if he has, is it not on a minuscule scale? Is he not being judged far more harshly than his actions and intentions merit? Is Samuel's brutality to be rewarded?[10]

And as for the Amalekites, are they truly the biblical equivalent of Nazis? If so, the narrator seems to quickly forget this charge. An incident later on, when David attacks a group of Amalekites (1 Sam. 30), illustrates this point. While David is away on a raiding expedition, the Amalekites sack and burn down the Philistine town of Ziklag where David dwells, killing the men and taking the women and children, including David's two wives. Returning with four hundred fighters, David slaughters the raiding party, "except 400 young men who mounted camels and got away." And that's the end of the story. Even under these circumstances, David does not pursue and then exterminate all the Amalekites. This is noteworthy for yet another reason. Since the narrative emphasizes David's distinction from Saul, wouldn't this have been the perfect opportunity for David to complete the job that Saul refused to finish? Yet if David is ignorant of God's command to wipe out all the Amalekites, why is Saul singled out for such exorbitant blame, especially since he did come close to accomplishing the instruction?

The inscrutable nature of Saul's transgressions that cause his downfall is, in a way, the point. Had Saul clearly deserved his fate, then his punishment would have reflected solely on himself and nothing larger. Instead, Saul's rejection and suffering are paradigmatic of the role he has been made to embody. God is pronouncing God's judgment on kings, and Saul has the misfortune to be the first one toppled.

More generally, the narrator is telling us that God has complete dominance over human affairs. Just as no person is too low to be raised up to any height, no person is too high to be cut down to the depths. Despite his height and strength, Saul embodies human vulnerability to God's designs.

The Hebrew poet Sha'ul Tchernichowsky (1875–1943) deeply identified with his namesake and wrote several poems about him. In "At Ein Dor," Tchernichowsky envisions Saul as challenging Samuel to justify God's capricious, cruel treatment of him:

> Oh man of God! What would God answer me?
> When He departs from me, what should I do? Answer me!
> Why, oh why, have you anointed me king?
> Why me, from behind the flocks, did you bring?[11]

Surely, in comparison to Israel's most prominent kings to follow, Saul appears considerably more worthy and obedient to God. David will commit adultery and murder; Solomon will marry one thousand wives and adopt their idols. Saul's transgressions do not merely pale in comparison; they seem incidental to his zeal to obey God. For example, when Saul's famished men defeat the Philistines, they slaughter the enemy's cattle and eat the meat with the blood, which kosher law forbids. Furious, Saul forces his men to slaughter their meat properly at an altar he erects to God (1 Sam. 14:31–35). He charges them, "You must not sin against the Lord and eat with the blood"—hardly the speech of a rebel.

The story of Saul may have been meant to send shivers down the spines of all his monarchical followers. Indeed, David goes on to study Saul and learns his lesson well. David remains ever mindful of God's dominance and the fragility of the power invested in kings. He is always treading lightly.

Who Is David?

The Goliath story in 1 Samuel 17 presents two different pictures of David, and correspondingly two ways of understanding David's role in defeating the Philistine giant. In the first scenario, the one prevalent in popular legend, David is the quintessential underdog, an adolescent weakling outmanned by an opponent of gargantuan strength and size—"six cubits and a span tall," nearly ten feet. Surely, this appears to be Goliath's own perspective on the contest: "When the Philistine caught sight of David, he scorned him, for he was but a boy, ruddy and handsome. And the Philistine called out to David, 'Am I a dog that you come against me with sticks?'" (1 Sam. 17:42–43). What's more, Goliath's helmet, breastplate, greaves (leg armor), and javelin are all of bronze, while his spear, "like a weaver's bar" in size, has an iron head weighing "six hundred shekels." He is an impregnable one-man army with the latest equipment. By contrast, David is a simple shepherd who hasn't even gone through basic training. When Saul places a helmet, breastplate, and sword on him, he takes them off because he is unable to walk.

The human characters in this version are also action figures for a divine battle. David's callowness is proof of God's power, while Goliath's physical strength belies the powerlessness of his divine protectors. Goliath "cursed David by his gods," and David replied, "You come against me with sword and spear and javelin; but I come against you in the name of the Lord of Hosts, the God of the ranks of Israel, whom you have defied" (1 Sam. 17:45). Thus, in a popular biblical irony, David's weakness is his greatest source of strength. God's infinitely superior might is invoked by such a fragile vessel as David—what a worthy instrument to reveal God's preeminence.

Yet underneath the picture of an undeveloped pretty boy capable of channeling God's power is another image of David. David's father, Jesse, sends him to the front to bring food to his brothers who are serving Saul. While there, he witnesses Goliath's taunting challenge of single combat and overhears the soldiers discussing Saul's promised reward: "The man who kills him will be rewarded by the king with great riches; he will also give him his daughter in marriage and grant exemption [from taxes] to his father's house in Israel" (1 Sam. 17:25). His ambition piqued, David immediately expresses interest in battle and asks again about the reward. David is then ushered to Saul, who tells David he has no chance against the mighty Philistine. David replies, "Your servant has been tending his father's sheep, and if a lion or a bear came and carried off an animal from the flock, I would go after it and fight it and rescue it from its mouth. And if it attacked me, I would seize it by the beard and strike it down and kill it. Your servant has killed both lion and bear; and that uncircumcised Philistine shall end up like one of them, for he has defied the ranks of the living God" (17:34–36). As much as God will act to defend David, David here acts to defend God against God's enemies.

Crucially, David's account of his own derring-do recalls the exploits of the most famous Israelite strongman, Samson. Both characters outfight a lion when attacked: "[When] a full-grown lion came roaring at him . . . [Samson] tore him asunder with his bare hands as one might tear a kid asunder" (Judg. 14:5–6). Far from an immature weakling, David comes off as a second Samson. David's battle with Goliath, who possesses Samson's physique and supernatural strength, allows the narrator to separate Samson's problematic and heroic aspects. David retains Samson's heroic qualities, strength included, while Goliath inherits Samson's brutal, uncontrolled excesses, his comic-book, larger-than-life countenance.

The "real David," then, is a person of "flesh and blood," and, like Samson, in possession of violent urges that periodically flash through the text. A telling example comes right after the Goliath episode. Somehow, David, who in the previous story had no military experience, rapidly rises to lead Saul's troops: "David went out [with the troops], and he was successful in every mission on which Saul sent him, and Saul put him in command of all the soldiers; this pleased all the troops and Saul's courtiers as well" (1 Sam. 18:5). Like Samson, David slaughters large numbers of Philistines. He rises simultaneously in popularity; the Israelite women cheer him on with a victory dance and a chant: "Saul has slain thousands, David, his tens of thousands!" The implication here—the people see David as qualified for kingship—is not lost on Saul, who becomes consumed by jealousy.

Later, fleeing Saul (in jealous pursuit of David whom he thinks—rightly—will usurp his throne), David escapes to Ziklag and becomes a vassal to the Philistine king Achish. There he stages brutal attacks in the spirit of Samson: "David and his men went up and raided the Geshurites, the Gizrites, and the Amalekites. . . . When David attacked a region, he would leave no man or woman alive; he would take flocks, herds, asses, camels, and clothing" (1 Sam. 27:8–9). Here, David emerges as a renegade warlord willing to sell his loyalty and services to any chief that can use him. He attracts a ragtag crew of what were known as *gibborim*, self-styled heroes from the dregs of society: "Everyone who was in straits and everyone who was in debt and everyone who was desperate joined him, and he became their leader" (22:2).

Elsewhere, and again like Samson, David reveals a promiscuous sexual drive. In 1 Samuel 25, immediately after God strikes down a husband, Nabal, David sends messengers to take Nabal's wife Abigail for himself (as he will for Bathsheba, later). In the next verse, we discover that Abigail is just one of several wives David has accumulated; he had "taken Ahinoam of Jezreel" and "Saul had given [David] his daughter Michal" (1 Sam. 25:43–44). Later, the story reports that "sons were born to David in Hebron," six sons to six different wives (2 Sam. 3:2). After he is anointed king, David takes "more concubines and wives in Jerusalem, and more sons and daughters were born to David" (2 Sam. 5:13).

David's Ambition

When Samuel selects David as king (1 Sam. 16), David is emphasized as an unlikely, almost arbitrary choice. Samuel is impressed by Jesse's first son, Eliab, but God tells Samuel to reject him. Samuel then proceeds to cycle through Jesse's next six sons before asking if Jesse has another and retrieving him from the sheepfold. David could not appear less enterprising. Yet once David overhears the soldiers talking of Saul's reward for the man who defeats Goliath, his persistent inquiry about the reward makes his intentions clear.

Shortly after David slays Goliath, David's betrothal to Saul's daughter Michal hinges entirely on David's ambition (1 Sam. 18:17–29). Saul had already promised to give his daughter to Goliath's slayer; now, perceiving David as a threat to his throne, "Saul thought, I will give her to him, and she can serve as a snare for him, so that the Philistines may kill him." Saul sends courtiers to seduce David; they whisper to him, "The king is fond of you.... So why not become the king's son-in-law?" At first David demurs: "Do you think that becoming the son-in-law of a king is a small matter, when I am but a poor man of no consequence?" The reader does not yet know: Is David merely being humble, or does he truly want to become Saul's son-in-law but cannot afford the bride price? Sensing the implicit negotiation, Saul suggests that David bring him one hundred Philistine foreskins in exchange for waiving the bride price. Saul imagines that his offer will succeed no matter the outcome: Most likely he will lose a potential rival to the throne, since the Philistines have the more powerful army, and, if not, enemy warriors will die. Seizing this opportunity, David fights with "his men" (perhaps adherents from David's previous battles on behalf of Saul) and kills two hundred Philistines, collecting their foreskins—twice the bride price—in exchange for Michal. When he first heard of Saul's offer, "David was pleased with the idea of becoming the king's son-in-law." By now, David's true ambition is no longer in doubt. The excess of foreskins is a token of David's enthusiasm for the crown—and perhaps for Michal as well.

For the next thirteen chapters, until the end of 1 Samuel, David assiduously cloaks his ambition to unseat Saul. During this extraordinarily long period between his anointment by Samuel and his assumption of the throne, he zealously insists on his subservience to Saul. He even recognizes Saul as king after he himself has been declared king! In so doing, David is dramatizing his own innocence regarding Saul's continued downfall. As Moshe Halbertal and Stephen Holmes point out in *The Beginning of Politics*, David "want[s] his personal horror at regicide to be publicly notorious."[12] The more that Saul pursues David and seeks his death, the more David insists that he is not responding in kind, even as he demonstrates that he is fully capable of doing so. Twice, David makes an extravagant show of sparing Saul's life (1 Sam. 24 and 26): once, after managing to penetrate Saul's ranks and approach Saul asleep, first staying his own hand; and the second time, halting his hot-headed soldier Avishai.

Apart from David's direct show of concern for Saul, he forms close bonds of care and kinship with Saul's family, thereby further tamping down any suspicion that he is plotting to unseat Saul and his royal dynasty. Saul's son Jonathan "loved David as himself" (1 Sam. 18:1); Saul's daughter Michal "had fallen in love with David" (18:20).[13] Later, as king, David publicly vows to keep faith with the House of Saul by restoring Saul's property and possessions to Jonathan's son Mephibosheth, who is lame (2 Sam. 9). David in effect adopts Mephibosheth by feeding him as a member of his house—which also shows David's grace, as he reverses the episode in which he himself was banished from Saul's table (1 Sam. 20).

Yet at other times a different picture of David emerges. After both Saul and Jonathan have died, the narrator openly acknowledges that Saul and David are enemies in an epic struggle: "The war between the House of Saul and the House of David was long-drawn-out; but David kept growing stronger, while the House of Saul grew weaker" (2 Sam. 3:1). Whereas the stories generally depict the conflict as driven by Saul's insane enmity and irrational jealousy of David, this sentence, written by the "objective" narrator—and its placement, after the deaths of Saul and Jonathan, Saul's main heir—indicate that their conflict is not just about two individuals competing for control but in fact a rational and prolonged struggle between two dynasties. Even more telling, when Shimei son of Gera, "a member of Saul's clan," sees David and his followers marching away from Jerusalem, he accosts them, hurling stones and accusations: "Get out, get out, you criminal, you villain! The Lord is paying you back for all your crimes against the family of Saul, whose throne you seized" (16:7–8). Shimei's lone voice breaks through the narrative's long-maintained façade of David's lack of kingly ambition and love for Saul's family. Yet this dissent is not permitted to last long; Shimei will recant his accusation and beg forgiveness (19:19–24).

One disturbing scene seems designed to bolster David's alibi in the slaughter of Saul's family, but David nonetheless comes off as passively complicit (2 Sam. 21). A famine is taking its toll on territories under David's control. David asks God what caused the famine, and God responds: *Saul's bloodguilt in killing many Gibeonites*. David then asks the Gibeonites how he can make expiation to remove the famine's curse, and they tell David to hand over seven of Saul's descendants to slaughter. David responds, "I will do so," and, true to his word, a brutal ritual massacre of the seven descendants soon ensues. Afterward, David brings the bones of Saul and Jonathan to be buried together with the bones of these descendants. Finally, "when all that the king had commanded was done," God removes the famine.

The text thus crowns David as the compassionate hero, while his enemies, members of the House of Saul, are mercilessly butchered. Yet, did the famine have to end this way? David never protests, to God or to the Gibeonites. He doesn't even consider applying his royal prerogative to protect the lives of Saul's seven remaining heirs. What a contrast to the lengths to which David went to protect Saul's life! Even if this story was intended to show David's innocence of wrongdoing, at best it portrays him as blithely indifferent to slaughter.[14]

Another passage seeks to assert David's nobility of character but is even more jarring in its implications (1 Sam. 29:6–11). As we saw earlier, David gleefully acted as a hired soldier for a Philistine warlord. Now the Philistines are arrayed against Saul's army, prepared to do battle. Achish's fellow warlords view David as a potential fifth column/turncoat and oppose his participation. Breaking the news to David, Achish expresses his personal opposition to the decision and his absolute faith in David's trustworthiness. In other words, Achish trusts that David will make a loyal soldier and commander against the Israelite army! David's response is even more astonishing. Not only does he disagree with the Philistines' conclusion that he should refrain from fighting, he appears insulted by the Philistines' lack of faith in him: "But what have I done, what fault have you found in your servant from the day I appeared before you to this day, that I should not go and fight against the enemies of my lord the king?" In other words, whereas once David was eager to fight against the Philistines, the enemy of the Lord, now he is crestfallen because the Philistines are preventing him from fighting against the Israelites! This perplexing and dizzying reversal, in opposition to the main thrust of the David stories, again lays bare David's ambition against Saul and his house. The Philistine army proceeds to rout the Israelites, killing Jonathan and inducing Saul's suicide. Only then, after his political opponents have perished, does David return to the Israelite camp to lead the mourning.

Making Sense of David's Behavior

No doubt, David is a difficult character to understand from the plain sense of the text. He is a creature of contradictions. He is built up to be a heroic king after the institution of monarchy has been denounced as an affront to God. After Samuel proclaims him king he spends years not as king, as if his anointment never transpired. Furthermore, the reader is rarely granted access to David's internal life, so the various contradictions bear no obvious resolution. Many stories relate David's stringent efforts to deny his ambition that other passages make evident.

Perhaps the most challenging contradiction lies in David's bumpy, careening moral character. In a great many stories, David piously relies on God for his success. When he is finally pronounced king, after Saul's and Jonathan's demise (2 Sam. 2:1–7), David consults God twice to determine where he should head: "Sometime afterward, David inquired of the Lord, 'Shall I go up to one of the towns of Judah?' The Lord answered, 'Go up.' David further asked, 'Which one shall I go up to?' And the Lord replied, 'To Hebron.'" Even though God gives him what may be the most laconic response in the entire Bible—both answers are one word in the Hebrew— David's asking God to provide him with a roadmap (and twice at that) betokens his piety. Later on, David offers the men of Jabesh-Gilead, who took the initiative to bury Saul, a double blessing: "May you be blessed of the Lord because you performed this act of faithfulness to your lord Saul and buried him. May the Lord in turn show you true faithfulness; and I too will reward you generously because you performed this act." By offering God's blessing to these men, David becomes a messenger of God, one who channels God's agency in human affairs. David also aligns his own beneficence toward these men with the Lord's.

The halo this episode wreathes around David is later besmirched by David's acts of adultery and murder (2 Sam. 11). One day, David espies a beautiful woman bathing nearby. David learns her name, sends messengers to bring her to the palace, and proceeds to lie with her. He then arranges for Bathsheba's husband, Uriah, to leave a military encampment in order to meet him in the palace. When Uriah arrives, David tells him to go home, presumably to sleep with his wife, which would cover David's own involvement should Bathsheba become pregnant. Uriah refuses, protesting that he will not lie with his wife while his army is encamped for battle. When Uriah returns to the ranks, David orders his general, Joab, to go to war but then withdraw troops, leaving Uriah exposed. David is manipulating his army solely to eliminate his romantic rival! Joab follows orders, Uriah dies in battle, and David marries Bathsheba.

Like another powerful Israelite leader, Samson, who is undone by his attraction to Delilah, David is undone by his desire for Bathsheba. David will never be the same character after this episode. He has lost the moral foundations on which his character stands: his loyalty to God, his respect for fellow human beings, his restraint and punctiliousness. Even the people no longer show him the same consistent reverence. For the first time, God accuses David of wrongdoing and suggests that their relationship will no longer be as close or protective. For the remainder of 2 Samuel, he suffers repeated humiliation and even rebellion at his children's hands. The equivalent of Samson's hair has been shorn.

Comparing David's behavior in these two stories, the reader inevitably asks, How can the same person be the humble servant of God in one chapter and a brazen adulterer and murderer soon thereafter? Does one or the other of these episodes represent the "real" David, or are they both equally real—and if so, how is the reader expected to make sense of David?

Many biblical scholars view the significant contradictions in his depiction as emanating from different sources in different historical periods, all woven together into the final document of 1–2 Samuel. However, David's disparate actions over the course of his story might otherwise be understood as logical and unified through the lens of the Freudian concept of defense mechanisms. Three defense mechanisms are especially noticeable in David's actions: repression, reaction formation, and projection.[15]

The first defense mechanism, "repression," is the most basic psychological reaction and the gateway to the other defense mechanisms to follow. The British website Psychologist World explains:

According to Sigmund Freud's psychodynamic theory, the impulsive desires of the psyche's id are prevented by being fulfilled by the ego, which observes the Reality Principle—that our actions are restricted by our environment, including social etiquette. Moreover, the super-ego acts as our moral compass, inducing feelings of guilt at having experienced the irrational desires that the id creates.

Tensions inevitably arise between the id, ego, and super ego, and the guilt induced by the latter can lead to feelings of anxiety and shame. In order to live with such feelings, Freud believed that our minds repress the thoughts at the source of our anxieties: instead of contemplating them consciously, they are "bottled up" in the unconscious mind, emerging in symbolic dreams and unexplained patterns of behavior.

We see the tensions in the human psyche described here—between David's id, his desire to kill and replace Saul; David's superego, his awareness that such desires are wrong; and David's ego, trapped between these conflicting forces and evidencing both guilt and seething hostility—in the cloak-cutting scene (1 Sam. 24). Saul, jealous of David's success and suspicious of his intent, learns of David's location and brings a posse to kill him. Saul walks into a cave to urinate, unaware that David and his men are hiding there. David's men give voice to his id: "This is the day of which the Lord said to you, 'I will deliver your enemy into your hands; you can do with him as you please.'" Instead of attacking Saul, however, David decides to sneak up to him and cut a corner of Saul's cloak. The text suggests there are different ways to interpret this gesture. When David confronts Saul a few minutes later, he produces the cloth as evidence that he has no intention to harm his king, for he could have done so if he wanted to: "Though I was urged to kill you, I showed you pity; for I said, 'I will not raise a hand against my lord, since he is the Lord's anointed.'" If this is meant to allay Saul's concerns, it might easily be taken otherwise; David asserts that he has the upper hand and spared Saul out of his own graciousness and conscience.

Immediately after he cuts the cloak, however, David himself interprets the cut differently, as a symbolic wound to Saul and his royal authority: "But afterward David's heart struck him for cutting off the corner of Saul's cloak. He said to his men, 'The Lord forbid that I should do such a thing to my lord.'" This suggests that David did not set out to warn Saul of his power and restraint; rather, driven by his men's urging, David initially moved to kill Saul with the knife—but in the midst of the action he had a change of heart and cut the cloak instead.

He is suddenly overcome with guilt, regretting not only his near assassination of Saul, but even the symbolic wound to the cloak. When David rushes after Saul to confront him, these conflicting emotions are freshly at combat in his psyche: "You must see plainly that I have done nothing evil or rebellious, and I have never wronged you. Yet you are bent on taking my life. May the Lord judge between you and me! And may He take vengeance upon you for me, but my hand will never touch you" (1 Sam. 24:12–13). In the same breath by which David protests his innocence and accuses Saul of seeking his death, he invokes God to destroy Saul! With David's hotline to God, as we've seen, such a threat is far from idle.

The next defense mechanism David exhibits, called "reaction formation," builds on his repression. Again, Psychologist World explains:

> When the insatiable desires of the id conflict with the ego and super ego, a person may formulate a reaction to those impulses. Often, this action is the direct opposite to the demands of the original desire, and helps to counteract impulses which may be unacceptable to act out or fulfill.
>
> For example, a man may experience feelings of love towards a married woman. The super ego recognises that the fulfillment of his desires would contradict social norms regarding acceptable behavior, and so a reaction formation would occur — the man may experience feelings of dislike towards her — the opposite of the original feelings.

Even as the aforementioned biblical passages might be construed as apologetics, defenses of David attributing Saul's downfall to God's punishment of Saul's missteps, we can also read David's extreme fidelity to his king as a reaction formation toward his repressed feelings of ambition. No greater proof exists than David's intimate embrace of Saul's children, Michal and Jonathan. David marries Michal and loves Jonathan like a brother; both of them sense David's authentic devotion and love him more strongly for it. David's love of Saul's children confirms the success of his own repression.

A third defense mechanism, "projection," similarly enlarges on tendencies toward repression by forcefully denying one's genuine emotions. Instead of a person exhibiting behaviors that are the opposite of the ones he or she would like to perform, he or she projects those illicit desires onto another person. Psychologist World elaborates:

> When we experience feelings or desires that cause anxiety, or that we are unable to act on owing to the negative impact that they would have on us or those around us, we may defend the ego from resulting anxieties by projecting those ideas onto another person. A person who is afraid of crossing a bridge with a friend might accuse them of having a fear of heights, for example, and in doing so, avoid accepting their own weaknesses.

David exhibits this defense mechanism at the beginning of 2 Samuel. A messenger arrives at Ziklag, the Philistine town where David has encamped for more than a year, and informs him that Saul and Jonathan have died. David's reaction suggests the news comes as a surprise to him: "How do you know . . . that Saul and his son Jonathan are dead?" The messenger claims that he is the one who personally helped them die: "[Saul] said to me, 'Stand over me, and finish me off, for I am in agony and barely alive.' So I stood over him and finished him off, for I knew that he would never rise from where he was lying. Then I took the crown from his head and the armlet from his arm, and I have brought them here to my lord" (2 Sam. 1:8–10). The messenger's account differs significantly from the objective narrator's report in the previous chapter: "Saul said to his arms-bearer, 'Draw your sword and run me through, so that the uncircumcised may not run me through and make sport of me.' But his arms-bearer, in his great awe, refused; whereupon Saul grasped the sword and fell upon it. When his arms-bearer saw that Saul was dead, he too fell on his sword and died with him" (1 Sam. 31:4–6).

The messenger is clearly lying. He did not kill Saul—Saul killed himself—and he was not even the arms-bearer whom Saul had asked to kill him. By inventing a different version of Saul's death, the messenger hopes that David will reward him for his alleged role. After all, the messenger has faithfully fulfilled Saul's wishes, putting the king out of his agony, and now, in equal fidelity to David, he has brought David

Saul's crown, perhaps at the risk of his life (he may have extracted it from the battlefield). For his service in support of both Saul and David, the messenger patently hopes to receive a reward. He may also be seeking recompense by stoking David's ambition: *Reward me for bringing you the emblems of kingship! Your opponents are dead; the crown now is yours! Even more, I was the one who killed Saul, albeit at his own request!*

For his part, David appears to believe the messenger's account, but instead of being pleased, his outrage is kindled: "How did you dare . . . to lift your hand and kill the Lord's anointed?" (2 Sam. 1:14). David then summons a servant to slay the messenger. Perhaps he thinks the messenger should not have killed Saul even if he had been ordered to. Perhaps David sees the messenger's version as a bald-faced, ambition-stoked lie and has him killed accordingly. David also discovers that the messenger is an Amalekite, a member of the people so committed to Israel's destruction that God mandates their extermination. So, his slaying the messenger may correct for Saul's unwillingness to kill the Amalekite king, Agag (despite David's ignorance of any injunction against the Amalekites).

If David does believe the messenger, though, then wouldn't killing the man be an overreaction that requires a different explanation? Can the messenger truly be faulted for obeying Saul's command and then seeking David's succession? Instead, David may be projecting his own feelings of guilt over his repressed ambition onto the messenger. David draws a stark distinction between himself and the messenger while in fact the two share uncomfortable similarities: Both the messenger and David seek to benefit from Saul's death while denying responsibility for it. Robert Polzin calls the messenger David's "double"; by having him killed, David casts his own sins on another, a symbolic cleansing reminiscent of the scapegoat ritual (Lev. 16:20–22).[16] The poor messenger thus provides a useful screen for David to project and exorcise his inner turmoil.

Guilt and Paralysis

Whereas at first—at least throughout the second half of 1 Samuel—David's character is established as ideal for the throne while Saul disintegrates into madness, this contrast falls apart when David takes the reins of power. From this point on, the biblical storyteller exposes the similarities between David and Saul.

This switch is especially apparent when comparing the narrative space devoted to the two kings' military and political triumphs. Once Saul becomes king, his military successes are delivered in just two lines: "He waged war on every side against all his enemies: against the Moabites, Ammonites, Edomites, the Philistines, and the kings of Zobah; and wherever he turned he worsted [them]. He was triumphant, defeating the Amalekites and saving Israel from those who plundered it" (1 Sam. 14:47–48). Similarly, David's military and political accomplishments are confined to one short chapter (2 Sam. 8), which attests that David "attacked the Philistines and subdued them"; that he did the same to the Amalekites; and that the Moabites, along with the nations of Edom and Ammon, "became tributary vassals of David." David "defeated Hadadezer son of Rehob, king of Zobah" and "struck down 22,000 of the Arameans" when they tried to rescue their ally Hadadezer. Hadadezer's enemy King Toi then sent gifts to congratulate David and form an alliance.[17]

Remarkably, an additional claim in this chapter—"The Lord gave David victory wherever he went" (2 Sam. 8:14)—might have colored the entire depiction of David's reign, but it is limited solely to this description of events. David's triumph, in other words, becomes a throwaway line, buried beneath the tragic narrative of the fight over David's succession that occupies the rest of David's story. In effect, even as the Bible acknowledges these kings' military and political triumphs, it dramatically reduces the space—and therefore attention—accorded to them, while proliferating stories that elaborate on their imperfect personal lives. Just as half of 1 Samuel concerns the decline of Saul and his house, half of 2 Samuel describes the decline of David, his family's internecine clashes, and the near disappearance of his house.

David's escapade that reveals his greatest moral failing happens in three steps: (1) adultery with Bathsheba, (2) assassination of her husband, (3) marrying Bathsheba. David's prophet, Nathan, traps him into acknowledging his sin through the use of a parable (2 Sam. 12:1–14). A rich man who possessed a large flock was the neighbor of a poor man with a single ewe. When a visitor came to the rich man, instead of feeding his guest from his own flock, he stole the neighbor's sheep and cooked it. The story arouses David's ire: The rich man "deserves to die!" David exclaims. "He shall pay for the lamb four times over."[18] Nathan then tells David, "That man is you!" Indeed, David, rich in wives and property, has taken Uriah's life and his wife.

Just as Saul's transgression of God's command—which, in contrast with David's, seems minuscule—evoked God's wrath and the eventual end of his reign, so do David's actions arouse God's full anger. For stealing Uriah's wife, God tells David, "The sword shall never depart from your House," suggesting that, akin to the House of Saul, after centuries of internal divisions, the House of David will eventually fall. God threatens more immediate consequences as well: Another man will take and sleep with his wives.

At this point, David cannot pay restitution: Uriah is dead. All he can do is acknowledge Nathan's verdict and accept God's punishment. This is exactly what David does, wholeheartedly: "I stand guilty before the Lord!" (2 Sam. 12:13).

David's confession seems to come as an enormous relief to him. Far from being the perfect choirboy, the blameless servant of God and Saul, David admits he is a fallible human animal, made of flesh and blood and here unmade by powerful desires and motives. Nathan acts not only as judge and mirror for David's ethical failings but as psychoanalyst. He helps David to recognize his vigorous, ceaseless efforts to be someone else. David no longer needs to pretend he is someone other than who he is.

David's admission of guilt can thus be seen as referring not only to Bathsheba and Uriah but to his entire campaign to usurp Saul's throne and destroy his family. In short, a newly liberated David acknowledges full responsibility and accepts God's justice.

Unfortunately for David, however, his punishment and liberation join hands. While celebrating the lifting of his long repression, he must suffer for the egregious harm he caused by the explosive release of his pent-up desires. Immediately after Nathan's reproof, David and Bathsheba's child falls ill and dies. David accepts this death as the beginning of the Divine verdict; he rises from mourning to prostrate himself before God. This second period of David's life then switches from his Samson phase to his Jacob phase. Just as Jacob's long trail of suffering from his children can be seen as a punishment for his own deceptions of his father and brother, so too David's profound suffering over his children's sibling violence appears as a form of retribution that balances the scales in the moral universe he inhabits. Contesting the succession to the crown, David's children reprise the infighting among Jacob's sons, only worse.

During this period, David's behavior evinces yet one further contradiction. Earlier in 2 Samuel 8, David is depicted as an outstanding leader who musters Israel's army to defeat enemies, gains advantage over neighboring powers, and arranges a well-functioning government. Yet during this succession narrative, which fills the second half of 2 Samuel up to 1 Kings 2, David acts with a degree of apathy. Readily duped by his children, he willingly lets them take charge even when he knows the wiser course would require upright leadership—which he can no longer provide.

This newly passive and impotent David emerges particularly in the story of Amnon's rape of Tamar and its aftermath (2 Sam. 13). Amnon develops a crush on his half-sister Tamar. Amnon's friend Jonadab advises Amnon to pretend to be sick and ask his father, David, to send Tamar to feed him. Already, the children sense David's pliability to their will. Amnon's intuition is correct: David appears thoroughly incapable of seeing through Amnon's plot or sensing the danger to come. "Amnon lay down and pretended to be sick. The king came to see him, and Amnon said to the king, 'Let my sister Tamar come and prepare a couple of cakes in front of me, and let her bring them to me.' David sent a message to Tamar in the palace, 'Please go to the house of your brother Amnon and prepare some food for him'" (2 Sam. 13:6–7). In promptly fulfilling Amnon's wish and then exiting the stage, David is nothing more than a naive enabler of his son's wicked plot. He is incapable even of protecting the safety of his daughter. In effect David acts as Jacob did when he sent Joseph to check up on his brothers, who then abducted Joseph and sold him. The text clearly suggests the parallel, for Tamar is dressed in "an ornamental tunic" (13:18), the same term used for Joseph's clothing.[19]

David's fecklessness recurs after Amnon carries through his plot, raping Tamar and then sending her away.[20] The standard Hebrew text informs us that "when King David heard about all this, he was greatly upset" (2 Sam. 13:21)—but did nothing. (The Septuagint, the earliest Greek translation of the Bible, goes on to add a clause, not found in the Hebrew version, spelling out this implication: "But he did not rebuke his son Amnon, for he favored him, since he was his firstborn.") Usually in the biblical narrative, David is referred to simply by his name. The use of David's title "king" here is ironic: The most powerful man in the kingdom, the man who conquers enemies and garners tribute, cannot bring himself to chastise his own son.

David's mistaken restraint leaves room for Tamar's brother Absalom to take charge and manipulate this incident to his own ends. Equally obtuse to Absalom's motives, David is just as reluctant to exercise leadership or caution.

> Two years later, when Absalom was having his flocks sheared at Baalhazor near Ephraim, Absalom invited all the king's sons. And Absalom came to the king and said, "Your servant is having his flocks sheared. Would Your Majesty and your retinue accompany your servant?" But the king answered Absalom, "No, my son. We must not all come, or we'll be a burden to you." He urged him, but he would not go, and he said good-bye to him. Thereupon Absalom said, "In that case, let my brother Amnon come with us," to which the king replied, "He shall not go with you." But Absalom urged him, and he sent with him Amnon and all the other princes. (2 Sam. 13:23–27)

The use of "king" again in this instance signifies Absalom's pretense of deference: "your servant," "your Majesty." Absalom skillfully casts the sheep-shearing event as a mere agricultural festivity among family (like a Thanksgiving feast). His reiteration of the invitation is meant to broadcast his special concern and love for David and his family—the opposite of his true intent. Again, David is quick to leave. He voices reluctance to interfere with his children's affairs, an ostensible by-product of his trust in his children, but his actions convey his desire to retreat from the exercise of power. Especially in his family, the last person he wants to be is "king."

David's reluctance to rule is especially evident at the end of this exchange. Absalom asks David's permission for Amnon to attend the festival. At first David declines. The text does not give a reason, but one may infer that David senses something amiss. He knows that Tamar is Absalom's full sister; perhaps he sniffs some hostile intent beneath Absalom's thick veneer of subservience. Still, David lacks the will to resist Absalom's importunity. His thin thread of resistance is easily cut. In the very next line, Absalom orders his men to kill Amnon. Once more, David serves as the passive enabler to his sons' violence.

A contrast with a similar scene, the rape of Dinah (discussed in chapter 5), makes the case for David being nearly as culpable as his children for their misdeeds. Jacob is clearly unaware that his sons Shimon and Levi are planning to kill Dinah's rapist, Shechem; Shechem's father; and all the males in the town for good measure. Learning of the plot soon after they have carried it out, he immediately reproves his sons, the killers. David, by contrast, goes beyond full ignorance to actually facilitate the crimes. He brings Tamar to Amnon's house and leaves her there; he retrieves Amnon and escorts him to Absalom's party, abandoning him as well to his fate. In neither case does he say a word of reproach after the crimes. He does not force Amnon to marry his half-sister to restore her honor. His silence is more glaring considering that these crimes take place within his family. Jacob's anger falls on his sons for ruining the family's standing among their neighbors; David watches silently as his family disintegrates before his eyes. Compared with Jacob, David is, strikingly, the more ineffective and pathetic figure. The mighty king is a powerless father and a ruined man.

In the meantime, Absalom has become the initiator in the family. His decisive, bloody deeds stand in stark contrast to David's inaction: "Now Absalom gave his attendants these orders: 'Watch, and when Amnon is merry with wine and I tell you to strike down Amnon, kill him! Don't be afraid, for it is I who give you the order. Act with determination, like brave men!'" (2 Sam. 13:28). Absalom already sounds like someone leading an army, which he will do shortly. His vengeance against his brother provides a launch pad to test his father and flex his leadership muscles.

The narrator is anxious to portray David as innocent of desiring to harm his rebellious son, just as the story insisted on David's innocence in Saul's downfall. David's general Joab sees that David's "mind was on Absalom" (2 Sam. 14:1). Presumably concerned that David is considering punishing or even killing his son, Joab enlists a "wise woman" from the town of Tekoa to approach David with a story, similar to Nathan's, designed to steer David to forgive Absalom. David is quick to agree, and Absalom proceeds to live in Jerusalem, plotting his next moves. Absalom works hard to win the people's support. Rising early, he stands before the city gates, convincing all who approach the king in judgment (by supporting them in their cause) that he himself would make a better judge than his father. David is silently acquiescent during these years — after all, someone must have told him of Absalom's vigorous undermining of his authority. Finally, after years of campaigning, Absalom manages to win a large enough following to have himself declared king. Absalom captures the capital for his reign; David must flee Jerusalem with his band of followers.

Only now that David's life and country are threatened does David manifest his former abilities — the cunning to devise successful strategies, and the patience to wait for the right moment to strike. The David of old, the one who slew Goliath, killed tens of thousands, raided Philistine cities, brought down the House of Saul, and established a thriving and powerful nation — that David is now determined to defeat his rebellious son. He sends an ally, Hushai the Archite, to serve as a double agent in Absalom's court. After pledging loyalty to the new king, Hushai first feeds him bad advice. Meanwhile, Hushai reveals Absalom's war plans to David via the king's new spy network of allies. As Absalom comes on the attack, David's well-prepared army routs his son's. David has asked his troops to spare Absalom himself, but when Joab encounters

Absalom hanging from his long hair caught in a tree, he and his men kill the rebel leader.

When David hears of Absalom's fate, he returns to form as Israel's chief mourner. Once he lamented Saul and Jonathan, tore his clothes over Amnon; now with Absalom he weeps and weeps until all his troops follow him into mourning. For his son who killed his brother, who spent years in conniving and then executed his father's overthrow, sending his father and allies into exile—for this son, David wishes he "had died instead of [Absalom]" (2 Sam. 19:1)! Again, David is in reaction formation territory: demonstrating excessive love for the son he had the least reason to love, and whose death comes indirectly from his own command.

Thus the David narrative lingers over his failures of leadership in managing his "house." When faced with evidence that his sons possess his same sexual urges and ambitions, he is frozen. Perhaps, recognizing himself in them, he feels incapable of imposing on them the same restraints that stifled him for years. Additionally, he regards his children's clashes fatalistically, as God's punishing decree and his own just desserts for his earlier sins.

David cuts a tragic figure worthy of Shakespeare: At the moment of his, and his people's, greatest political triumph, his personal weaknesses prevent him from enjoying the fruits of his success and induce the near-total collapse of his dynasty. Just as Saul's descendants perished in battle with the Philistines or with David, several of David's own sons die fighting each other or their father. Ironically, David increasingly comes to resemble the king from whom he spent so many years distinguishing himself.

Deathbed Reversal II

At the very end of his life (1 Kings 1–2), David, like Jacob lying on his deathbed, is called to make a fateful decision for his heirs.[21] For his part, Jacob intentionally reverses the order of blessings for Joseph's sons, paying greater honor to the younger son and asserting his own vision over Joseph's wishes in the process. David, too, has to decide between two sons, and has a much weightier judgment to pass: who will inherit the throne. Yet again, at first, he appears as a weak figure, easily deceived and manipulated by both sides in the struggle for kingship.

The story starts with a shocking detail. As part of his condition in old age, David cannot feel warm; on their own accord his courtiers send messengers throughout the land seeking a "young virgin . . . a beautiful girl" to "wait upon Your majesty . . . and lie in your bosom." The process seems more like the beauty contest in Esther than an act of hiring a nurse. Clearly, David's strong erotic desires have not diminished. While the text goes on to tell us that David "was not intimate with her," the selected girl, Avishag the Shunammite, nonetheless becomes more than a nurse or attendant to the king.

While Avishag is attending to David, Adonijah, David's older son, decides to proclaim himself king. Unbeknownst to David, Adonijah forms alliances with David's general, Joab, and one of his priests, Abiathar, thus arming himself with both temporal and spiritual power. Since Adonijah was "born after Absalom," presumably he is next in line for the throne and believes it is his prerogative to seize what belongs to him by right. Most likely he does not trust that David will act on his behalf, and thus steps into the power vacuum to force David's hand with a fait accompli. As usual, David is ignorant of his children's machinations. Now, however, for the first time, the narrator explicitly blames David for Adonijah's behavior: "His father had never scolded him, 'Why did you do that?'"

In the interim, Bathsheba and Nathan plot to curry David's favor on behalf of David's younger son Solomon. Whereas Adonijah does not realize, or accept, that he needs David's imprimatur, Solomon's handlers recognize David's power and exercise all their cunning to bend it to their intended heir. No matter how diminished he is in body and spirit, David as king still possesses authority and requires courtly formalities of respect. Nathan directs an elaborate scene reminiscent of Esther's preparations before her encounter with Ahasuerus: First, Bathsheba is to approach David, asserting that David had promised Solomon would be his heir, and reporting Adonijah's actions; then Nathan himself will enter and confirm Bathsheba's words. Sure enough, their repeated announcement of Adonijah's deeds and questioning of David's intended successor have the desired effect: The king is roused to action.

From the story itself, and the simple fact that to date the biblical text has never told us this seemingly important piece of information, it's not evident that David had ever promised Solomon the throne. David may be reacting angrily to Adonijah's attempted usurpation behind his back. He may be swayed by his love of Bathsheba as well as his respect and/ or fear of Nathan, his faithful prophet. He may prefer Solomon for the same reason that Jacob preferred Joseph: Both Solomon and Joseph are the children of David's and Jacob's favorite wives. Or, David's weakened state may render him vulnerable to a forceful argument. The reader's choice depends on interpreting David's character at this point in his life. Is David a vital king and father asserting his will or an empty puppet pulled by strings? The strength of David's subsequent proclamation— "The oath I swore to you . . . that your son Solomon should succeed me as king . . . I will fulfill this very day!" (1 Kings 1:30)—suggests the former, whereas his weakened condition and pusillanimous treatment of his sons until now argues for the latter. Nevertheless, David's decisive orders arranging for Solomon's enthronement indicate a change is afoot (1 Kings 1:32–40). Now, as he raises one son and punishes another, he is the choreographer instead of the audience.

David's final scene (1 Kings 2:1–9) allows no doubt that he, like Jacob, undergoes a deathbed revival. One might easily imagine Marlon Brando reprising his role in *The Godfather* as he recites David's dying words to Solomon instructing his heir as to whom he should let live (the sons of Barzillai) and whom he should destroy (Adonijah's general, Joab, and Shimei). David makes no provision for Adonijah to be permitted to withdraw and accept his brother as David's choice. The fact that David does not mention Adonijah suggests he is leaving Solomon to do what he wants with him—and David, like a dying mafioso, knows Solomon wants Adonijah dead.

After David dies, Solomon, sure enough, does not exhibit even the slightest restraint in doing away with his brother. And so, once again,

David's son kills his half-brother. There's no room here for the tears and hugs of Joseph and his brothers. Reunion brings nothing but bloodshed.

David the Psalmist: Hero of the Spirit

> David, king of Israel, lives and thrives!
> —popular Jewish song

What makes David a hero? The answer seems to derive more from his role as a king in Israelite history and less to do with who he was as a man. As a king, he was successful. He is credited with expanding the nation's borders, triumphing over its military enemies, and erecting a solid scaffold of government. He established a dynasty of monarchs who ruled for centuries, and his reign lives on in traditional Jewish memory as the pinnacle of Jewish political power. Sometimes, too, the text shines light on David's admirable traits: his restraint as Saul seeks to kill him, his willingness to admit his failings when Nathan confronts him. Overall, however, the historical account presents a murky portrait of David even by the standards of the Bible's flawed heroes.

Fortunately for David's reputation, an entire body of biblical texts portray him as heroic, in a vastly different way. The Psalms expand on references in 1 Samuel to David as a musician and singer who soothes the troubled mind of Saul. The text of 2 Samuel gives several examples of David's prowess as a poet: the majestic dirge over Saul and Jonathan, "How are the mighty fallen!" (chapter 1); the long psalm of praise to God, a personal capstone and summary (chapter 22, identical to Psalms 18 with some variants); and a poem of the "last words of David" (chapter 23), placed a few chapters before David's death, that boasts of the "eternal pact" God has granted to his house. Among the Psalms, about half are overtly attributed to David.

The Psalms present a picture of David up close, speaking from the heart, confessing his faults, laying bare his fears and struggles. Whereas in the books of Samuel, David's exclamation "I stand guilty before the Lord!" offers one of few moments of spiritual authenticity in which the biblical reader encounters a living person behind the mask, in the

Psalms practically the entire book gives voice to that genuine inner life. Rendered in first-person, these prayers — David's conversations with God — speak directly, authentically, and powerfully to his contrition and fear, rage and joy. Like all great lyric poetry, their personal quality has enabled readers through the ages to identify with his feelings. David's "I" is simultaneously him and the multitudes who make these prayers their own. In so doing, the Psalms recast David as a far more compelling and comprehensible hero.

Several of the Psalms claim to have been written at specific moments of David's life as described in 1–2 Samuel. Of these, Psalm 51 gives expression to David's thoughts and emotions at a pivotal moment of his career, "when Nathan the prophet came to him after he had come to Bathsheba." The poem exposes David's spirit when he utters his great admission, "I stand guilty before the Lord." One can easily imagine David harboring the feelings in this prayer and voicing them internally:

> Have mercy upon me, O God,
>> as befits Your faithfulness;
>> in keeping with Your abundant compassion,
>> blot out my transgressions.
> Wash me thoroughly of my iniquity,
>> and purify me of my sin;
>> for I recognize my transgressions,
>> and am ever conscious of my sin.

David is fully cognizant of his sin, yet he needs to throw himself on God's mercy, for God alone can forgive him. As we saw in the story, David's confession is only marginally liberating, given that it is followed by his awareness of the severity and justness of God's punishment:

> Against You alone have I sinned,
>> and done what is evil in Your sight;
>> so You are just in Your sentence,
>> and right in Your judgment.

David acquiesces to his punishment and is paralyzed in terror by it simultaneously. In the psalm, he asks God to restore their relationship, lift from him the burden of his sin, and give him the ability to begin anew.

> Hide Your face from my sins;
>> blot out all my iniquities.
> Fashion a pure heart for me, O God;
>> create in me a steadfast spirit.
> Do not cast me out of Your presence,
>> or take Your holy spirit away from me.

Between the lines of David's faith in God's power to redeem him, we can hear David's anxieties. A steadfast spirit is precisely what David lacks. Indeed, he proves unable to control his manipulative, competing sons. David's greatest fear is that his "house" will suffer the same fate as Saul's at God's hands.

Toward the end of the psalm, David returns to the strategy that won him God's favor for so long:

> True sacrifice to God is a contrite spirit;
>> God, You will not despise
>> a contrite and crushed heart.

"A contrite and crushed heart" beautifully expresses David's state of mind after Nathan's accusation and God's promise of punishment. David is hopeful that God will reward a king—even this king—with genuine contrition and humility. The psalm shows David spiritually reorienting himself: acknowledging his mistakes and casting himself on God's mercy. It transforms the flawed, opaque figure of biblical history into a hero of spiritual life—a man who wrestles with pangs of conscience, voices genuine penitence, and finds hope in his faith in God's justice. It also helps to transform our relationship to David, revealing a glimpse of warm blood in the cold heart of this ambitious, conflicted king.

7

GOD

Archetype or Antitype?

> The Lord is king,
>> He is robed in grandeur;
>> the Lord is robed,
>> He is girded with strength.
> The world stands firm;
>> it cannot be shaken.
> —Psalm 93:1

While Jewish tradition acclaims God's greatness, it is not clear whether or not the God of the Bible is an "archetype"—the paradigm of a biblical hero. Is God a heroic biblical character who resembles other human biblical heroes, only in a greater way? Or is God an "antitype"—a being so removed from human constraints that the notion of a "hero" cannot apply?

From the perspective I have advanced here, the biblical God can't be a hero in the sense of a human exemplar. But from the Bible's perspective, it often seems that *only* God can be a hero—all people are reduced to size. Which is it?

In sources other than the Bible, ancient heroes are portrayed as half-god, half-human. They are like us, but more advanced models— able to rise above common mortals, but incapable of achieving divine immortality. Their advantages imbue them with the power to attain high accomplishments, but their ambitions often lead them to forget their vulnerability and overreach at their peril.

The Bible, however, does not believe in advanced models—which in itself causes difficulties in rendering a human as a hero. Thus, the Bible's position might be construed as:

1. There is no such thing as a hero; people are too flawed, God is too far beyond us.

This book, however, takes a second position:

2. There is such a thing as a human hero, but we need to shrink our expectations. Biblical protagonists can be heroes while being highly flawed in character.

Meanwhile, there is a third possibility as well:

3. God is the world's hero. Only God is sufficiently above human capacity to be able to accomplish heroic deeds. Or, in the vacuum of heroes created by biblical theology, God steps in to fill the role.

Does position 1 require position 3? If people are no longer candidates for heroic status in the Bible, does God inevitably step in to take the prize? The great sage Hillel once said, "In a place where there are no men, try to be a man" (Pirkei Avot 2:6). Is the Bible a place bereft of "men"? Does God then take the place of a "man"?

The prevailing notion of monotheism (or, in some biblical passages, monolatry[1]) further complicates any conception of the Bible's God as a hero.

Complication #1: The Hero as a Human Character with a Body

The first complication lies in the conception of a hero as a human character who uses a body to act, lead, think, and speak. Depicting God as a literary character places the Bible in the bind of saddling this character with the physical attributes and motions attributed to characters in all stories. Does the Bible's portrayal of God allow for or elude the creatureliness of literary characters?

How God is physically conceived in biblical storytelling is hard to discern, especially in comparison to the abundantly evident physicality of the Greek gods and divine pantheons of the ancient Near East. In the traditional Jewish conception as well as our own times, God cannot be said to possess form or corporeal features. God indeed exists, but the meaning of "exists" is different for God than for mortals. God exists in another sense or dimension. God can exist everywhere at once. God is not limited by space or time or the needs that attend to physical beings.

However, this conception of God is far from a given. Benjamin Sommer puts it this way in *The Bodies of God*, his pathbreaking study of the subject: "The God of the Hebrew Bible has a body."[2] Indeed, an abundance of anthropomorphic imagery attaches to God in the Bible. God is said to possess a variety of body parts: an arm, hand, face, nose, back, heart, eye.[3] Furthermore, the Bible presents God as taking numerous actions—speaking, seeing, hearing, walking, sitting, descending, and so on—suggesting some sort of body responsible for such agency. God sits on a throne (Isa. 6:1) and rests God's feet on a footstool (Ps. 99:5). The most common phrase in the Torah is surely "And God said to Moses." Psalm 27:4 also tells us that the highest goal of life is to "gaze upon the beauty of the Lord," and it is not clear that this is meant metaphorically.[4] What is more: God is anthropopathic, exhibiting human emotions, including anger, satisfaction, and regret.

In effect, by presenting a character named God in the narrative, the Bible introduces notions of God that challenge the dominant philosophical conception in monotheistic faiths.[5] In one form or another, a character in a story resembles a person. The animal characters in *The Wind in the Willows* or *The Tale of Peter Rabbit*, for example, appear to be people in furry garb; the Greek gods Zeus and Athena are no less human in stories about them.

Yet, plenty of evidence suggests that biblical references to God's corporeality are not to be interpreted in the same mortal way. To take one example: in the Tower of Babel story, the Lord "came down to look at the city and tower that man had built" (Gen. 11:5). God comes across like a human leader who leaves the capital to survey the insurrection scene firsthand. But aside from the troubling anthropomorphisms in this sentence—"came down," "look," God's apparent ignorance and consequent need to come close in order to see—is the question of where God came down from. The passage assumes that God dwells in the heavens, but what does that really mean? How can a being dwell "on high"? What kind of physical existence would enable God to inhabit the skies, or beyond? Through what mode of transportation would God "descend"?

We don't really know. Biblical anthropomorphisms are often sufficiently attenuated as to drape a large swath of gauze over the reader's impression of God's physical presence. We never "see" the Bible's God in the same way we see other divinities of the ancient Near East and Mediterranean. The reader stands with Moses in the cleft of the rock, staring at God's back, while God's "face will not be seen." Without such an understanding of God's substance, it can be challenging to comprehend how God might be a hero who takes action in the material world.

Complication #2: Monotheism's Challenge to Biblical Storytelling

A second complication lies in the challenge monotheism presents to biblical storytelling. Narrative is predicated on conflict, and ancient narrative primarily tells the stories of conflict between and among gods: Marduk slays Tiamat, Chronos castrates his father Uranus, Zeus defeats and dethrones Chronos, Athena fights for the Greeks in the Trojan War, and so on. In the ancient world, warfare occurs on two levels—the earthly field and between divine protectors—simultaneously. What, then, is the biblical narrator to do? How can the Bible find narrative interest without the clash of divinities? Most critically, if there is only one supreme God, and that God is on the side of the Israelites, how can there be meaningful conflict? Wherein lies God's heroism when there are no opponents?[6]

The Bible addresses these issues by reenvisioning the nature of narrative conflict in multiple ways:

1. *The human plane is stacked against the Israelites.* Israel is chosen precisely for its weakness in numbers and military might. Israel's overwhelmingly more powerful enemies include the leading empires of the ancient Near East: the Egyptians, Philistines, Assyrians, Babylonians. Even the aged, unwarlike Abraham gathers a small posse of servants and friends to join in battle among "nine Canaanite nations." God's impressive feat is to overcome the Israelites' low odds on earth. The defeat of the powerful proves God's rule in the heavens and on earth.

2. *The conflict exists* among *the Israelites.* In this scenario, victory is not at all assured, for people, not God, control human destiny. And the Israelites do lose at times. They are brought low by their own "stiff-necked" proclivities: immorality, unfaithfulness, social dissension. Their "battleground" lies in the war of these qualities against their opposites: righteousness, loyalty, justice. Thus, victory or defeat lies entirely in the people's hands. When Israel loses, it is the people's fault, not God's. While this view assigns blame after the fact to the defeated people, in other narratives it endows them with supernatural powers acquired through their proper exercise of moral choice.

3. *God has also triumphed over enemy gods (in buried memory).* The biblical scholar Jon Levenson notes that the Creation account contains elements of an "Israelite myth" in which God battles hostile divine forces and, instead of destroying them, contains them, limiting their impact. Generally, these forces are envisioned as aquatic deities—for example, Yamm (the god of the sea), and Leviathan and Tannin (giant sea beasts)—who threaten a reversion to a time when the earth was covered with water. At certain times, during periods of natural disasters or national catastrophe, those hostile forces revive and spill back over the boundaries God has set for them. In other passages, God battles not actual divinities but the perceptions of gods rampant among Israel's neighbors. During Israel's wars with Egypt, for example, God mocks Pharaoh's pretensions to divinity in his encounters with Moses, as well as the

Egyptians' faith in the Nile as a god in the time of Ezekiel. In short, God triumphs over real or even imaginary opposing forces.

The rest of this chapter explores the argument regarding God's heroism from both sides: archetype and antitype. In the first part I consider God the hero of the Bible and weigh how we might better understand the biblical text accordingly. In the second part I take the opposite approach: God is not the hero. The conclusion attempts to reconcile these conflicting views into a coherent vision of the Bible's position.

Archetype: God Alone Is Hero

In his Pulitzer-winning book, *God: A Biography*, Jack Miles considers the biblical God a hero in the mold of Hamlet—and as such the archetype of the Western hero. God contains different aspects and numerous internal contradictions. God is both creator and destroyer; friend, father, lover, and even wife; a predictable lawgiver and terrifying fiend. God also undergoes unpredictable changes from Genesis to Chronicles. The Bible begins with God occupied intently with the earth and people; over the course of centuries, God's involvement grows attenuated, as if God loses interest.[7]

Within God's multifaceted character, a number of aspects render God as the hero, namely: God as ethical paradigm, God as king, and God as savior. These aspects are regarded here not as contradictions internal to God but as interlocking and in some ways overlapping qualities arising from a cohesive vision of God's behavior as manifested in the world.

Ethical Paradigm

Rabbi Hama, son of Rabbi Hanina, said, What does the Torah mean when it says: "You shall walk in the ways of the Lord" (Deut. 13:5)? Can a person really walk in the shadow of the Divine Presence? Rather, it means that you should imitate the ways of God. Just as God clothed the naked, as it says, "And the Lord God made garments of skins for Adam and his wife, and clothed them" (Gen. 3:21), so you shall clothe the naked. Just as God visited the sick, "The Lord appeared to him"

(Gen. 18:1; Abraham, after his circumcision), so you should visit the sick; just as God buried the dead, as it says, "[God] buried [Moses] in the valley" (Deut. 34:6), so you should bury the dead; and just as God comforts the grieving, as it says, "After the death of Abraham, God blessed his son Isaac" (Gen. 25:11), so you too should comfort the grieving.

—Talmud Sotah 14a

In this famous passage, a host of biblical stories are assembled to cast God as a Jewish hero in the Rabbinic mold. God appears to be the perfect role model, establishing many of the behaviors that have become central to Jewish morality: clothing the poor, visiting the sick, burying the dead, and comforting the bereaved. According to Rabbi Hama, the expression "You shall walk in the ways of the Lord" indicates that the Bible represents God as a hero, the paradigm for the ways people ought to act. Just as other heroes exemplify the ideals of their culture, such as nobility, courtesy, and bravery, God exemplifies the ideals of Israelite culture—commanding them in word and embodying them in deed.

Yet, if the idea of the hero requires the character to behave in human ways, because mortals can be inspired only by relatable heroes, then the God of the Bible appears out of contention. While Rabbi Hama makes note of God's humble, comforting, humanlike gestures, much more often the God of the Bible is supreme, robed in majesty and glory, mightier than all. God is capable of actions no other can approach: creating a world, forming dry land out of sea and returning the sea over the land, laying mountains low and impelling the hills to dance, shattering mighty armies and shaping nations' destinies—and, of course, commanding people to live by a perfect code of law. Everything else in the world "shall all wear out like a garment" (Ps. 102:27), but God endures forever.

Nonetheless, many people are deeply inspired by the biblical God. God's ethical ideals, God's expectations of each of us, are foundational to the Bible, and many people who read the text view their own moral actions as fulfillment of God's will.

In the Prophets and Psalms, these foundations are restated explicitly and repeatedly. God's establishes Creation on ethical principles: "The world is built upon lovingkindness" (Ps. 89:3). God's expectations are clear and straightforward: "[This is] what the Lord requires of you: Only to do justice and to love goodness, and to walk modestly with your God" (Mic. 6:8). Reward comes to those who follow the Lord's precepts: "Light is sown for the righteous, joy for the upright" (Ps. 97:11). Recurring terms include *tzedek* and *tzedakah*, "righteousness" and "righteous behavior"; *mishpat*, "justice"; *chesed*, "loving-kindness"; *emunah*, "faithfulness"; *emet*, "truth"; *yashar*, "upright"; *tov*, "good." In the Creation story in Genesis 1, the repetition of the phrase "And God saw that it was good" conveys the notion that goodness is an essential criterion for the design of the universe.

Once established, these ideals have taken on a reality of their own, independent of their Creator. They have been used not only to judge people but to judge God. Most famously, standing before Sodom and Gomorrah, Abraham questions whether God is acting faithfully according to God's own principles: "Will You sweep away the innocent along with the guilty? . . . Shall not the Judge of all the earth deal justly?" (Gen. 18:23, 25). If God is to act as a judge, God's judgments are expected to reveal the same moral probity God expects of human actions. Similarly, Moses challenges God to live up to God's standards, and succeeds in blunting the extent of God's wrathful judgment. Fed up with the Israelites after the creation of the Golden Calf, God offers Moses a deal: "Now let Me be, that My anger may blaze forth against them and that I may destroy them, and make of you a great nation" (Exod. 32:10). "Let Me be" indicates that Moses has the power to prevent God's assault, and sure enough, Moses throws his lot with his people: "If You will forgive their sin [well and good]; but if not, erase me from the record which You have written!" (32:32). In essence, Moses is saying. *God, I will not be part of a Torah in which cruelty and harsh justice override loving-kindness.* God responds by revising God's verdict: "He who has sinned against Me, him only will I erase from My record" (32:33).

While such challenges to God's justice are rare in the Bible, their existence in early pivotal scenes provides space for readers to exercise their own judgment on the Judge. Readers are not meant to believe that, a priori, God's actions throughout the Bible must be just. Rather, somewhat akin to Abraham and Moses, readers are to weigh the biblical evidence and determine for themselves whether or not God is acting in accord with God's own precepts.

Signally, the questioning of God's judgment and justice serves to enhance rather than diminish God's qualifications as hero. Part of God's heroic composition lies in the fact that God's ethical standing is not merely a given but something God must continue to achieve. Through the window of the two aforementioned exchanges, we see God deliberating over the ethical validity of God's actions. God is willing to listen to another point of view and potentially change a decision. On occasion, God also shows remorse over a previous action: "And the Lord regretted that He had made man on earth, and His heart was saddened" (Gen. 6:6). God's ability to reflect on prior actions, to self-judge, to allow others to judge God, and to use that feedback to change course—all these are acts of a God serving as ethical exemplar.

Another, related aspect of God serving as an ethical exemplar lies in God's being open to human questioning about the world God has created. Many Psalms give voice to feelings of despair about why God permits the wicked to prosper while the righteous suffer:

> How long shall the wicked, O Lord,
> how long shall the wicked exult,
> shall they utter insolent speech,
> shall all evildoers vaunt themselves?
> They crush Your people, O Lord,
> they afflict Your very own;
> they kill the widow and the stranger;
> they murder the fatherless,
> thinking, "The Lord does not see it,
> the God of Jacob does not pay heed." (Ps. 94:3–7)

Even as the poet expresses hope in God and confidence in God's protection, he criticizes God for the (unspecified) crisis of misfortune he regards as fully unjust. He calls on the "God of retribution" to restore the triumph of justice and protection of the righteous: "Shall the seat of injustice be Your partner, that frames mischief by statute?" (94:20). After all, the current state of affairs threatens to overturn the rule of justice God alone established for the world.

King

Clearly and consistently, the Bible portrays God as in control of the depicted world. The Bible's vision of a supreme deity is couched in the political language of its day, often through the institution of kingship. Heroes in ancient times were frequently drawn from the ranks of kings, and kings were very often conceived of, or conceived of themselves, as partly divine (see the introduction). To the ancient mind, then, to portray God as king is to represent God as the archetypal hero.

If a king, like a god, is elevated above his subjects, then when the Bible calls God a king, the effect is not to lower God to the human level but to cloak God in the raiment of sovereign power. The Bible starts with the reader's perception of a king's power and majesty and uplifts the reader to an appreciation of those qualities in God. As the Rabbis of the Talmud observed, the Torah speaks in human language: God is like the greatest king, to the highest level.[8]

Nonetheless, the Bible does not acknowledge God's kingship as merely metaphorical. There is a tension in the Bible between God-as-king and the-king-as-metaphor-for-God—the same tension to be observed in God-as-hero versus God-surpassing-heroism. As we'll see, the Bible takes God's kingship as real—at times, even more real than the human variety. Yet other passages, such as the prophet Isaiah's vision of God in Isaiah 6, convey the impression that the Bible employs kingship as a vehicle to push our understanding to the breaking point and beyond: "I beheld my Lord seated on a high and lofty throne; and the skirts of His robe filled the Temple. Seraphs stood in attendance on Him. Each of them had six wings: with two he covered his face, with two he covered his legs, and with two he would fly. And one would call to the other, 'Holy, holy, holy! The Lord of Hosts! His glory fills all the earth!'"

This vision is at once a king seated on a throne and a reality far beyond human, terrestrial experience.

If we conceive of God in the figure of king, in what ways is God heroic? Psalm 149 provides one model of God's heroic kingship:

Let Israel rejoice in its maker;
let the children of Zion exult in their king.
Let them praise His name in dance;
with timbrel and lyre let them chant His praises.
For the Lord delights in His people;
He adorns the lowly with victory.
Let the faithful exult in glory;
let them shout for joy upon their couches,
with paeans to God in their throats
and two-edged swords in their hands,
to impose retribution upon the nations,
punishment upon the peoples,
binding their kings with shackles,
their nobles with chains of iron.

Read as a companion piece to Psalm 94, Psalm 149 tells us that God has arrived and retribution has been carried out. But God's role here seems to have shifted. In the earlier psalm, addressed to "God of retribution," God appears as a distant, forgetful savior who needs to be woken up and summoned to the rescue. In Psalm 149, God indeed acts as king. Just like a human king, God turns a ragtag army of the "lowly" and "faithful"—no one's first recruits—into fearsome gladiators. The reader can imagine God giving speeches, training the army, commissioning weaponry, surveying the battlefield, rallying the troops . . . and, loyal to their "king," the people carry out the retribution gleefully and brutally. Note that the psalm never mentions an Israelite king, because God has taken over the role. There is no room for a human king, because God is the ultimate commander-in-chief.

The first section of 1 Samuel (discussed in chapter 6) offers us a different vision of God as king acting heroically in human events. Hannah's prayer seems addressed at a God who is both an all-powerful reigning monarch in the heavens and an ethical legislator who ensures the rule of justice and righteousness on earth. God has built the earth like a king constructs a palace: "For the pillars of the earth are the Lord's; He has set the world upon them" (1 Sam. 2:8). The purpose of God's cosmic construction project is not self-glorification, but rather the establishment of an order based on moral behavior, here specifically the protection of the poor and the needy:

He raises the poor from the dust,
Lifts up the needy from the dunghill,
Setting them with nobles,
Granting them seats of honor....
The Lord will judge the ends of the earth. (1 Sam. 2:8, 10)

The text seems to be telling us that society is rigged against the poor. Humans are incapable of reining in the rich and powerful, and thereby maintaining the social order that will uphold the high ethical expectations God has imposed. Only God is capable of checking the arrogance of the mighty, of creating an order ruled by justice instead of power. God as hero thus metes out justice singlehandedly, passing judgment and carrying out God's verdict by exercising power against the powerful. This biblical depiction shows God as acting similarly to legendary human heroes throughout history: possessing the power of right and swooping in to overturn the rule of the wicked and restore legitimate authority. Hannah's God is akin to Robin Hood and caped superheroes.

Furthermore, Hannah's prayer provides a prelude to the rise of human kingship by establishing the contrasting nature of God's kingship. As we've seen, human monarchy is built on the abuse of centralized power: "[God said], 'This will be the practice of the king who will rule over you: He will take your sons and appoint them as his charioteers and horsemen, and they will serve as outrunners for his chariots. . . . He will take your daughters as perfumers, cooks, and bakers. He will seize your choice fields, vineyards, and olive groves, and give them to his courtiers. . . . He will take a tenth part of your flocks, and you shall become his slaves'" (1 Sam. 8:11–17). When the people choose a human king, God avers, "It is Me they have rejected as their king." God is the true king and the true hero; human kingship is the people's misguided attempt to substitute a counterfeit hero for the real coin.

God's reign as king is also heroic because the role requires God's active engagement in human affairs. The divine king must continually intervene to reprove the human king as he falls for the temptations of power.

Savior

God's active role in human affairs leads to the final aspect of God's heroism: God as savior. God fulfills this role most spectacularly during the Exodus from Egypt. The Bible describes God's actions in language saturated with anthropomorphisms and anthropopathisms: "God heard their moaning [of the Israelites under Egyptian slavery], and God remembered His covenant with Abraham and Isaac and Jacob. God looked upon the Israelites, and God took notice of them" (Exod. 2:24–25). After the Children of Israel pass through the Sea of Reeds and their Egyptian pursuers are drowned, Moses, Miriam, and the Israelites sing the "Song of the Sea":

> The Lord is my strength and might,
> He is my salvation. . . .
> The Lord, the Warrior —
> Lord is His Name! (Exod. 15:2–3)

God's saving power is exercised on a global stage. Beyond the Egyptians, other nations hear of this mighty deed and are put on notice:

> Agony grips the dwellers in Philistia,
> Now are the clans of Edom dismayed;
> The tribes of Moab — trembling grips them;
> All the dwellers in Canaan are aghast. (Exod. 15:14–15)

Saving the Israelites accomplishes several goals at once. God sets the Israelites on a path to worshipping God, receiving the Covenant, and inhabiting their land. God upends a great injustice and simultaneously asserts the moral principles on which God established the world. Just as importantly, God lets the whole world know of God's supreme power. God creates a record that other nations cannot ignore.

Note the song's exclamation of God as "my salvation." The biblical verb *hoshi'a* (meaning deliver someone from peril, usually the peril of war or slavery), appears more than two hundred times, nearly always in reference to God, and betokens salvation specifically as God's defeat over enemies, usually Israel's oppressors. God as savior achieves triumph no matter the size and strength of the Israelite forces: "Jonathan said to the attendant who carried his arms, 'Come, let us cross over to the outpost of those uncircumcised fellows [Philistines]. Perhaps the Lord will act in our behalf, for nothing prevents the Lord from winning a victory [*hoshi'a*] by many or by few" (1 Sam. 14:6). The men of the Philistine outpost taunt Jonathan — "Come up to us, and we'll teach you a lesson" — but God delivers as expected, enabling Jonathan and his companion to slaughter twenty Philistine warriors.

God's salvation, often accomplished through bloodshed, induces terror. God is called a "warrior" (literally, a "man of war") in the "Song of the Sea." In Isaiah's description of a God who "speaks in righteousness and is mighty in salvation [*hoshi'a*]," God appears as a terrifying superhero gone amok, wearing clothes splattered in blood from the enemies on whom God has stomped:

> Why is your clothing so red,
> Your garments like his who tread grapes?
> "I trod out a vintage alone;
> Of the peoples no man was with Me.
> I trod them down in My anger,
> Trampled them in My rage;
> Their life-blood bespattered My garments,
> And all My clothing was stained." (Isa. 63:2–3)

And yet, despite God's resounding, definitive victory over enemies, God's salvation is repeatedly invoked, implored, and demanded throughout the Bible. In other words, the Bible shows God's salvation as partial, not complete or absolute; enemy forces are always present and hatching plots for resurgence.

Moreover, as Levenson demonstrates in *Creation and the Persistence of Evil*, time and again in the Bible, God is called on to play the role of savior just like a human hero, because biblical monotheism is not nearly as absolute as later manifestations of monotheistic religions. According to Levenson, God is not entirely alone among a host of primordial powers. Instead, agents of chaos in the natural world, and of evil in the human world, are constantly threatening to overwhelm the sphere of Creation, the order and benevolence God created. God's role is to contain them like torrential waters held by a dam, but sometimes (often because of human malfeasance) they break through the dam and return the world to ruin and evil. God is thus the hero in the Bible both for establishing a world of harmony and justice, because such a world is never a given, and for perennially battling the negative powers in the universe. God's triumph over these powers must be renewed daily, and the outcome of the struggle is not entirely assured.

The mythological vision of God's heroic battles features prominently in biblical poetry. In Psalm 74, for example, God's ancient victory over aquatic monsters leads to the establishment of dry land and water sources, continents and seas, day, night, and seasons:

O God, my king from of old,
who brings deliverance throughout the land;
it was You who drove back the sea with Your might,
who smashed the heads of the monsters in the waters;
it was You who crushed the heads of Leviathan,
who left him as food for the denizens of the desert;
it was You who released springs and torrents,
who made mighty rivers run dry;
the day is Yours, the night also;

it was You who set in place the orb of the sun;
You fixed all the boundaries of the earth;
summer and winter—You made them. (Ps. 74:12–17)

Citing God's promise to Noah, Psalm 104:9 asserts that God "set bounds [the waters] must not pass, so that they never again cover the earth." Yet the claim that the waters are held within bounds set by God suggests that they are capable of passing beyond them, and thus are restrained only by God's vigilant exertions. Both the literal waters of destruction, and the metaphorical waters of injustice, can and will return should God fail to maintain the levee.

Passages such as these present a fundamentally different vision of reality than the main narrative thrust of the Bible. Most of the Bible takes place on the human plane; the Divine is in the backdrop. More to the point, human behavior is pivotal in determining history. God, the architect, has fashioned the world to respond to human determinations. People hold the steering wheel of history.

In these poetic accounts, however, the human drama recedes. Unlike in the rest of the Bible, what matters is not the particulars of laws and their observance, not the delicate relationships among family members, not the railings of prophets, the obeisances of priests, or the decisions of kings. Everything of importance takes place in the heavens, well beyond human concerns or influence. The destiny of the universe depends solely on who wins the cosmic battle.

The shift from an anthropocentric to a theocentric view of reality takes place at the climax of the book of Job. Job's friends explain that his suffering—the death of Job's children, the destruction of his property and possessions, a painful skin affliction—must be God's punishment for his own transgressions. Job disagrees. Still, he believes that God will offer him an alternative, understandable explanation that will justify God's treatment of him. Both Job and his friends comprehend human destiny as shaped by God's justice and expect to be able to perceive God's actions through the powers of human reason.

God's speech to Job "out of the whirlwind" (Job 38–41) denies humans this ability. The camera zooms out, with God speaking from far beyond the precincts of human intimacy. Whereas elsewhere in the Bible, God's control of the sea is meant to provide human comfort (God has dominion over the wicked on earth), in Job the same motif is employed to assert human incapacity to fathom God whatsoever:

Who closed the sea behind doors
When it gushed forth out of the womb,
When I clothed it in clouds,
Swaddled it in dense clouds,
When I made breakers My limit for it,
And set up its bars and doors,
And said, "You may come so far and no farther;
Here your surging waves will stop"? (38:8–11)

God's exertions take place on such a monumental scale that the human mind cannot possibly encompass them. God's power is so awesome that God's mighty sea is like a newborn baby, swaddled in clouds. During this speech, God's description of the sea monster Leviathan also contrasts the scale of God's power to human impotence: "Divine beings are in dread. . . . No sword that overtakes him can prevail. . . . There is no one on land who can dominate him" (Job 41:17, 18, 25). God's speeches thus reframe the human perspective on life: Human suffering dissolves in the face of a cosmic reality of such overwhelming immensity. At most, however, removing the focus from the pain of the human condition offers very cold comfort. Yes, by "being but dust and ashes" (42:6)—reduced to such insignificance by God's rhetoric—Job is no longer tormented by the search to understand the causes of his suffering. Yet his relief comes at the expense of the vision of a God of justice that governs the biblical worldview.

Is the God of Job a hero or a bully? If people are puny in comparison to God, then who is God a hero for? In Job, the God who speaks from the whirlwind is indeed a hero, but one whom no one can appreciate as such—a hero beyond human ken. People are far too small to be heroes, and God is too great for us to grasp God's heroism. God is a giant among ants; all we can do is observe with awe.

Job pushes the biblical notion of God's heroism to its outer limit, and so provides a fitting bridge to the opposing position.

Antitype: God Cannot Be a Hero

In his book *The Heroic Heart*, Tod Lindberg argues why gods cannot be considered heroes:

> Death being an impossibility for an immortal, the gods are likewise incapable of risking death. Insofar as greatness of the kind Achilles embodied entails the willingness to risk one's life, the gods are incapable of it. . . . Next to the living Achilles, the gods seem childlike, innocent in their ignorance of the full meaning for living mortals of both death and greatness.[9]

In Lindberg's view, a god or God cannot be a hero by definition, because the essence of heroism is the willingness to achieve something great by risking one's life. If gods are understood to be immortal, then deities cannot lose their lives, and so cannot put themselves at risk.[10]

The Greek philosopher Aristotle offers another rationale for why a god or God cannot be a hero. Writing about tragedy, the most prestigious form of literature in his time, in his *Poetics*, Aristotle describes the hero as limited in his understanding of his situation. Starting off as noble-born, high on the social ladder, the hero experiences a downfall caused by his own mistake, arising in turn from constraints on his knowledge and character.

In both views, boundaries are necessary for heroism to emerge. Heroism can exist only through the ability to accomplish great things in the face of personal and external obstacles.[11]

As such, because heroes are defined by their impediments as well as achievements, for God to be a hero, God would need to face and overcome great obstructions, such as another god beyond God, an even more powerful para-god who could impose a boundary on God's powers. After all, the monotheistic God of the Bible possesses such immense power, anything God wishes to accomplish can be done without effort. God can change the world and bring salvation in an instant:

> For He is angry but a moment,
> and when He is pleased there is life.
> One may lie down weeping at nightfall,
> but at dawn there are shouts of joy. (Ps. 30:6)

In short, God cannot risk life and limb. God's calculations never arise from regard for God's own well-being. Even when God does show concern over God's reputation,[12] or over justice, the fate of nations, and the welfare of God's creations, God inevitably does so from a great height, removed from the midst of the action where the hero must exist to take a stand.

To consider God a hero, in other words, would be to put God back in the pantheon of divine myth that biblical monotheism emerged from and rejected. In effect, the hero is too confining a role for God. God's role is, instead, to cultivate, advise, and mentor heroes (and sometimes to destroy them).

Given this understanding, we can liken God's role in human affairs in the Bible to the musical term "counterpoint." Counterpoint indicates a musical line played alongside the main melody. In the work of Bach and his contemporaries, while the right hand generally plays the main composition theme, the left hand plays a completely different theme — one that both supports the theme and stands apart from it. This genuine melodic line in its own right is often repeated and developed throughout the piece. In contrapuntal music, there's a degree of freedom in which several musical lines can emerge and unfold in different forms over the course of the composition, shuttling back and forth between the hands. Counterpoint goes beyond harmony. Being independent from the main melody, it often stands in a degree of productive tension with it.

The biblical God can be seen as the counterpoint of heroes. God often supports the protagonists, providing guidance, sustenance, encouragement; but just as often, God stands in tension with or in outright opposition to them. God reminds human beings of their constraints and responsibilities: urging Abraham to listen to Sarah, telling Moses when it's time for him to die, confronting David with his sins of murder and adultery. Even when God's presence is not explicit in the storytelling—Joseph and his brothers, Esther—the arc of the story conveys the biblical authors' sense of God's design for human destiny. Shakespeare's Hamlet captures the impression of those biblical narratives: "There's a divinity that shapes our ends, / Rough-hew them how we will."[13]

To use a different metaphor, God is the Bible's dramaturge, setting the scene and establishing rules within which human actors play their parts. This function is explicit in humanity's opening sequence: "The Lord God planted a garden in Eden, in the east, and placed there the man whom He had formed" (Gen. 2:8). God literally sets the stage: creating the characters (Adam from the soil, Eve from Adam's rib) and the props (garden, trees, rivers); cultivating the characters' powers of reasoning and autonomy (Adam's naming the animals); establishing dramatic tension (the mandate not to eat of the Tree of Knowledge of Good and Evil and the snake's subsequent deception); withdrawing from the action at the pivotal moment (Adam and Eve's conversation with the serpent), then returning to it; and finally wrapping up the narrative storylines (through the two protagonists' punishment and banishment). Crucially, God retreats and allows the two humans to take center stage. The one day of rest that God takes after creating the earth might also be understood as a withdrawal—God stepping back to allow God's creatures to come forward.

Elsewhere, God also takes a supporting role in relation to the Bible's human actors. In many stories, God's actions can be seen as adapted to reflect the person featured in the narrative. Abraham pursues justice—God responds by asserting the justice of God's actions and commanding Abraham to put his faith in God's ultimate justice. Samson is bound up in his strength—God gives him that strength, creates conditions for him to lose it, then restores his strength so he can defeat the Philistines. Esther hides her identity beneath her makeup during the beauty contest—God helps Esther hide her intentions of exposing Haman's treachery toward the Jews.

Synthesis: God as Co-Hero

> I the Lord am your God who brought you out of
> the land of Egypt, the house of bondage.
>   —Exod. 20:2
> The Lord spoke to Moses, "Hurry down, for your people, whom
> you brought out of the land of Egypt, have acted basely."
>   —Exod. 32:7

So which is it? Is God the hero of the Bible or not? Does God or Moses take the Israelites out of Egypt?

The question hinges on a literary issue. Who is the Bible's protagonist: God or people? God is, after all, the only consistent character running through the long chain of works in the biblical corpus. Is the story that the Bible tells, as Miles proposes, ultimately "about" God, about a single Divinity who creates the world, gives shape to a creature who is like God, attempts to establish the world according to principles and ideals, is repeatedly disappointed, intervenes at times and steps back at others, and eventually leaves the field in the hands of human plenipotentiaries? Or, instead, is the Bible the story of the maturation of a people: their birth as the culmination of a benevolent process of natural development, and the growth of families, nations, agriculture, warfare, government, and religion, as they struggle—and often fail—to carry out God's intentions?

In the ancient Near Eastern epic the *Enuma Elish*, people are created in order to serve the gods. The gods clearly remain in control, and humanity is allotted merely a walk-on role in the drama of the universe. In the Bible, though, God appears to serve people as much as people are expected to serve God. God fashions the first person with exquisite care, places him in a lush garden that supplies almost all his needs, and searches for and eventually creates a companion so he will not be lonely. And the people are much more than servants of God. People are the agents of God on earth. They are expected to administer the resources of life with the same care God put into shaping the terrestrial garden.

Both sides are endowed with great independence and freedom of action. God commands — "But as for the tree of the knowledge of good and bad, you must not eat of it" (Gen. 2:17); "Go forth from your native land and from your father's house to the land that I will show you" (Gen. 12:1), and so on — but the people are granted extraordinary latitude over whether and how to obey. And God, too, has the freedom to exercise interpretive choice. Consider God's very first command to humans: "For on the day you eat of [this fruit], you shall surely die." Adam and Eve disobey God's injunction, and, according to Genesis 5:5, Adam lives a total of 930 years, nearly all of them after the expulsion from Eden!

In short, in most Bible stories, people are foregrounded as the protagonists; God is the leading character in a minority of situations. But in one extended sequence — arguably the most important one in the Bible — God and people are true partners in heroic action. In the Exodus, God and Moses need to act in concert for salvation to manifest. Moses' extreme reluctance to lead, his extended pleading for God to find a replacement (Exod. 3–4), serves as God's entrée into playing a greater, more explicit role than God has taken thus far. Moses plays a role that God cannot — a human leader. God lends Moses authority, strength, and numerous supports — Aaron as his spokesman, the turning of his staff into a snake, the proper Name of God to report to the people, the words to tell Pharaoh, and of course the plagues. Moses and Aaron raise their rods and arms — God inflicts desolation.

In this case, God is not content to let Moses perform all the actions and take the credit. Contrast the plagues of Egypt with the trials of Abraham. God's tests of Abraham are designed to reveal Abraham's greatness, whereas God's plagues demonstrate God's greatness. The story elicits recognition of the dominance of Israel's God among Israel's enemies. Pharaoh says, "The Lord is in the right, and I and my people are in the wrong" (Exod. 9:27).

Even though the plagues derive from God's overwhelming might, human agency is nonetheless critical. Only after the Israelites "cried out" does it say that "God heard their moaning, and God remembered His covenant with Abraham and Isaac and Jacob" (Exod. 2:23–24).

God and humans are co-heroes in this epic account. Without God, there would be no story of liberation, but without Moses and Aaron repeatedly emphasizing God as the cause of the plagues, there would be no story of the defeat of false beliefs. In the first verse of the Ten Commandments, God asserts that God is the One who brought the people out of Egypt; in the episode of the Golden Calf, God tells Moses that the people *who he, Moses, brought out of Egypt* are acting basely. In this human-divine co-production, both parties carry the glory, and the blame.

Ultimately, there may be different levels at which humans and God are heroes. God defines and embodies what is heroic: sometimes abstract qualities of justice, truth, righteousness; at other times, strength, majesty, dominion. Humans, even the most heroic humans, fall significantly shy of attaining God's qualities or acting in harmony with God's ethical design.

Most critically, these two planes of heroism exist in relation to one another. God's heroism resides in envisioning and modeling a world of harmony and justice, but God also needs people to execute a harmonious and just world. Likewise, people can achieve a life of "moral grandeur and spiritual audacity" (in the words of Rabbi Abraham Joshua Heschel writing to President John F. Kennedy)[14] by drawing strength and guidance from God. Furthermore, according to the Bible, people can rarely achieve great things without God's assistance. God refines Jacob's character, and thereby makes him a worthy father to a new nation. God seats David upon the throne for his humility and recognition of God's kingship.

Thus, whether or not we ultimately deem God a biblical hero, we might conclude that God is heroic on a grand scale independently from and interdependently with humans. Only after the Bible has drawn a thick charcoal line between God and humanity will the narrator lift humans back up to a heroic perch, helping them achieve something worthy of remembrance forever in the Book.

CONCLUSION

The Biblical Hero Today

Meet Jonah, a biblical antihero. No sooner does he receive God's call than he flees. Instead of embracing his prophetic mission to warn the inhabitants of Nineveh to repent and change their ways, he takes a ship in the opposite direction. He arrives in Nineveh anyway, against his will, inside the belly of a traveling whale. Then he complains to God that his mission is pointless. Since the people will indeed repent, they will not see God's threatened destruction carried out—and what kind of prophet is he if God doesn't strike? If Jonah has any heroism, it resides in his serving as an unwilling and unwitting channel for God. Through his cowardice, evasions, and stubbornness, Jonah allows God's patience and mercy to shine contrastingly through.

In this book, Moses, Samson, Esther, Abraham, Jacob, and David have been identified as biblical heroes. Surely, as we have seen, each of them has been guilty of less-than-stellar behavior. Why, then, should they be considered heroes, whereas Jonah is not?

Taking into consideration the biblical portraits of nobility and fallibility in this book, the Bible teaches us five consistent messages about its heroes:

1. Through their thoughts and actions, we can glimpse the qualities of God. According to the biblical worldview, people cannot be full-blown heroes in and of themselves; rather, they are admirable to the degree that they reveal God's will unfolding in history. Whether or not they are aware of it, God has chosen them for a mission: founding, continuing, leading, warning, or saving their people, the Children of Israel. They are judged according to how faithfully they carry it out.

In essence, biblical heroes are recognizable by their responsibility. They are responsible for their actions, their families, their nation. When they act immorally—because surely they do—they are responsible for owning up to it, as David does when he says to the prophet Nathan, "I stand guilty before the Lord."

2. All biblical heroes are collective heroes. Today's heroes, whether a basketball legend like LeBron James or a Supreme Court justice such as Ruth Bader Ginsburg, are largely revered in a vacuum, for achieving excellence on their own, through force of will or native genius. By contrast, biblical heroes are cultivated by their surroundings; God singles them out to perform a mission in the world, and only then can they take heroic action for their society. Moses is saved by midwives, his mother, his sister, and Pharaoh's daughter—all before he's given a name; and his first act is to save a Hebrew slave from being beaten to death. David, the last of seven brothers, is chosen by God as king material; his story too begins with him saving the Israelite army by slaying Goliath. Only through their actions on behalf of other people does their true heroism emerge.

3. Biblical heroes are as human as we are. Heroes of the Bible are flawed, complicated creatures—a stew of noble qualities and assorted shortcomings. Unlike the heroes of fables and legends, one cannot boil these heroes down to a single character trait or message. What is more, the biblical storyteller often withholds explicit judgment on these characters, rendering their moral stature as highly ambiguous. Is there any moral basis by which David, the military hero, can steal Uriah's wife, Bathsheba, while sending Uriah to die on the front lines? Does Jacob act unethically by tricking his brother Esau out of his birthright and blessing, or is he correctly fulfilling his mother's will? When Samson destroys the Philistine temple, killing all the people gathered to celebrate their victory over him, is his revenge justified, and does his final act outweigh a lifetime of troubling behavior? The narrator's silence awakens the readers' moral imagination.

In this particular sense, biblical characters are akin to characters of great literature. The greatest characters of nineteenth-century literature, such as Emma Bovary, Anna Karenina, Lord Jim, and so on, are heroic despite their moral failings, or in defiance of their society's moral strictures. Similarly, biblical heroes are each uniquely unpredictable and evade attempts to make them fit moral or social expectations.

Often, too, the Bible shows its heroes as struggling with their inner demons. Jacob wrestles with the angel to expurgate twenty years of pent-up fear and animosity toward his brother. After Nathan accuses David of adultery and murder, David suffers under the burden of guilt for the rest of his life.

Consequently, the Bible seems to be telling us, people should not load their heroes with unrealistic expectations. We are to acknowledge that *something*, but not *everything*, is extraordinary about a hero. Esther saves her people from Haman's genocidal intentions even as she consents to marry a corrupt, dissolute king. Abraham protests God's intention to exterminate the inhabitants of two cities even though he is mysteriously compliant when God commands him to sacrifice his own son. The inner torments these characters bear enrich our ability to identify with them as heroes. We should appraise our heroes using a degree of tolerance for their failings and a seasoning of skepticism over their accomplishments.

4. Many different people can be heroes, and heroes can embody different roles. The Bible radically democratizes its heroes. People of all walks of life can qualify—some are prophets, others are wives and mothers, and the majority start out as shepherds. They may come from the throne or the hinterland. They may be men or women, children or elders. No ailment, disability, or characteristic disqualifies someone from heroic status. Some heroes are blind, stuttering, lame, or lepers (2 Kings 7).

Several heroes adopt multiple functions during their lives. Throughout his long career, David passes from shepherd to warrior, musician to highwayman, vigorous king to enfeebled father. Esther travels from orphan to beauty pageant contestant to queen to national savior (by contrast, in just a few chapters). Joseph is alternately spoiled son, dream interpreter, enslaved brother, household supervisor, favored prisoner, government minister, and family counselor. Biblical heroes' heterogeneous identities exemplify our own increasingly meandering career paths and our sense of our inner multiplicity.

5. The Bible's heroes are meant to serve as forerunners of our own tortuous moral lives. While many readers look to biblical characters as exemplars of spiritual traits, a more realistic assessment finds these heroes bristling with rough edges, just as we are. Rashi interprets the verse in the *Shema* (Deut. 6:5) "You shall love the Lord your God with all your heart" to mean with your two inclinations, for good and for evil. Like us, biblical heroes possess twinned inclinations and forked motives. The Bible has rewarded the intensity of its readers' gaze over the centuries precisely because it does not offer one simple truth. Biblical truths must be won through prolonged reflection and familiarity—and especially, in the Jewish tradition, by focusing on the rough edges, the parts we find difficult to understand.

Fortunately for us, our tolerance for less in our heroes can also allow us to see the heroic in more individuals and circumstances. The Bible teaches us that even the people we revere the most likely have a skeleton or two in the closet and people we never think of as heroic just might possess a degree of heroism. Contextualized within the often-monochromatic messaging of our modern era, the Bible's treatment of its heroes offers us a requisite recast to see the humanity, godliness, and potential for heroism in one another.

Notes

Preface

1. Gordon Wood (*Revolutionary Characters*, 7) describes the same phenomenon in the study of America's founding fathers: "Although criticizing the founding generation has been going on for more than a century, there does seem to be something new and different about the present-day academic vilification. Historians' defaming of these elite white males seems much more widespread than it used to be. Sometimes this criticism has taken the form of historians' purposely ignoring the politics and the achievements of the founders altogether, as if what they did were not all that important."
2. Plato, *Protagoras*, in *The Dialogues*.
3. Klapp, *Heroes, Villains, and Fools*, 17.
4. MacIntyre, *After Virtue*, 216.
5. The three scholars do agree, however, that all stories about heroes are variations, at root, of one mythic structure known as an "Ur-story." Rank and Raglan are taken from Segal, *In Quest of the Hero*, 3–175.
6. Edward L. Greenstein ("The Fugitive Hero," 17–35) proposes a scheme similar to Raglan's for a type of hero who is found, occurring only in ancient Near Eastern mythology. He sees this type as being especially prevalent in biblical stories, including those about Jacob, Joseph, Moses, and David.

Introduction

1. Heidel, *Babylonian Genesis*, 46.
2. "A *ṣalmu*, then, did not merely direct the worshipper's mind toward a god who dwelled in some other sphere; it did not *depict* the god. Rather, . . . the divine presence entered into the statue, and the *ṣalmu was* the god" (Sommer, *Bodies of God*, 21).
3. The Bible's depiction contrasts, perhaps polemically, with the ancient depiction of the king being a representative of a god. Whereas a king alone reigns over his subjects, in Genesis the entire human race has "dominion" (King James) over all other living creatures.

4. Campbell quotes verbatim from Louis Ginzburg's *Legends of the Jews*. Ginzburg himself took this version of the midrash from Adolph Jellenek's anthology *Beth Ha-Midrasch*.

5. James Kugel (*Bible as It Was*) thoroughly illustrates the way midrashic elaborations answer questions implicit within the biblical source texts.

6. Matthew 2 tells a similar story about Jesus's birth, likewise combining biblical elements with the classical profile of a hero.

7. However, it is believed that in some cases Chronicles inserts early material that was not included in Kings.

8. Chronicles was written during the Second Temple period, most likely the fourth century BCE. Most scholars hold that Kings was compiled toward the end of the First Temple period (late seventh–early sixth century BCE), with a second author (or group) appending and editing it into its current shape during the Babylonian exile of the mid-sixth century.

9. Homer, *Odyssey* 10:390.

10. This holds true just as much, if not more, for non-Western mythologies. In the classic Chinese epic *Monkey*, for example, the heavenly court resembles the earthly Chinese empire in various ways, from the manners at court to the details of its bureaucracy, while the traffic flows heavily in both directions between heaven and earth, and magical powers are bestowed almost equally on residents of both worlds.

11. Homer, *Iliad* 5:382–91.

12. Homer, *Iliad* 21:194–99.

13. Jacobsen, *Treasures of Darkness*, 39.

14. An obscure passage in Genesis suggests that the earliest biblical material portrayed the boundary between man and God in the porous terms of ancient myth: "It was then, and later too, that the Nephilim appeared on earth—when the divine beings cohabited with the daughters of men, who bore them offspring. They were the heroes of old, the men of renown" (6:4). In the rest of the Bible, heroes would need to arise without divine blood, though there is a hint of divinity in Moses (Exod. 7:1).

15. In his *Hero in America*, Dixon Wecter observed how presidents preserve the people's esteem in a democracy: "No hero must announce that he is infallible. He must be greater than the average, but in ways agreeable to the average. He may know their collective will better than they know it themselves . . . but he must keep his personal modesty, his courtesy toward the People who gave him that power. The hero is an instrument" (11).

16. Wills, *Cincinnatus*, 23.

17. Walt Whitman, "Song of Myself," in *Leaves of Grass*, 24, accessed at https://en.wikisource.org/wiki/Leaves_of_Grass/Book_III.

18. Whitman, "Song of Myself," 18.

19. Lewis, *American Adam*, 128.

20. As the name suggests, this variety of hero is mostly masculine.

21. Boorstin, *Image*, 66–73.

22. Braudy, *Frenzy of Renown*, 6–7.

23. Sternberg, *Poetics of Biblical Narrative*.

1. Moses

1. Philo, *Life of Moses*.

2. Muffs, *Love & Joy*, 9–48, called this episode an example of "prophetic intercession": the prophet not only serving as a vessel for God's message but also working in the opposite direction, arguing with God on the people's behalf.

3. Wildavsky, *Moses as Political Leader*, 8.

4. See Redford, "The Literary Motif of the Exposed Child." Gary Rendsburg ("Moses as Equal to Pharaoh," 205–8) traces the striking parallels between the accounts of Moses' birth and the Egyptian god Horus's.

5. Foster, *Before the Muses*, 819. Scholars believe that the account of Sargon's birth derived from a much later period, ca. first millennium BCE, than his actual life.

6. Foster, *Before the Muses*, 819.

7. The pattern, found in Raglan's *The Hero: A Study in Tradition, Myth, and Drama*, Part II, is taken from Segal, *In Quest of the Hero*, 138.

8. Some Jewish and Christian interpreters prefer to imagine Moses' direct ascension into heaven. See Kugel, *Bible as It Was*, 544.

9. See Fishbane, *Kiss of God*, 14–50, for a discussion of this theme in TANAKH and Jewish tradition.

10. A full analysis of this passage can be found in Rabin, *Understanding the Hebrew Bible*, 20–29.

11. Here NJPS reads "ruler" rather than my substitution of "judge." As I see it, the Hebrew *shofet* here clearly implies judge, that is, "Who are you to judge us?"

12. Alter, *Art of Biblical Narrative*, 47–62.

13. Joseph Campbell (*Hero with a Thousand Faces*, 97–192) describes the hero's journey toward an encounter with a goddess and god, resulting in the hero wresting an "ultimate boon" (such as fire, writing, medicine) for humanity.

14. Exod. 23:17, 34:23; Deut. 16:16; and so on. The grammatical use of the passive ("shall be seen the face of the Lord") is awkward; some scholars suggest that pious editors modified the original active verb, "see" (Brettler, *God Is King*, 94). If so, the distinction between Moses as privileged visionary and his followers is further undermined.

15. Discussed in Kugel, *God of Old*.

16. According to Marc Brettler (*God Is King*, 83), the stone is lapis, "probably reflecting a partial etiology of the sky's blueness." The commentators discussed here disagree over the meaning of the Hebrew term *livnat*, which may derive from *leveinah*, "brick," or *lavan*, "white."

17. This assertion seems to contradict the statement made just a few verses before (Exod. 33:11), that "the Lord would speak to Moses face to face, as one man speaks to another." Robert Alter (*Five Books of Moses*) resolves this tension by attributing this statement to the perspective of the Israelites standing before Moses' Tent of Meeting, a perspective established in the prior verses. At the least, one can say that the proximity of these contradictory assertions suggests that the second passage is meant to serve as a corrective to the first.

18. Rendsburg ("Moses as Equal to Pharaoh," 201–18) reviews the details of Moses' depiction, from his birth and staff to his horns, in light of Egyptian literary and artistic parallels, to show how the Bible portrays Moses as an Israelite "pharaoh" and hence a worthy opponent.

19. See Levenson, *Creation and the Persistence of Evil*; also Cross, *Canaanite Myth and Biblical Epic*.

20. Moses holds "the staff of God," a common agent of victory in the ancient Near East, but the text insists that his upright arm is decisive (Gordon, "Homer and the Bible," 92).

21. Pardes, *Biography of Ancient Israel*.

22. The philosopher and poet Yehuda Halevi (1075–1141) argued in his book *The Kuzari* that the events at Sinai are uniquely believable among ancient revelations because an entire nation was present to witness them.

23. A talmudic saying (Makkot 24a) holds that the people heard only the first two commandments—the ones given by God in the first person—and received the rest from Moses.

24. Campbell, *Hero with a Thousand Faces*, 193.

25. In the words of the sociologist of religion Peter Berger: "The roots of secularization are to be found in the earliest available sources of ancient Israel. In other words, we would maintain that the 'disenchantment of the world' begins in the Old Testament" (*Sacred Canopy*, 113).

26. Drawing on a midrash, Aviva Zornberg (*Moses*, 99–100) offers a different interpretation of Moses' smashing the tablets: Moses sins with the tablets to equate himself with the people who have sinned with the Golden Calf. God considers Moses to be above the people and offers to "destroy them, and make of you a great nation." Moses asserts that he is not above the people;

his sin is an act of solidarity, a gesture signaling to God that Moses is inseparable from the people.

27. Stephen Garfinkel ("The Man Moses," 25) draws a connection between Moses' striking the rock, rather than speaking to it as God instructs, with Moses' early insistence that he is not a "man of words" (Exod. 4:10). However, God promises to give Moses the words he needs. By striking the rock instead of using words, Moses abrogates his verbal contract with God.

28. A hint of Moses' legacy, however, can be found in Judges 18:30: "Jonathan son of Gershom son of Menasheh, and his descendants, served as priests to the Danite tribe until the land went into exile." The name "Menasheh" is written with the nun suspended above, suggesting an earlier reading of "Mosheh," Moses.

29. Quoted in Segal, *Quest of the Hero*, 62.

30. For a fuller discussion, see Rabin, *Understanding the Hebrew Bible*, 35–39.

31. King Josiah is notably praised in these terms: "There was no king like him before who turned back to the Lord with all his heart and soul and might, in full accord with the Teaching of Moses; nor did any like him arise after him" (2 Kings 23:25).

2. Samson

1. Translated from the French. "L'Albatros," in *Fleurs du mal*. Available at https://fleursdumal.org/poem/200.

2. Edward L. Greenstein ("The Riddle of Samson") regards Samson as an allegorical figure representing Israel as depicted throughout the book of Judges.

3. In this respect, the story fits in perfectly with the cycle of stories in Judges, where the "battle of the sexes" often plays out in gruesome ways.

4. Manoah confuses the angel with God—a confusion that at times is encouraged by the biblical narrator (see the alternation of angels and the Lord in Genesis 18:9–15). He correctly fears the consequences of glimpsing God: "[God said,] You cannot see My face, for man may not see Me and live" (Exod. 33:20).

5. The Bible portrays Samuel as being like Samson in its declaration "No razor shall ever touch his head" (1 Sam. 1:11). However, the narrator does not explicitly call Samuel a nazirite. According to the Talmud, David's long-haired son Absalom is also a nazirite.

6. The Mishnah (Nazir 1:2) describes three separate categories of nazirite: an ordinary nazirite of limited duration (minimum thirty days), a Samson-style nazirite, and an eternal nazirite. These last two categories, both of which endure for a lifetime, differ as follows: a Samson nazirite never cuts his hair

but may come in contact with the dead; an eternal nazirite can cut his hair every twelve months, but can never come in contact with the dead.

7. Gordon, "Homer and Bible," 84–85.

8. Apollodorus, *The Library*, 2.5.1.

9. Some modern commentators speculate that this phrase was added by an editor, so as not to attribute divine powers to Samson himself.

10. Gregory Mobley (*Empty Men*, 171–223) calls Samson "animalistic" in his association with lions and jackals. He also regards Samson as a "wild man" in the mold of Enkidu, the protagonist's best friend in the Gilgamesh Epic, as well as the *lahmu*, the long-haired "chaos monster" in the *Enuma Elish*, the Babylonian epic of creation.

11. Apollodorus, *The Library*, 2.7.6–7.

12. Mobley (*Empty Men*, 190) cites scholars who note that the solution to this unanswered riddle is love: "What is sweeter than honey, and what is stronger than a lion?" (Judg. 14:18). The riddle proves prophetic when Samson, the lion, is defeated by his love for Delilah.

13. In his relationship with the Philistines, alternately his friends and archenemies, Samson shares characteristics of the trickster, including his riddles, boastfulness, independence, perpetual contests with a range of enemies, and larger-than-life actions and struggles. Note that the Philistines respond to Samson's riddle (Judg. 14:14) with a riddle of their own (14:18), demonstrating that their combat is engaged through wit and brawn simultaneously.

14. The English pronunciation, de-lie-lah, sounds like the Hebrew word for night, *lailah*. This common association evokes images of Delilah as dark, sinister, mysterious—images that may be appropriate, even if from a linguistic perspective the connection does not make etymological sense based on the Masoretic vocalization. Herbert Marks (*English Bible*, 476) notes the contrast between Samson's sun and Delilah's night.

15. Jean-Pierre Sonnet and André Wenin ("La mort de Samson," 372–81) similarly find that the text offers three competing explanations for the return of Samson's strength: the regrowth of his hair, God's response to Samson's prayer, and Samson's own resolve and desire for vengeance.

16. "The plagues may be understood as attacks on the Egyptian gods. The early plagues . . . attack minor deities of the Egyptian pantheon. These would include Hapi, the Nile River god, and Heqet, the frog-goddess of life. The later plagues not only are more intensive, they also are an attack on the chief god Re [the sun god]. Thus the eighth plague of locusts blots out the sun in midday, and the ninth plague of darkness . . . darkens the sky for three days" (Gordon and Rendsburg, *Bible and the Ancient Near East*, 145–46).

3. Esther

1. Since scholars hold that the book of Esther was composed during the Second Temple period, probably in the fourth or third century BCE, and the earliest tales of the *Arabian Nights* were not written down for more than a millennium thereafter, the resemblances cannot be ascribed to a direct influence, at least of a written document. At best we might conjecture an ancient oral tradition that formed the basis of the Scheherazade story, which Jews encountered under Persian rule. Despite some speculation along these lines in the nineteenth century, later scholars have tended to trace the origins of the frame to Sanskrit literature from India.

2. Lane, *Stories from the Thousand and One Nights*, 5–13. In this chapter, I use common spellings (Scheherazade, vizier) instead of the spellings that appear in Lane (Shahrazad, Wezir).

3. For example, Midrash Rabbah on Esther 6:1: "'On that night, the king tossed in his sleep'—The heavens tossed the throne of the King of Kings, the Holy One, Blessed be He, who saw Israel in trouble. But does God sleep? Doesn't it say, 'Behold, the Guardian of Israel neither slumbers nor sleeps' (Ps. 121:4)? However, at times when Israel is immersed in trouble and the nations of the world in tranquility, of that it is written, 'Awake, why do You sleep oh God' (Ps. 44:24)." The fact that God is not mentioned at all in the book of Esther made this kind of code reading all the more pressing.

4. Compare 1 Kings 6–7, the construction of Solomon's Temple, and Exodus 25–27, 35–38, on the composition of the Tabernacle. Solomon also builds a massive, ornate palace for himself, the Lebanon Forest House, but there is no description of its interior decoration.

5. The color of the slaves seems intended to heighten the sense of betrayal.

6. See John Barth's lifelong obsession with Scheherazade in works such as the novella "Dunyazadiad" in *Chimera*.

7. Note that Rachel and Esther are both described as "shapely and beautiful" (nearly identically in the Hebrew too).

8. Coontz, *Marriage, a History*, 59.

9. Coontz, *Marriage, a History*, 89.

10. Coontz, *Marriage, a History*, 90.

11. Cyrus Gordon and Gary Rendsburg (*Bible and the Ancient Near East*, 306–7) connect Esther's disguise with the Iranian practice of dissimulation (*kitmân* or *taqiyya*), an ancient survival technique practiced by Shiites and Sunnis in each other's territory, and practiced by Christians, Baha'is, and Jews in Muslim lands. The authors speculate dissimulation may extend back to pre-Islamic Iran.

12. Joseph attributes his success to God several times, but God does not appear as a character in his story. In the book of Esther, God is completely absent from the text.

4. Abraham

1. A midrash emphasizes this aspect of Abraham's wanderings: "Rabbi Berachiya said, How was Abraham our father like a bottle of balsam extract covered by a tight lid, left in the corner, whose smell did not waft! When the bottle is moved, its smell wafts. Thus said the Holy One Blessed be He to Abraham our father: Move yourself from place to place and your name will grow great in the world" (Bereishit Rabbah 39:2).

2. My sense of the "fortunate fall" is very different from that of early Christian doctrine, in which Adam and Eve's sin established the proper conditions for Jesus's salvation.

3. Bereishit Rabbah 38:13.

4. The narrator does not mention a child either, only Abraham's nephew Lot, unmarried but wealthy in his own right, whom he is still watching over.

5. See, for example, from the last book of the TANAKH: "O our God, you dispossessed the inhabitants of this land before Your people Israel, and You gave it to the descendants of Your friend Abraham forever" (2 Chron. 20:7).

6. I don't claim that pilgrim characters influenced the depiction of Abraham — the influence here runs in the opposite direction.

7. Christian writers such as Dante embraced Virgil in part because they sensed in Aeneas a different heroic sensibility than was found in other ancient tales. In the words of R. D. Williams, the editor of a Latin edition: "We see in him [Aeneas] an honest and honourable endeavour to shoulder his immense social, religious, and military obligations. But he is a new type of hero, an 'unheroic' type. His strength is limited, his resolution sometimes frail; he gropes his way forward through darkness and uncertainty. We are never sure, as the poem develops, whether he will succeed" (1:155). In these ways, Aeneas is more biblical than Roman.

8. Virgil, *Aeneid*, trans. Fitzgerald, 6:1151–54.

9. Indeed, Christians have often regarded Abraham as the model pilgrim: "Christian writers have also looked back to the Old Testament to find inspiration for the idea of pilgrimage in the example of Abraham. . . . Abraham's summons is the archetypal call of the pilgrim — the irresistible prompting to exchange the familiar with the strange, the secure with the unknown, a life of ongoing domesticity with one charged with divine meaning." Harpur, *Sacred Tracks*, 10–11.

10. Bunyan, *Pilgrim's Progress*, 18.

11. Bunyan, *Pilgrim's Progress*, 220–21.

12. According to James Harpur (*Sacred Tracks*, 11), Bunyan's allegory captures the deeper meaning of Christian pilgrimage: "Underlying all these motives for Christian pilgrims is the idea that to make a journey to a sacred centre is to enact a concrete ritual representing the journey of the soul through the travails of mortal life to heaven."

13. Bunyan, *Pilgrim's Progress*, 266–67.

14. A group of Irish monks regarded pilgrimage in terms reminiscent of Abraham: "What made these early Irish pilgrims different from later medieval ones was the fact that they did not have a predetermined destination and that they were prepared, having set out, never to see their homeland again" (Harpur, *Sacred Tracks*, 37).

15. Pirkei Avot 5:4: "With ten tests did God test our father Abraham, and he withstood them all, to make known how great was our father Abraham's love."

16. Scholars connect this scene with the ancient Near Eastern ritual of cutting an animal to seal a treaty. Implied is a curse: *May the one who breaks this treaty be broken in parts.* This curse is alluded to in Jeremiah 34:18–20, in which people pass through a split calf in order to affirm their commitment to a covenant. In biblical Hebrew, to make a covenant is expressed as "to cut a covenant," alluding precisely to this ritual. (See Rabin, *Understanding the Hebrew Bible*, 55–57.)

17. Jon Levenson (*Death and Resurrection of the Beloved Son*, 3–17, 111–24) argues convincingly that God's command for Abraham to sacrifice his son, and Abraham's willingness to carry it out, represent not aberrations but rather the ideal of child sacrifice—returning our most precious gift to God—that existed until the time of the prophets.

18. The midrash in which Truth and Peace urge God not to create man (Bereishit Rabbah 8:5) picks up on this sense conveyed by the early chapters of Genesis that humanity, instead of being the pinnacle of Creation, causes Creation to go awry.

19. According to Jewish law, there are three things one must sacrifice one's life for rather than commit: idolatry, murder, and forbidden sexual relations. Over the centuries many Jews have also given their lives when faced with forced conversion.

20. Shalom Spiegel's classic exploration of Jewish commentary on the *Akedah*, *The Last Trial*, shows how Jews suffering persecution portrayed themselves as Isaacs who actually underwent the trial of human sacrifice.

21. Daniel Hillel (*Natural History of the Bible*, 61) regards their conflict as a not-unexpected result of the ecology in which they live: the semiarid steppe. As "seminomadic shepherds" of the "pastoral domain" in the Land of Israel,

Abraham and Lot dwell in a region where they are unable to put down roots and cultivate crops. Once their flocks graze for a short time, the vegetation is exhausted and they must move on. From this perspective, it is quite plausible that the land could not support both men's flocks. Lot chooses to move to the "floodplain of the Jordan," the closest equivalent in Israel to the fertile river region of the Nile, whereas Abraham remains in the rugged semi-desert savannah near Beer-sheba.

22. Indeed, the Rabbis of the Talmud considered Abraham's strategic side as sinful and even a cause for the Israelites' enslavement in Egypt: "Rabbi Abbahu said in the name of Rabbi Elazar: Why was Abraham punished and his descendants enslaved in Egypt for 210 years? . . . Rabbi Yohanan said: That he prevented people from entering beneath the wings of the Divine Presence [namely, Pharaoh and Abimelech]" (Nedarim 32a).

23. In Meir Sternberg's analysis, the negotiations compose a "network of indirection" that "cohere into a pattern of doubletalk that makes for a double reading" ("Double Cave, Double Talk," 31).

24. Abraham reveals his devotion to Sarah through his loyalty, which extends after her death. He sets the model for other biblical figures who take great care of their loved ones by granting them a proper burial. God performs this same act of kindness after Moses' death.

25. These men are strange in more ways than one. First, the text says that the Lord appeared to Abraham; when he looks up, he sees three men; then he calls them "my lords," using an expression that is also used to refer to God. Abraham switches between the singular and the plural in his address to them. When the men leave Abraham they look toward Sodom; in the next sentence, the Lord imparts to Abraham God's intention to destroy that city. Within a few verses there seems to be a disturbing metamorphosis between the Lord, celestial beings, men, and back again. Biblical scholars have drawn attention to similarities between this episode and a divine visit in the Ugaritic *Tale of Aqhat*.

26. Midrash provides an additional reason for Abraham's recumbency: He is recuperating from his circumcision in the previous chapter.

27. On the rarity and difficulty of travel in the ancient Mediterranean, see Casson, *Travel in the Ancient World*.

5. Jacob

1. My understanding of the trickster is informed by Lewis Hyde's far-ranging discussion in *Trickster Makes This World*, along with the earlier study by Paul Radin, *The Trickster*. Interestingly, Hyde does not discuss Jacob, perhaps because of the conflict between trickster values and the biblical ethos. The

Bible's depiction of Jacob is quite possibly indebted to the ancient trickster tradition, since his affiliation with this popular character is so unmistakable.

2. The original meaning of the name likely derived from *Ya'akov-El*, "God-will-protect" (Garsiel, *Biblical Names*, 21).

3. This alternate etymology of Jacob's name is made explicit in Jeremiah 9:3: "For every brother acts deceitfully" (*'akov ya'kov*).

4. Mobley, *The Empty Men*, 156.

5. Darnton, *Great Cat Massacre*, 54.

6. Lyons, *Man of Wiles*, 242.

7. "Our ideas about property and theft depend on a set of assumptions about how the world is divided up. Trickster's lies and thefts challenge those premises and in so doing reveal their artifice and suggest alternatives." (Hyde, *Trickster Makes This World*, 72.)

8. Quoted in Hyde, *Trickster Makes This World*, 71.

9. In both cases, scholars believe that the stories were written down around the eighth to seventh century BCE but recounted events that occurred many centuries earlier, in fact or in legend.

10. Cyrus Gordon lays out the numerous similarities weaving together Homer, the Bible, and Ugaritic texts into an "East Mediterranean literature." Regarding the trickster motif, he writes: "Deception has a reputable place in the *mores* of the epic (in sharp contrast to the ethics of an Amos or a Socrates)" ("Homer and the Bible," 74).

11. Homer, *Odyssey* 19:449.

12. Homer, *Odyssey* 19:464.

13. Homer, *Odyssey* 13:493–96.

14. Given the stark contrast in narrative style between Homer and the Hebrew Bible as famously described by Erich Auerbach in *Mimesis* (3–23), the extent of the resemblance between Odysseus and Jacob is all the more striking.

15. "There may well be a complicating irony in the use of this epithet [*tam*, "simple," or "innocent"] for Jacob, since his behavior is very far from simple or innocent in the scene that is about to unfold" (Alter, *Five Books of Moses*, 130).

16. Understanding Genesis 25:28, *tzayid be-fiv*, "game in his mouth," as "snare in his mouth," or verbal deception (see Rashi quoting midrash). The Rabbis came to regard Esau/Edom as codenames for Rome/Christianity or other dominant, persecuting civilizations, and they interpreted the alleged progenitor through the lens of their antipathy.

17. See Hyde, *Trickster Makes This World*, 17–38.

18. Hyde, *Trickster Makes This World*, 19.

19. The popular medieval trickster Reynard similarly deceives his opponents by appealing to their appetite for food, treasure, and power. Here is his obser-

vation of his chief enemy/victim, Isengrim the wolf: "I never saw him not hungry, not even when he was completely full. I can't think where the food he consumes goes." (Simpson, *Reynard the Fox*, 202.)

20. As Reynard puts it, "Even though the King and all the court had sworn my death, I'll come out on top of the lot of them. . . . The court can't do anything without me and my wily cleverness" (Simpson, *Reynard the Fox*, 136). Reynard has his own Rebecca, Rukenawe the She-Ape, whom Reynard calls "aunt"; she choreographs Reynard's moves during his contest with Isengrim.

21. One strain of Rabbinic interpretation finds Jacob carrying out his mother's directives in silent opposition; for example, "'He went and took and brought [food] to his mother'—compelled, bent and weeping" (Bereishit Rabbah 65:15). Given Jacob's track record, this author finds the apologetic line to be forced, but it does point out the degree to which Jacob is manipulated by his mother.

22. Stacey Sher, co-executive producer of *Pulp Fiction*, quoted in Lynn Hirshberg, "Quentin Tarantino, Pre-*Pulp Fiction*," *Vanity Fair*, July 1994.

23. Gary Rendsburg ("Notes on Genesis XXXV," 364–65) regards Rebecca as a trickster who, like her son, suffers a measure-for-measure punishment. In her case, she disappears from the story, and is unique among the Matriarchs and Patriarchs in that her death and burial are not noted. Rendsburg reads in the mention of the death of "Deborah, Rebecca's nurse" in Genesis 35:8 a reminder to the reader of Rebecca's vanishing narrative.

24. Westcott, "The Sculpture and Myths of Eshu-Elegba," quoted in Hyde, *Trickster Makes This World*, 117.

25. Radin, *Trickster*, 133.

26. Jacob takes after Abraham in this respect (the men/angels/Lord who visit him before the destruction of Sodom and Gomorrah). But whereas the biblical line between heaven and earth, Divine and human, holds firmer in Abraham's stories, that line buckles more in Jacob's saga—perhaps more than anywhere else in the Bible, with the exception of the Prophets.

27. Alter, *Five Books of Moses*, 149. The word *sullam* appears solely here in the Bible (a phenomenon called a hapax legomenon), making it difficult to certify its meaning.

28. Aside from the prophets, later Jewish mystics often had visions of such an ascent to the various heavenly orbs; see Jacobs, *Jewish Mystical Testimonies*.

29. One might say this is an aspect of the idea of humanity being created "in the image of God": the characteristics of the biblical Patriarchs have their counterparts within God's self, that is, Abraham's righteousness, Isaac's fidelity, Jacob's trickery.

30. See Rendsburg, "The Mock of Baal"; and Hurowitz, "The Baal Is Busy."

31. David Marcus ("David the Deceiver") finds a pattern of measure-for-measure punishment for deceitful action, what he terms "retributive deception," throughout the TANAKH, and most prevalent in the Jacob and David sagas.

32. Erdoes and Ortiz, *American Indian Trickster Tales*, 48–49 (Navajo).

33. The ancient Rabbis who established Jewish interpretation of the Torah naturally took Jacob's side; they considered Laban as someone who sought to "uproot all," a kind of archenemy of the Jews (as described in the Passover Haggadah). In the view of Louis Finkelstein ("The Oldest Midrash," 299–304), the midrash in the Haggadah projects Laban as a symbol of the Seleucid Empire in Syria in order to balance the text's obvious anti-Egyptian message. However, the biblical text portrays him much more equivocally, as one trickster opposing another.

34. Gordon and Rendsburg (*Bible and the Ancient Near East*, 133–34) note that the chain of deceptions throughout the Jacob and Joseph sagas often involve a goat and a garment. Here, Laban and Leah deceive Jacob with a veil; later, Jacob outsmarts Laban with goats.

35. Another midrash imagines the baffling marriage scene in the tent differently, with Rachel as the trickster. According to Bava Batra 123a, Rachel is the one who tricks Jacob, out of her compassion for her sister. She gives Leah a special sign so Jacob will think she is Rachel; she sneaks into the marriage tent, hiding under their bed and speaking instead of Leah. Rachel thus serves as a Cyrano for her sister, selflessly acting behind the scenes on her behalf to ensure that the illusion is preserved throughout the night. In so doing, she is also reprising Jacob's deception of his father. Jacob had the wrong voice but the right sign, hairy hands; with Rachel's help, Leah has both the right voice and the right sign.

36. Zakovitch, *Jacob: Unexpected Patriarch*, 64. Zakovitch also points to numerous parallels between Laban and Pharaoh that cast a dark shadow over the reader's evaluation of Laban: Both begin as welcoming, then entrap their guests and exploit their labor; both Jacob and the Children of Israel attempt to flee; both are overtaken by their oppressors and then saved with God's help (88–90).

37. Contrast the way the narrator characterizes the growth of Jacob's flock in Genesis 30:37–43, attributing it to Jacob's ingenuity, with how Jacob describes it to his wives in 31:8–13, as a gift from God.

38. Hyde, *Trickster Makes This World*, 91.

39. This incident is repeated in the book of Judges (chapter 11), where Jephthah's foolish oath unwittingly condemns his daughter to death.

40. As Herbert Marks notes (*English Bible*, 76), the text is not clear whether Jacob remained on the side opposite his family, or instead he crossed over with them and sent them somewhere further along.

41. A third line of interpretation taken by some Jewish commentators is that this scene is a prophetic political allegory, alluding to future struggles of the Jewish people in exile (see Leibowitz, *Studies in Genesis*, 369–70).

42. Simpson, *Reynard the Fox*, 237.

43. Matthew Thiessen (*Contesting Conversion*, 47–51) considers this story to be about the question of whether non-Israelites, especially ones from the proscribed Canaanite tribes (see Deut. 7:1–3), are permitted to intermarry with Israelites through performing the ritual of circumcision.

44. Such laws have existed up to relatively recently. For example, the law of *matrimonio riparatore*, "rehabilitating marriage," allowing a rapist to "preserve the honor" of his victim by marrying her, and in the process avoiding criminal liability, was only revoked in Italy in 1981.

45. A later event may call Shechem's intentions into question. After the brothers commit their carnage, they take Dinah out of Shechem's house, indicating that Shechem may have been holding her captive (a point seen as crucial by Meir Sternberg, *Poetics of Biblical Narrative*, 467–68). Alternatively, perhaps Shechem was affirming his love and obligation toward Dinah by insisting she remain in his house. The ambiguities of judgment lurking beneath the narrator's neutrality remain potent.

46. See Rabin, *Understanding the Hebrew Bible*, 37–38.

47. Here's an example of Amos's scathing satire against the rich (4:4–5): "Come to Bethel and transgress; to Gilgal, and transgress even more: Present your sacrifices the next morning and your tithes on the third day; And burn a thank offering of leavened bread, and proclaim freewill offerings loudly. For you love that sort of thing, O Israelites—declares my Lord God."

6. David

1. A single biblical book may present vastly different perspectives on the same king and his historical significance. Indeed, many biblical scholars attribute the tension in the depiction of biblical kings to the alternation between narrative threads derived from two main sources: an earlier court history, perhaps written during the king's reign or shortly thereafter, and a later version that elevates the role of the prophet over the king. The different strands often appear in conflict. The court history aims to embellish the reputation of the greatest kings; the prophetic writers, coming after the court historians and often biased against them, explain why the entire line of kings came to ruin at the hands of foreign powers. As figures caught between certain writers who would bolster their images and others who would shatter them, the kings appear in fractured portraits. Like the hundreds of classical statues beheaded by Christian iconoclasts, the biblical kings are thus built up and

then torn down, over and over. The effect is jarring but also fascinating—an antiquated equivalent to postmodern texts that are intentionally self-deconstructing. The ancient biblical editors insisted on preserving a certain respect for the original sources while at the same time weaving together other sources in blatant opposition—comparable, say, to cutting passages of Karl Marx and Edmund Burke into a single account of the French Revolution. See discussion in McCarter, *I Samuel, The Anchor Bible*.

2. Halpern, *David's Secret Demons*, 73–103.

3. Letter to Atticus, March 1, 49 BCE, quoted in Freeman, *Julius Caesar*, 250.

4. Quotations from Plutarch come from Harrison, *Julius Caesar in Shakespeare, Shaw and the Ancients*, 78–101.

5. Freeman, *Julius Caesar*, 353.

6. Originally they formed one book, the book of Samuel; at a later point they were split in two, because they could no longer fit onto one scroll.

7. Polzin, *Samuel and the Deuteronomist*, 18–79.

8. Rosenberg, *King and Kin*, 153.

9. Notably, this same term for a prophet was given when the downfall of Eli's house was proclaimed. A "man of God" is one who announces God's plan for human destiny.

10. Halbertal and Holmes (*Beginning of Politics*, 27) consider Samuel's overreaction against Saul as evidence of Samuel's smoldering, unjust blame of Saul for destroying his dynasty: "Samuel used his religious prestige to demoralize and deflate the person he viewed, with very little justification, as his undoer."

11. Translated from the Hebrew, which is available at https://benyehuda.org /tchernichowsky/beein_dor.html.

12. Halbertal and Holmes, *Beginning of Politics*, 48.

13. Moshe Garsiel (*Biblical Names*, 242) connects the motif of people loving David (Saul, Jonathan, Michal, Saul's servant, and later all Israel and Judah) with David's name, which can mean "love" (vocalized "dod"). David's son Solomon is likewise given the name Yedidya, meaning "beloved of God" (1 Kings 3:3). Robert Alter (*David Story*, 115) points out that Michal's profession of love is the only time the Bible describes a woman as loving a man.

14. Cyrus Gordon ("Homer and Bible," 90–91) offers a different perspective on David's action, comparing it to Achilles' slaughter of twelve Trojan noblemen as sacrifice for the death of Patroclus (Homer, *Iliad* 23:176).

15. The psychological definitions given here and below come from "31 Psychological Defense Mechanisms Explained," https://www.psychologistworld .com/freud/defence-mechanisms-list.

16. Polzin, *David and the Deuteronomist*, 6–7.

17. Biblical scholars hold that the events telescoped in this chapter took place throughout the years of his reign.

18. David appears to be citing the law of restitution in Exodus 21:37 against himself: "When a man steals an ox or a sheep, and slaughters it or sells it, he shall pay five oxen for the ox, and four sheep for the sheep." As observed in the Talmud (Yoma 22b), David is indeed punished fourfold for stealing the "lamb," Bathsheba: Three of his sons die in his lifetime, and his daughter is raped.

19. Famously translated in the King James Bible as "a coat of many colors."

20. As Tamar tells Amnon, sending her away is "even worse" than raping her, since she is no longer a virgin and hence unmarriageable. According to biblical law (Deut. 22:28–29), a man who rapes a virgin must marry her, and he can never divorce her.

21. David Marcus ("David the Deceiver") points to the similarities between Jacob and David as trickster figures who deceive at first and then are deceived in a measure-for-measure pattern. He does not discuss the death-bed revival scenes, however, which complicate this pattern.

7. God

1. The belief that various gods exist but only one is worthy of worship. See, for example, Exodus 15:11, "Who is like You, Oh Lord, among the gods" (usually translated as the "mighty," "celestials," and so on); and Psalms 82:1, "God stands in the divine assembly, among gods He pronounces judgment."

2. Sommer, *Bodies of God*, 1. Sommer shows that the early strata of the Bible, particularly passages from the Northern Kingdom, reveal notions of "multiplicity of divine embodiment and fluidity of divine selfhood" (56) — that is, that God can exist in multiple discrete places and forms at the same time. Later strata, specifically the Priestly and Deuteronomistic writings, oppose this view, resulting (again) in a tension visible throughout the Bible.

3. The idea that these descriptions may have been meant literally finds confirmation in an early work of Jewish mysticism, *Shiur Komah* ("The Measure of [God's] Size"), which purports to convey the size of God's appendages, as mentioned in the Bible, using sizes so enormous that they surpass human understanding.

4. Jon Levenson ("The Jerusalem Temple," 45–46) trots out scholarly speculation that there may originally have been an icon in the Temple representing God.

5. The opening section of Maimonides' *Guide for the Perplexed* argues that the Bible's anthropomorphic language is metaphoric, designed to reach people according to their understanding.

6. God's "victory is only meaningful if his foe is formidable, and his foe's formidability is difficult, perhaps impossible, to imagine if the foe has long since vanished" (Levenson, *Creation and the Persistence of Evil*, 27). Malcolm Lyons (*Man of Wiles*, 218) remarks on a similar challenge to medieval Arab storytellers: "As the invincibility of Islam restricts the narrators' ability to ratchet up tension in battles, one solution is to allow the enemy to shelter from the heroes behind walls."

7. In Miles' view (*God: A Biography*, 408), the troubling contradictions in God's character provide a paradigm enabling us to understand this same division in ourselves: "God is the divided original whose divided image we remain. His is the restless breathing we still hear in our sleep."

8. Marc Brettler (*God Is King*, 49) relates the Bible's strategies for differentiating God's kingship from the human variety, including the use of different terminology and piling on of superlatives: "Through morphological, syntactic and contextual modifications, the biblical authors clarify that God's kingship is qualitatively different from human kingship." Brettler considers "king" *only* as a metaphor for God in the Bible (24). I disagree. One can say that all language for God is metaphorical, a projection of human imaginative resources on an unknowable, all-powerful being. Nonetheless, the term "king" is applied so pervasively to God throughout the Bible, and is so integral to the ancient Israelite understanding of God's power and role in the world, that often when it is used, there is no conscious distinction between the vehicle and tenor, between "king" and "God" as separate entities that are being compared. God *is* king, *the* king.

9. Lindberg, *Heroic Heart*, 28.

10. However, it should be noted that some ancient gods, such as the Greek Chronos and Babylonian Apsu and Tiamat, are killed by other gods.

11. The term "antitype" in this section's heading has a specific meaning in biblical exegesis, referring to a system of correspondences between the Old and New Testaments worked out by Christian interpreters centuries ago. Here, the term is used simply to mean "the opposite type": If the hero archetype is a person who is both limited by mortality and exercises those limits to the fullest, then God defines a contrasting condition, a being removed from human constraints.

12. For example, "Let not the Egyptians say, 'It was with evil intent that He delivered them, only to kill them off in the mountains and annihilate them from the face of the earth'" (Exod. 32:12).

13. Shakespeare, *Hamlet*, Act 5, Scene 2, 11–12.

14. See https://jwa.org/media/telegram-from-abraham-joshua-heschel-to
-president-john-f-kennedy-june-16-1963.

Bibliography

Alter, Robert. *The Art of Biblical Narrative*. New York: Basic Books, 1981.

———. *The David Story: A Translation with Commentary of 1 and 2 Samuel*. New York: W. W. Norton, 1999.

———. *The Five Books of Moses*. New York: W. W. Norton, 2004.

Apollodorus. *The Library*. Translated by Sir James George Frazer. Loeb Classical Library, vols. 121 and 122. Cambridge MA: Harvard University Press, 1921.

Auerbach, Erich. *Mimesis: The Representation of Reality in Western Literature*. Translated by Willard R. Trask. Princeton NJ: Princeton University Press, 1953.

Berger, Peter. *The Sacred Canopy: Elements of a Sociological Theory of Religion*. New York: Doubleday, 1967.

Boorstin, Daniel J. *The Image or What Happened to the American Dream*. New York: Atheneum, 1961.

Braudy, Leo. *The Frenzy of Renown: Fame and Its History*. New York: Vintage, 1986.

Brettler, Marc Zvi. *God Is King: Understanding an Israelite Metaphor*. Sheffield, England: Sheffield Academic Press, 1989.

Bunyan, John. *The Pilgrim's Progress from This World to That Which Is to Come*. Everyman's Library. New York: E. P. Dutton & Co., 1907.

Campbell, Joseph. *The Hero with a Thousand Faces*. Princeton NJ: Princeton University Press, 1949.

Casson, Lionel. *Travel in the Ancient World*. London: George Allen & Unwin, 1974.

Ch'êng-ên, Wu. *Monkey*. Translated by Arthur Waley. London: Penguin, 1961.

Coontz, Stephanie. *Marriage, a History: From Obedience to Intimacy, or How Love Conquered Marriage*. New York: Viking, 2005.

Cross, Frank Moore. *Canaanite Myth and Biblical Epic*. Cambridge MA: Harvard University Press, 1973.

Darnton, Robert. *The Great Cat Massacre and Other Episodes in French Cultural History*. New York: Basic Books, 1984.

Erdoes, Richard, and Alfonso Ortiz, eds. *American Indian Trickster Tales*. New York: Penguin, 1998.

Finkelstein, Louis. "The Oldest Midrash: Pre-Rabbinic Ideals and Teachings in the Passover Haggadah." *Harvard Theological Review* 31 (1938): 291–317.

Fishbane, Michael A. *Kiss of God: Spiritual and Mystical Death in Judaism.* Seattle: University of Washington Press, 1994.

Foster, Benjamin R. *Before the Muses: An Anthology of Akkadian Literature.* Bethesda MD: CDL Press, 1993.

Freeman, Philip. *Julius Caesar.* New York: Simon & Schuster, 2008.

Garfinkel, Stephen. "The Man Moses, The Leader Moses." In *Jewish Religious Leadership: Image and Reality*, vol. 1, edited by Jack Wertheimer, 17–33. New York: Jewish Theological Seminary, 2004.

Garsiel, Moshe. *Biblical Names: A Literary Study of Midrashic Derivations and Puns.* Ramat-Gan, Israel: Bar-Ilan University Press, 1991.

Gordon, Cyrus H. "Homer and the Bible: The Origin and Character of East Mediterranean Literature." *Hebrew Union College Annual* 26 (1955): 43–108.

Gordon, Cyrus H., and Gary A. Rendsburg. *The Bible and the Ancient Near East.* New York: W. W. Norton, 1997.

Greenstein, Edward L. "The Fugitive Hero Narrative Pattern in Mesopotamia." In *Worship, Women, and War: Essays in Honor of Susan Niditch*, edited by John J. Collins, T. M. Lemos, and Saul M. Olyan, 17–35. Providence RI: Brown Judaic Studies, 2015.

———. "The Riddle of Samson." *Prooftexts* 1 (1981): 237–260.

Grossman, David. *Lion's Honey: The Myth of Samson.* Translated by Stuart Schoffman. New York: Canongate, 2006.

Hallo, W. W. *The Context of Scripture: Canonical Compositions from the Biblical World.* Leiden, Netherlands: Brill, 1997–2002.

Halbertal, Moshe, and Stephen Holmes. *The Beginning of Politics: Power in the Biblical Book of Samuel.* Princeton NJ: Princeton University Press, 2017.

Halpern, Baruch. *David's Secret Demons: Messiah, Murderer, Traitor, King.* Grand Rapids MI: William B. Eerdmans, 2001.

Harpur, James. *Sacred Tracks: 2000 Years of Christian Pilgrimage.* Berkeley: University of California Press, 2002.

Harrison, G. B. *Julius Caesar in Shakespeare, Shaw and the Ancients.* New York: Harcourt, Brace, 1960.

Heidel, Alexander. *The Babylonian Genesis: The Story of the Creation.* Chicago: University of Chicago Press, 1942.

Hillel, Daniel. *The Natural History of the Bible: An Environmental Exploration of the Hebrew Scriptures.* New York: Columbia University Press, 2006.

Homer. *The Iliad.* Translated by Richmond Lattimore. Chicago: University of Chicago Press, 1951.

———. *The Odyssey.* Translated by Robert Fagles. New York: Viking, 1996.

Hurowitz, Victor A. "The Baal Is Busy, Do Not Disturb! A New Look at 1 Kings 18:27." In *Teshura Le-Zafrira: Studies in the Bible, the History of Israel and the Ancient Near East*, edited by Mayer I. Gruber et al., 155–63. Beer Sheva, Israel: Ben-Gurion University of the Negev Press, 2012.

Hyde, Lewis. *Trickster Makes This World: Mischief, Myth, and Art.* New York: Farrar, Straus and Giroux, 1998.

Jacobs, Louis. *Jewish Mystical Testimonies.* New York: Schocken, 1977.

Jacobsen, Thorkild. *The Treasures of Darkness: A History of Mesopotamian Religion.* New Haven CT: Yale University Press, 1976.

Kierkegaard, Soren. *Fear and Trembling.* Garden City NY: Anchor, 1954.

Klapp, Orrin E. *Heroes, Villains, and Fools: The Changing American Character.* Englewood Cliffs NJ: Prentice-Hall, 1962.

Kugel, James L. *The Bible as It Was.* Cambridge MA: Harvard University Press, 1997.

———. *The God of Old: Inside the Lost World of the Bible.* New York: Free Press, 2004.

Lane, Edward William, trans. *Stories from the Thousand and One Nights: The Arabian Nights' Entertainments.* Revised by Stanley Lane-Poole. New York: P. F. Collier, 1909.

Leibowitz, Nehama. *Studies in the Book of Genesis, in the Context of Ancient and Modern Jewish Biblical Commentary.* Translated and adapted from the Hebrew by Aryeh Newman. Jerusalem: World Zionist Organization, 1972.

Levenson, Jon D. *Creation and the Persistence of Evil: The Jewish Drama of Divine Omnipotence.* Princeton NJ: Princeton University Press, 1988.

———. *The Death and Resurrection of the Beloved Son: The Transformation of Child Sacrifice in Judaism and Christianity.* New Haven CT: Yale University Press, 1993.

———. "The Jerusalem Temple in Devotional and Visionary Experience." In *Jewish Spirituality from the Bible Through the Middle Ages*, edited by Arthur Green, 32–61. New York: Crossroad Publishing Company, 1987.

Lewis, R. W. B. *The American Adam: Innocence, Tragedy, and Tradition in the Nineteenth Century.* Chicago: University of Chicago Press, 1955.

Lindberg, Tod. *The Heroic Heart: Greatness Ancient and Modern.* New York: Encounter Books, 2015.

Lyons, Malcolm C. *The Man of Wiles in Popular Arabic Literature: A Study of a Medieval Arab Hero.* Edinburgh: Edinburgh University Press, 2012.

MacIntyre, Alisdair. *After Virtue: A Study in Moral Theory.* 2nd ed. Notre Dame IN: University of Notre Dame Press, 1984.

Marcus, David. "David the Deceiver and David the Dupe." *Prooftexts* 6, no. 2 (May 1986): 163–71.

Marks, Herbert, ed. *The English Bible, King James Version.* Vol. 1, *The Old Testament.* New York: W. W. Norton, 2012.

McCarter, P. Kyle, Jr., trans. *I Samuel. The Anchor Bible*. Garden City NY: Doubleday, 1980.

Miles, Jack. *God: A Biography*. New York: Vintage, 1995.

Milton, John. *Complete Poems and Major Prose*. Edited by Merritt Y. Hughes. New York: Macmillan, 1957.

Mobley, Gregory. *The Empty Men: The Heroic Tradition of Ancient Israel*. New York: Doubleday, 2005.

Muffs, Yochanan. *Love & Joy: Law, Language and Religion in Ancient Israel*. New York: Jewish Theological Seminary, 1992.

Pardes, Ilana. *The Biography of Ancient Israel: National Narratives of the Bible*. Berkeley: University of California Press, 2000.

Philo. *The Life of Moses*. From *The Works of Philo Judaeus, The Contemporary of Josephus*, vol. 3. Translated by C. D. Yonge. London: Henry G. Bohn, 1855.

Plato. *The Dialogues of Plato*, vol. 1. Translated by Benjamin Jowett. New York: Macmillan, 1892.

Polzin, Robert. *David and the Deuteronomist*. Bloomington: Indiana University Press, 1993.

——. *Samuel and the Deuteronomist*. San Francisco: Harper & Row, 1989.

Rabin, Elliott. *Understanding the Hebrew Bible: A Reader's Guide*. Jersey City NJ: KTAV, 2006.

Radin, Paul. *The Trickster: A Study in American Indian Mythology*. New York: Schocken, 1972.

Redford, Donald B. "The Literary Motif of the Exposed Child." *Numen* 14, no. 1 (1967): 209–28.

Rendsburg, Gary A. "The Mock of Baal in 1 Kings 18:27." *Catholic Bible Quarterly* 50, no. 3 (July 1988): 414–17.

——. "Moses as Equal to Pharaoh." In *Text, Artifact, and Image: Revealing Ancient Israelite Religion*, edited by Gary Beckman and Theodore J. Lewis, 201–19. Providence RI: Brown Judaic Studies, 2006.

——. "Notes on Genesis XXXV." *Vetus Testamentum* 34, no. 3 (July 1984): 361–66.

——. "Unlikely Heroes: Women as Israel." *Bible Review* 29, no. 1 (Feb. 2003): 16–23, 52–53.

Rosenberg, Joel. *King and Kin: Political Allegory in the Hebrew Bible*. Bloomington: Indiana University Press, 1986.

Segal, Robert A., ed. *In Quest of the Hero*. Princeton NJ: Princeton University Press, 1990.

Simpson, James. *Reynard the Fox: A New Translation*. New York: Liveright, 2015.

Smith, Mark S. *The Early History of God*. 2nd ed. Grand Rapids MI: William B. Eerdmans, 2002.

Sommer, Benjamin D. *The Bodies of God and the World of Ancient Israel*. Cambridge: Cambridge University Press, 2009.

Sonnet, Jean-Pierre, and André Wenin. "La mort de Samson: Dieu bénit-il l'attentat suicide?" *Revue théologique de Louvain* 35, no. 3 (2004): 372–81.

Spiegel, Shalom. *The Last Trial*. Translated by Judah Goldin. New York: Schocken, 1969.

Sternberg, Meir. "Double Cave, Double Talk: The Indirections of Biblical Dialogue." In *"Not in Heaven": Coherence and Complexity in Biblical Narrative*, edited by Jason P. Rosenblatt and Joseph C. Sitterson Jr., 28–57. Bloomington: Indiana University Press, 1991.

———. *The Poetics of Biblical Narrative: Ideological Literature and the Drama of Reading*. Bloomington: Indiana University Press, 1985.

Thiessen, Matthew. *Contesting Conversion: Genealogy, Circumcision and Identity in Ancient Judaism and Christianity*. New York: Oxford University Press, 2011.

Virgil. *The Aeneid*. Translated by Robert Fitzgerald. New York: Random House, 1983.

———. *The Aeneid of Virgil*. Books 1–6. Edited by R. D. Williams. London: Macmillan, 1972.

Wecter, Dixon. *The Hero in America: A Chronicle of Hero-Worship*. New York: Charles Scribner's Sons, 1941.

Weiss, Dov. *Pious Irreverence: Confronting God in Rabbinic Judaism*. Philadelphia: University of Pennsylvania Press, 2017.

Wildavsky, Aaron. *Moses as Political Leader*. Jerusalem: Shalem Press, 2005.

Wills, Garry. *Cincinnatus: George Washington and the Enlightenment*. Garden City NY: Doubleday, 1984.

Wood, Gordon S. *Revolutionary Characters: What Made the Founders Different*. New York: Penguin, 2006.

Zakovitch, Yair. *Jacob: Unexpected Patriarch*. New Haven CT: Yale University Press, 2012.

Zornberg, Aviva Gottlieb. *Moses: A Human Life*. New Haven CT: Yale University Press, 2016.

General Index

Abraham, xix, xx, 4–6, 22, 39–40, 70, 74–75, 81, 86; and Adam, 123–26; consistency of character, 130–31; God's promises, 128–29; as hero, 121–23, 154–55; and Isaac (*Akedah*), 145–48; as pilgrim, 131–37; practical side of, 148–54; and Sarah, 133, 135, 143–44, 150–51, 153, 154; spiritual pilgrimage of, 137–40; tensions of, 126–29, 140–45. *See also* Christian (hero of John Bunyan's *Pilgrim's Progress*); Hagar; Ishmael

Achilles, xii, xiv, 10, 11, 38, 44, 54, 69, 72, 78, 157, 262, 287n14

Adonijah, 239–40

Aeneas (hero of Virgil's *Aeneid*), xx, 9, 67, 131–34, 139, 280n7

Alter, Robert, 33, 180, 276n17, 287n13

Amalek, 53–55, 72, 217–18, 221, 231–32

Aristotle, 1, 262

Ark Narrative, 212, 214–15

Austen, Jane, 166

Balaam, 46, 170

Baudelaire, Charles, 73

Braudy, Leo, 17

Campbell, Joseph, xiii–xiv, 4–5, 57, 66, 274n4, 275n13, 276n24

Christian (hero of John Bunyan's *Pilgrim's Progress*), 134–40

Coontz, Stephanie, 107, 109

Coyote (Native American trickster), xx, 174–75, 178, 188, 194, 196

Creation, 1–2, 48, 49, 147, 163, 249, 251–52, 259, 281n18

Dante, 137

Darnton, Robert, 159

David, xix, xx, 17, 20, 22, 37, 72, 75, 95, 198; and Absalom, 235–38; ambition of, 222–25; and Bathsheba, 226, 232–33, 239–40; and Bible's ambivalence toward kings, 199–205; as cipher, 206; contradictions of, 206–7, 225–27; deathbed reversal, 238–41; decline of, 231–38; and Goliath, 219–20; and Julius Caesar, 207–11; as Psalmist, 241–43; psychological defense mechanisms in, 227–31; as second Jacob, 234–36, 238–40; as second Samson, 220–21. *See also* Amalek; Ark Narrative; Hannah; Jonathan; Michal; Nathan; Samuel (character); Saul; Solomon

Dinah, 21, 22, 161, 185–88, 236, 286n45

Elijah, 18, 22, 45, 72, 171–73, 198

Enuma Elish, 2, 265, 278n10

Esther, xix, xx; beauty contest, 107–9; eunuchs, 105, 109–10; as hero, 97, 120; intrigue and disguises in royal court, 109–12; and Joseph, 112–14; passivity of, 104–7; and Scheherazade, 98–104; takes charge, 117–19; transformation, 114–17. *See also* Mordecai; *The Thousand and One Nights*

Forster, E. M., xvii

Garcia-Marquez, Gabriel, 129
Gilgamesh, 11, 78, 278n10
God, xvi; anthropomorphism in the Bible, 246–48; as co-hero, 265–67; as counterpoint of a hero, 262–65; as ethical paradigm, 250–54; as king, 254–57; narrative challenge of depiction, 248–50; question of heroic status, xviii, 245–46; as savior, 257–62; as trickster, 163, 170–73

Hagar, 74, 123, 130, 131, 133, 143–45, 154, 163, 179
Halbertal, Moshe, 223, 287n10
Halpern, Baruch, 206
Hannah, 74, 212–16, 256
heroes: American, 13–17; Biblical, 1–8, 11–13, 17–23; Classical, 8–11
Holmes, Stephen, 223, 287n10
Homer, 283n10; *The Iliad*, xii, 9, 38, 287n14; *The Odyssey*, 9, 38, 283n14
Hyde, Lewis, 164, 178, 282n1

Ibsen, Henrik, 124
Ishmael, 74, 123, 130, 144–45, 154, 163

Jacob: and angel, 183–84; assessment as a hero, 196–98; as boundary-crosser, 167–70, 182–85; deathbed reversal, 192–96; and Esau, 163–66, 182–85; father of tricksters, 185–89; and Laban, 173–78, 180–81; trickery among sons, 189–92; as trickster, 157–62. *See also* Coyote (Native American trickster); Dinah; Leah; Odysseus; Rachel; Rebecca; Reynard the Fox (medieval trickster)
Jacobsen, Thorkild, 11
Jonah, 77, 269
Jonathan, 223–25, 229–30, 238, 241, 258

Klapp, Orrin, xii

Leah, 176–79, 181, 187, 194, 213, 285n34–35
Levenson, Jon, 249, 259, 281n17, 288n4, 289n6
Lewis, R. W. B., 16
Lindberg, Tod, 262
Lindbergh, Charles, 17
Louis XIV, 8

MacIntyre, Alasdair, xii
Michal, 221–23, 229, 287n13
Midrash, 4–6, 20, 102, 127–28, 176, 183, 276n26, 279n3, 280n1, 281n18, 282n26, 283n16, 285n33, 285n35
Miles, Jack, 250, 265
Milton, John, 78, 91–93
Mordecai, 102–3, 105, 110–19
Moses, xix, 6, 17, 18; and Aaron, 44–45, 49–50; arm (might), 49–53; arm (weakness), 53–55; assessment as a hero, 25–27, 65–70; birth, 27–29; breaking the tablets, 57–59; at Burning Bush, 35–38; death, 29–31; diminished stature of, 19–21; and Pharaoh, 44–49; saving slaves,

31–33; visions of God, 38–44; in the wilderness, 59–64; and Zipporah, 33–35. *See also* Sargon; Sinai (Covenant and vision)

Nathan, 22, 232–33, 239–42, 270, 271
Nazirite, 73, 74, 76–78, 89, 277n5–6

Odysseus, xx, 38, 68, 160–61, 193, 283n14

Paine, Thomas, 199
Pardes, Ilana, 56
Philo, xvi, 25
Plato, xi
Polzin, Robert, 212, 231
Protagoras, xi
Proust, Marcel, 116

Rabbi Ishmael, 30–31
Rachel, 21, 33, 34, 107, 161, 173–74, 176, 178–81, 188, 190, 193, 213, 279n7, 285n35
Raglan, Lord, xiii, xiv, 29, 273n6
Rank, Otto, xiii, 68
Rebecca, 33, 34, 74, 83, 84, 161, 164, 165–66, 173, 176–77, 194, 284n20, 284n23
Reynard the Fox (medieval trickster), xx, 185, 283n19–20

sacred marriage (Mesopotamian ritual), 10–11
ṣalmu. See *tzalmu*
Samson, xix, xx, 18; annunciation, 74–76; as antihero, 71–74; assessment as hero, 94–95; and Heracles, 79–82; among Israelites, 89–90; among Philistines, 82–89; triumphal death, 90–94. *See also* Milton, John; Nazirite
Samuel (character), 75, 212, 213, 215, 277n5; rejection of Saul, 217–18, 287n10; selection of David, 222–23, 225; selection of Saul, 201–5, 216
Sargon, 27–29
Saul, 47, 72, 95; and Amalekites; and David, 219–26, 228–33, 241; downfall of House of Saul, 207, 217–19, 223–24, 232–33, 237, 287n10; selection as king, two stories, 201–5, 216–17
Shakespeare, William, 47, 106, 198, 207, 209, 238, 264
Sinai (Covenant and vision), 3, 20, 40–44, 55–58, 66, 276n22
Solomon, xvii, 7–8, 20, 75, 81, 107, 218, 239–40, 279n4
Sommer, Benjamin, 247, 273n2, 288n2
Sternberg, Meir, 21, 282n23, 286n45

Tamar, 234–36, 288n20
Tchernichovsky, Sha'ul, 218
The Thousand and One Nights, 98–102, 279n1
type-scene, 33, 34, 75
tzalmu, 3, 273n2 (introduction)

Whitman, Walt, 14–15, 18
Wildavsky, Aaron, 26
Wills, Garry, 14
Wood, Gordon, 273n1

Zakovitch, Yair, 177, 285n36
Zornberg, Aviva, 276n26

Source Index

Hebrew Bible

Genesis

1, 252
1:2, 48
1:21, 48
1:26, 2
2:16–17, 124
2:17, 266
2:24–25, 125
4, 28
5:5, 266
6:4, 274n14
6:6, 253
6:9, 95
8:21, 147
10:8–12, 6
11:5, 248
11:10–26, 127
11:26, 4
11:31, 127
12, 146
12:1, 127
12:1–3, 126
12:4, 134
12:6–9, 139
12:8, 169
12:10–20, 150
13:2, 153
13:5–13, 149
13:14–17, 129
14, 141, 148–49, 182

15, 129, 142
15:13, 139
16, 74
16:5, 6
17, 129
17:5, 134
17:15, 134
17:18, 144
18:1–8, 152
18:9–15, 74, 277n4
18:10, 129
18:16–33, 140–42
18:23–25, 252
20:1–18, 150
21:8, 165
21:10, 163
21:12, 163
21:25, 130
22, 145–47
22:15–19, 129
23, 151–52
24:10–61, 33
25:1–6, 153
25:23, 74
25:27, 163
25:28, 283n16
25:32, 164
26:30, 165
26:34–35, 84
27:12–13, 165

27:35, 188
27:42, 166
28:10–22, 167–70
29, 173–77
29:1–20, 33
29:16–18, 107
29:26, 176
29:31–34, 178–79
30:1–24, 179–80
30:28–43, 177–78
30:37–43, 285n37
31:8–13, 285n37
31:10–35, 180–81
32:7–8, 23
32:10, 32
32:10–13, 183
32:28–33, 183–84
32:31, 21
33:1–17, 184–85
33:20, 277n4
34, 185–89
35:8, 284n23
41:42–43, 113
42:37, 193
44:29, 193
45:5, 116
47:9, 193
48:10, 193
48:12–19, 194
49, 195–96

Exodus
2:1–10, 27–29
2:11–15, 31–32
2:14, 18
2:16–17, 33
2:15b–21, 34
2:23–24, 267
2:24–25, 257
3–4, 35–38
3:1–6, 39
3:10, 36
3:11, 36
3:13, 36
3:14, 37
4:1, 36
4:10, 277n27
4:10–14, 35
4:24–26, 67
7:1, 44, 274n14
7:8–8:15, 45–46
8:24, 50
9:27, 266
13:17, 80
14:16, 51
14:21, 51
14:27–28, 52
14:31, 49
15:2–3, 257
15:6, 12
15:11, 288n1
15:14–15, 257
16, 148
17:7, 148
17:11–13, 53
17:8–16, 217
19:9, 56
19:18–19, 55
19:20, 55, 66
19:24, 66
20:2, 202, 265

21:2, 176
21:37, 288n18
23:2–3, 19
23:17, 275n14
24:9–11, 40–41
25–27, 279n4
31:16–17, 2
32:7, 265
32:10, 252
32:12, 290n12
32:25–35, 203
32:32–33, 252
33:11, 276n17
33:18–23, 41–42
34:23, 275n14
35–38, 279n4

Leviticus
10:3, 63
16:20–22, 231

Numbers
6:1–21, 74–78
11:4, 62
11:11–15, 62
11:18–20, 204
11:20, 63
12:1–2, 61
12:3, 25
13–14, 61
14:11–19
14:39–45, 61
16, 61
17, 61
17:16–26, 50
20, 30
20:9–12, 63
20:14–21:35, 61–62
22–24, 170–71
25, 61

25:14, 88

Deuteronomy
1:34–37, 64
6:5, 272
7:1–3, 286n43
15:12, 176
16:16, 275n14
16:20, 19
17:18–20, 12
21:1–9, 167
22:28, 187
22:28–29, 288n20
26:8, 50
32:50–51, 30
34:1, 29
34:5–6, 29–30
34:10, 43

Judges
1:7, 158
4, 198
7:2, 72
11, 285n39
13, 74–78
13:5, 76, 94
14:1–3, 83
14:5–6, 220
14:8–9, 88
14:10–19, 85
14:14, 278n13
14:18, 278n12–13
15:2, 85
15:9–13, 89
15:18, 90
16:1–3, 86–87
16:4, 87
16:15, 87
16:23, 94
16:28, 94

16:30, 92
16:31, 94
21:25, 201

1 Samuel
1:6, 213
1:8, 213
1:11, 277n5
1:12–13, 213
1:17–20, 75
2:1–10, 213
2:8–10, 256
2:27–36, 212
3:18, 212
4–6, 212–15
7:3, 215
8:7, 201
8:11–17, 257
9–10, 216–17
10:17–27, 202–5
14:6, 258
14:31–35, 219
14:47–48, 232
15:3, 217
16, 222
17, 219–20
18:1, 223
18:5–7, 221
18:17–29, 222–23
18:20, 223
20, 223
22:2, 221
24, 223
25, 221
26, 223
27:8–9, 221
29:6–11, 225
30, 217–18
31:4–6, 230

2 Samuel
1:1–16, 230–31
1:17–27, 241
2:1–7, 226
3:1, 223
3:2, 221
5:13, 222
6, 213
8, 234
8:2, 208
9, 223
11, 226–27
12:1–14, 232–33
12:7–12, 212
12:10, 22
13, 234–37
14:1, 237
16:7–8, 224
19:1, 238
19:19–24, 224
21, 224
22, 241
23, 241

1 Kings
1–2, 238–41
3:3, 287n13
6–7, 279n4
10:23, 7
11:1–4, 7
11:3, 107
11:43, 7
16:31, 107
16:32–33, 171
18:4, 171
18:17, 18
18:20–40, 171
18:27, 172
21:25, 171

2 Kings
7, 271
23:25, 277n31

Isaiah
6, 254
6:1, 247
63:2–3, 258

Jeremiah
1:5, 75
9:3, 283n3
34:18–20, 281n16

Ezekiel
32:2–3, 49

Hosea
12:3, 158

Amos
4:4–5, 286n47

Micah
6:8, 252

Zechariah
4:6, 73

Psalms
8:4–6, 1
18, 241
20:8–9, 54
27:4, 247
30:6, 263
44:24, 279n3
51, 242–43
74:12–17, 260
82:1, 288n1
89:3, 252

93:1, 245
94:3–7, 253
94:20, 254
97:11, 252
99:5, 247
102:27, 251
104, 48
104:9, 260
113:7, 163
115:4, 48
115:4–8, 172
118:5, 55
121:4, 279n3
149, 255

Job
38:8–11, 261

41:17–25, 261
42:6, 261

Song of Songs
5:2, 138
7:6, 88–89

Esther
1:1–3, 100
1:6–7, 100–101
1:8, 102
1:13–15, 101–2
2:7, 105, 111
2:8, 105
2:10, 105, 111
2:10–11, 103
2:15, 105

2:21, 109
3:8, 120
4:4–5, 109
4:11, 115
4:13–14, 114
5:2–3, 117
6, 118
6:8, 113
6:11, 113
7:2–4, 118–19
7:5–6, 119
7:8, 119
10:3, 113

2 Chronicles
9:22–31, 7
20:7, 280n5

Rabbinic Literature

Babylonian Talmud
   Bava Batra
      15a, 43
      123a, 285n35
   Bava Metzia
      86b, 282n26
   Menahot
      29b, 20
   Nedarim
      32a, 282n22
   Sotah
      14a, 41
   Yoma
      22b, 288n18

Bereishit Rabbah
   8:5, 281n18
   38:13, 280n3
   39:2, 280n1

65:15, 284n21
70:19, 176
77:3, 183

Esther Rabbah
   3:13, 102
   4:9, 102
   6:1, 279n3

Mishnah
   Nazir
      1:2, 277n6

Pirkei Avot
   2:6, 246
   5:4, 281n15

Rashi
   Gen. 6:9, 95

Gen. 25:28, 283n16
Exod. 24:10, 41
Deut. 6:5, 272
Deut. 34:5–6, 30–31
Deut. 34:10, 43

Ramban
   Deut. 34:10, 43

Rashbam
   Exod. 24:10, 41

Targum Onkelos
   Deut. 34:5, 30

Targum Yonatan
   Deut. 34:10, 43